GLOBAL SQUEEZE

The Coming Crisis for First-World Nations

RICHARD C. LONGWORTH

Foreword by Adele Simmons, President, The MacArthur Foundation

CONTEMPORARY BOOKS

HF
1359
.L66
1998

Library of Congress Cataloging-in-Publication Data

Longworth, Richard C.
    Global squeeze : the coming crisis for first-world nations /
Richard C. Longworth ; foreword by Adele Simmons.
        p.   cm.
    Includes index.
    ISBN 0-8092-2974-9 (cloth)
    1. International economic relations.   2. Economic
development.   3. United States—Foreign economic relations.
4. Germany—Foreign economic relations.   5. France—Foreign
economic relations.   I. Title.
HF1359.L66   1998
337—dc21   97-46457
                                                                CIP

Jacket and interior design by Scott Rattray

Published by Contemporary Books
A division of NTC/Contemporary Publishing Group, Inc.
4255 West Touhy Avenue, Lincolnwood (Chicago), Illinois 60646 -1975 U.S.A.
Printed in the United States of America
International Standard Book Number: 0-8092-2974-9
15   14   13   12   11   10   9   8   7   6   5   4   3   2   1

To the memory of my mother and my father

CONTENTS

FOREWORD

INGVAR CARLSSON, THE former Prime Minister of Sweden, and I went recently to the offices of the *Chicago Tribune* to meet with Dick Longworth and his colleagues about the report of an international commission on which we both served. The report, titled *Our Global Neighborhood*, described a fundamentally changed world in which the old Cold War paradigms were gone and suggested that humanity needed to find new, collaborative ways to manage its common concerns.

Our report talked about the extraordinary technological advances in communications and transportation that are revolutionizing the way the world interacts and conducts its business. We noted that these changes are most evident in the economic arena as the world moves beyond interdependency to confront a wholly new phenomenon: globalization.

Dick had just published a series of articles in the paper, reporting on discussions and conversations he had undertaken in Europe, Japan, and this country about the very same issue. The timeliness of the topic was self-evident. So was the fact that nobody fully understood its meaning or impact. Dick said that he had more information than he was able to convey in the newspaper and was contemplating a book.

At the MacArthur Foundation, we have developed the practice of inviting people working in areas of interest to us to spend time at our offices, meet with staff, and continue ongoing work or focus on a specific project. Dick came to the foundation as a Distinguished Visitor and completed the manuscript of the book you hold.

As Dick points out in his initial chapter, globalization is a revolution still in progress. We are learning as we go along, and one of the difficult lessons is that the impacts are both good and bad. Some people are better off, and others clearly are not. What is particularly disturbing, however, is the feeling that globalization is a phenomenon over which people have no control. One of the important, consistent points in this book is that we do have choices.

Another significant theme is that understanding economic globalization requires more than just economic analysis. Making public policy choices that will produce a vibrant economy requires attention to an array of political, social, environmental, and personal dimensions of people's lives. Interdisciplinary approaches to problem solving are essential. Scholars of economic theory need to incorporate insights from other disciplines into their work. For example, trade economists need to begin to consider the possibility that trade has something to do with jobs and wage disparities. The result will be richer theoretical insights, better analysis of complex issues, and improved contributions by economists to social policy. We need to encourage innovative social and economic thinking and the application of new ideas.

Issues of income inequality, an aging population, and the changing nature of work are all important and must be considered in the context of the global economy. The emergence of a global marketplace for goods, services, capital, and investment requires that we look at these developments in much more comprehensive and integrative ways. Adding the rapid pace of change and the increasing interconnectedness of the world to the mix only increases the complexity of the situation.

Globalization also means that we have to improve our understanding of the various national contexts within which decisions about the global economy are going to be made. Despite the oft-stated decline in the role and influence of states, globalization is far from signaling the end of nationhood. States continue to be the dominant political force in the world, and decisions made within national borders will continue to have serious consequences for the health and vitality of the world as a whole. People expect their governments to serve their interests and to make decisions that will improve their opportunities to achieve a more secure and stable existence.

The challenge for policy makers, public and private, is to shape the forces of globalization in positive ways and to work together, across all kinds of boundaries, to reduce the inequalities that will inevitably lead to social chaos and conflict. More inclusive economic development should be our common goal. As Dick so rightly says, economic globalization exists, and we have to learn to control and guide its progress and results. This book represents an important contribution to the debate.

Adele Simmons
President, John D. and Catherine T. MacArthur Foundation

ACKNOWLEDGMENTS

No BOOK IS published without the help and hand-holding of many supporters, from family to publisher. Any author of a book, particularly one of reportage, is acutely aware of his debt to those who have shared their time and wisdom with him. What follows is a short list of persons to whom I am particularly grateful; a more complete list would run for pages. None of these willing helpers bears responsibility for any errors, nor would many of them, I suspect, share all my judgments. But my gratitude to them all is profound.

My editors and colleagues at the *Chicago Tribune* supplied invaluable help, both practical and psychological. Special thanks go to the editor, Howard Tyner, and to Joe Leonard for their enthusiastic support and their generosity in letting me use material that appeared in earlier stories and series in the *Tribune*. Jim O'Shea gave me the original idea for this project. Sharman Stein was a valued associate in my reporting on the American middle class. Barbara Sutton helped greatly, as did Mike Jett, Howard Witt, Clarence Petersen, Lara Weber, Jeannie Adams, Steve Franklin, and the late Jim Yuenger.

The John D. and Catherine T. MacArthur Foundation offered not only a splendid place to write but warm hospitality and the intellectual stimulation characteristic of that great institution. Adele Simmons, the foundation's president, encouraged me to write the book, and her colleagues—Vic and Marti Rabinowitch, John Hurley, Kathy Lakie, Elise Berg, Sharon Furiya, Sydney Sidwell, Russ Daniels, Teresa Polk-Henderson, and many others—helped make it happen.

Many persons who shared their knowledge with me are mentioned in the text, but there are others who deserve my thanks.

In the United States, these include Gary Burtless, Chalmers Johnson, John Abowd, Art Kelley, Stephan-Gotz Richter, Karim Pakravan, Clyde Prestowitz, Greg Stanko, Jeremy Rifkin, Mark Primoff, Larry Mishel, Ben Page, Buzz Palmer, David Ranney, Tom Geoghegan, Kevin Phillips, Christopher Jencks, Jin Lee, John Cavanagh, Sylvester Schieber, Peter Diamond, Michael Tanner, and Willis Rowell.

In Germany, I was helped by Karl Schon, Dieter Koepke, Albert Schunk, Peter Stutz, Uwe Neuhaus, Rainer Hank, Axel Nitschke, Norbert Wieczorek, Peik von Bestenbostel, Dietmar Herz, Ursula Mertzig-Stein, Jürgen Müeller, Horst Teltschik, Martin Seeleib-Kaiser, G. Michael Roeskau, Bernard Veltrup, Martin Gehlen, Werner Willms, and especially Dominik Wichmann and John and Susan Schmid.

In France, thanks to Jonathon Kundera, Julian Nundy, Francis Kramarz, Pascale Furlong, David Voskuhl, Norman Bowers, Brigid Janssen, Valerie Ohannessian, Barry James, Bill Pfaff, Jacques Attali, and especially to Jeanne de Champagnac.

In Japan, I owe thanks especially to Asako Takaesu and to Mike and Carla Lev, Glen Fukushima, Ken Courtis, Tsuneo Katsuyama, Noboru Hatakeyama, Kenichi Ohmae, Nami Hoshijima, Keiichi Kimura, Nobumitsu Kagami, Ken Fukuchi, Akio Mikuni, Sam Jameson, Bob Neff, and Eamonn Fingleton.

Rich Hagle, my editor at NTC/Contemporary Publishing, has been a tower of support and guidance. Finally, this book never would have happened without the patience and love of my wife, Barbara.

PART I

New Forces, Old Values

1. ONE VAST CASINO

WHAT IS THE purpose of an economy? If it is not solely for the well-being of the people who live within it, what is an economy for?

For most of the past fifty years, the rich nations of the world have been able to fudge that question. Blessed by the greatest expansion in history, these nations had enough money to make sure that almost everyone within their borders shared in the economic growth. Prosperity cut a lot of slack.

For the United States, Japan, and Western Europe, economic growth bought a half-century of social stability. For the first time, the majority of people owned their own homes, bought cars, took vacations, enjoyed access to good health care. Secure jobs became plentiful, and they paid more every year. Better health care prolonged lives, and social security networks guaranteed a comfortable old age. Wider travel and longer education expanded horizons; so, for better or worse, did television.

Perhaps the most important product of this era was a sense of confidence. Life, being predictable, could be planned. Across much of the noncommunist world, hundreds of millions of persons saw a secure future and invested in it. They bought homes, raised families, built communities, shared their wealth through broad social programs or private philanthropies. Trusting in the future, they chose democracy, which is a political system based on trust.

In short, they created civilizations. In Japan and Western Europe, these civilizations were literally raised from the ruins of war. These civilizations had an economic base, a structure generous enough to enable its beneficiaries to build the kinds of lives they wanted. These lives weren't perfect. Substantial numbers of persons in these nations, especially in the United States, could not or did not share the wealth. Crime and blight did not disappear, nor did pollution and the more noxious by-products of commerce. But for nations that had spent the first half of this century in economic depression or at spearpoint in two world wars, the benefits of the last fifty years have been nothing short of miraculous.

That era is ending. A new force called globalization is sweeping across these fat and happy lands and threatens the economic base of their civilizations. The process is just beginning; the big story of the twenty-first century will be globalization's impact on the nations of the world. But already, secure jobs at ever-rising wages are becoming a thing of the past. This is true mostly for Americans, but Europeans and Japanese are acutely aware of American trends and fear them. As this sense of security vanishes, so do confidence and trust—in government, employers, neighbors. These trends also are visible now. As confidence and trust go, so do social stability and, finally, democracy.

Globalization, like any wind of change, blows equally at each door and window and sends the same waves crashing against each coast. But if the major nations of the world feel the same pressures, they are reacting to them differently, in their own way. The United States is not Europe nor Japan. Each has its own economy and political system—its own civilization—which is shaped by its own history and culture. Each responds to threats or opportunities in its own way. The choices that each makes now will shape its civilization through the next century.

This possibility of choice will be a persistent theme of this book. The global economy is not an act of God, like a virus or a volcano, but the result of economic actions taken by human beings and thus responsive to human control. There is no need to say, as many American economists and businesspeople do, that the market knows best and must be obeyed. This cultural capitalism is confined mostly to the United States and the other English-speaking nations. Other nations, in Europe and in Asia, see the market as the source of both bountiful benefits and lethal damage, and are determined to temper this force to their own priorities.

Each nation can choose the policy that enables it to channel the force of globalization to its people's advantage. The choice is a political one, and making it is what politicians are elected to do.

Issues and Choices

The impact of globalization on these wealthy nations and their responses to this impact are the subject of this book. In the next chapter, I intend to look more closely at the components of the global economy: at technology, trade, global investment, and, most important, the global capital market that drives this revolution. Chapter 3 will describe the way globalization is changing jobs and the way people work. From downsizing and instability in the United States to epidemic unemployment in Europe, this impact of globalization on the workplace is the real heart of the global debate. Economists argue over exactly how globalization delivers this impact, but we will look at the evidence and try to reach some conclusions.

In the following three chapters, I will outline the epochal changes affecting the United States, Japan, Germany, and France. I will describe the experience of each with the force of globalization, how each perceives this force, and how each is coping with it. Most Americans assume there is one common Western capitalism, based on the American model; I will show that this is far from true, just as the fears and aspirations of Europeans and Japanese differ from those of Americans.

Chapter 7 will deal with the issues of equality, inequality, and fairness in the global economy. These issues are most acute in the United States, where the gap between rich and poor has widened, but are beginning to be felt in Europe, too. Chapter 8 will focus on the key issue of efficiency. The global market worships efficiency at any cost, and this chapter will show why that cost is often high. Chapter 9 will consider the key demographic fact of the next century, which is the aging of the workforce of the industrial nations, the competition with the younger workers of the poorer nations, and the way the global economy will make it increasingly hard to care for this growing army of the old.

Finally, I will propose solutions. Some can be undertaken by national governments, but many are possible only in cooperation with other nations—both the wealthy nations with whom we've shared the economic miracle of the past half century and the once-poor nations that hope to benefit from new miracles of the century to come.

The Search for a New Order

These solutions will be based on a set of core beliefs. First, this economic revolution, like the Industrial Revolution of the nineteenth century, is a fact that cannot be denied nor ignored. It holds the potential for much good. But it also threatens the complex but stable civilizations that the United States and its wealthier allies have built since World War II. These civilizations have provided generations of Americans, Europeans, and Japanese the framework for rich, rewarding lives. They must not be thrown away in the name of an ideology that recognizes only the market.

The forces of this market will not and should not be repealed in favor of a sterile equality that would fail elsewhere as surely as it failed in the Soviet Union. If the last half of the twentieth century taught us anything, it is that market capitalism is by far the most productive and liberating channel for the realization of human ambitions and needs. The poor Russians and their neighbors were the guinea pigs in a mammoth experiment to prove the opposite, and they suffer still in its ruins. But the last fifty years also taught us that the market, unrestrained, can wreak the whirlwind. The success of the United States, the West Europeans, and the Japanese since World War II has risen from their ability to harness the market, to direct it down a road lined with laws and regulations. Like any game, market capitalism works only when all players know the rules and follow them. This seems obvious, but many enthusiasts of the global market argue that its genius lies in the way that it escapes both national boundaries and national regulations and seeks maximum returns, freed from any political or social control.

The old controls won't work anymore. The laws with which the wealthy societies have guided the market in the past are being swamped by the supranational power of the global market. Only nations acting together can write the new rule book.

The task in the decades to come is to control, shape, and guide these economic forces so they can enrich these civilizations and the lives of the people within them, while preserving the best of the old economic system that we are leaving behind us.

Globalization Defined

Globalization can be a vague and demagogic word. To its prophets, it promises a glorious future and unending riches. To its critics, it bodes doom. It is a catchall word that has become shorthand for a menu of economic and social changes. It certainly has to do with the growth of global trade and investment. It is most clearly seen in the development of a global financial market. It is blamed, often correctly, for waves of downsizing. Its fingerprints can be seen on millions of pink slips issued to factory hands and middle managers alike. It is both more and less than the dawn of the Information Age. Not everything ascribed to globalization can be credited to technology, but it would not exist without the development of the computer, the microprocessor, and the communications satellite.

I define globalization as the creation of a global economy. More specifically, it is a revolution that enables any entrepreneur to raise money anywhere in the world and, with that money, to use technology, communications, management, and labor located anywhere the entrepreneur finds them to make things anywhere he or she wants and sell them anywhere there are customers.

Clearly, this is still a revolution in progress. We aren't there yet. In some areas of this revolution, we aren't even close. A truly global economy would be a worldwide version of national economies like the American one. In such an economy, money, goods, services, jobs, and people would move as easily from country to country as they do now from, say, Illinois to Ohio.

As the global economy exists now, only money moves this freely. Money, in fact, flows like the trade winds. More than $1.3 trillion moves every day through the money markets of the world (see Exhibit 1.1). This daily flood is rising fast: it was only $20 billion in 1973, $207 billion in 1986, $820 billion in 1992. At its present level, the flow of money amounts to some $400 trillion each year, which is fifty times more money than the $8 trillion needed to finance all the world's foreign trade and investment. All the rest is speculation.[1]

Exhibit 1.1

Global Foreign Exchange Market Turnover, Per Day

1989	$590 Billion
1992	$820 Billion
1995	$1.19 Trillion
1996*	$1.35 Trillion
1997*	$1.54 Trillion

* Projections
Source: Bank for International Settlements.

As the French Nobel Prize–winning economist Maurice Allais has said, "The world has become one vast casino whose gambling tables are scattered from one end of the globe to the other."[2]

Even this capital market is not complete. Currency trading is virtually without barriers, and bond trading is becoming so, but worldwide trading in stocks is still fairly limited, to about $25 billion each day.[3]

Money may move without limits, but it often cannot be freely used. Almost every country restricts foreign investment in some ways. Most limit foreign control over key industries, such as those in defense, airlines, or sometimes the media. Others forbid foreigners to buy land. Japan virtually blocks foreign majority control of high-tech or manufacturing industries. China lets foreigners buy factories but insists that their output be exported, to prevent competition with Chinese companies. In Russia, the rules change from day to day and city to city.

World trade amounts to more than $6.3 trillion every year in goods and services. It would be billions more without the tariffs, quotas, inspections, rules, and other barriers that each country erects. From potato chips to computer chips, the move to free trade is more process than reality. Despite this, world trade is growing by 8 percent per year, or about three times as fast as the world economy itself.

Increasingly, jobs, too, are moving. Once-secure manufacturing jobs in Tulsa or Toulouse, in Hamburg or Houston, are vanishing as employers pick them up and transfer them abroad, in search of lower wages, weaker unions, or more congenial government regulations.

The easiest to move are those demanding the fewest skills, where strong backs count for more than strong minds. Most of those are gone already; simple assembly work has virtually disappeared from the richer nations, even Japan. But more complex assembly work is going, too. So are jobs in computer programming, data entry, travel agencies, steelmaking, auto manufacturing, banking. Some service jobs may be immovable but others are not. It's hard to get a bridge fitted by anyone except your local dentist. But the bridge itself can be made halfway around the world by technicians, earning one-tenth the American or European wage, using modern technology, working from an impression transmitted by satellite, and shipping the finished bridge by overnight courier. A local architect still designs your house, but the drawings themselves most likely will be done in a Bangkok back office by highly skilled Thai draftsmen who earn in a month what their American counterparts make in a week or less.

In this new global economy, technology—the power of the computer chip, the reach of the global satellite—is the key. Only when technology made the global economy possible did the relentless drive for profit make it happen.

If jobs move freely, people don't. A laid-off worker in California can go to Texas or Michigan in search of a new job; even Germans or Japanese, less footloose than Americans, move within their own countries. But they probably can't chase their old jobs to Indonesia or Guatemala. In many countries, laws against foreign workers, outside a few privileged categories, are all but insurmountable. Few workers have the knowledge or, especially, the languages to work in another country. To these barriers, add family ties and outright fear of the unknown, and workers seldom stray far from home. In the Midlands of England, where closed coal mines have left whole towns and villages unemployed, parents urge their sons to go on the dole rather than make the momentous move to London, let alone abroad. Even in a globalized era, fewer than 2 percent of the world's people live outside their native countries, and most of these expatriates are refugees.

In sum, globalization is happening, but it is still much easier to start a company, sell goods, or find a job inside one's own country than outside it.

There even is a globalization of ideas. At the top of the global pyramid is a village of global citizens, constantly in touch with each other by computer and satellite across oceans and continents. They are CEOs, traders, economists, corporate analysts, international lawyers, star journalists, better known to colleagues halfway around the world than they are to their nonglobal neighbors with whom they share little except a passport. Norbert Walter, the chief economist for Deutsche Bank in Frankfurt and one of the stars of this tribe, described how he edits a magazine: "We have fifty authors in fifteen places around the globe who contribute to this publication, all using the same software, sending their articles to a printer who could be anywhere, who then sends this publication back around the globe, anywhere."[4]

The rhetoric of globalization is probably a more potent force than globalization itself. An employer doesn't have to move jobs to Asia to persuade those left behind to take pay cuts. The mere possibility that, in this global age, he can do it is enough. "The possibility creates the reality," Walter said.[5] In Stuttgart, Jürgen Müller, a manager at Daimler-Benz, told me how his company's workers swiftly accepted previously taboo changes after Daimler opened more plants abroad, including one in Tuscaloosa, Alabama. "You wouldn't believe how useful the example of Tuscaloosa was in discussions with our workers here," he said.[6]

"The rhetoric of globalization already resounds from every rooftop," said David Marquand, a British political scientist. "Why deregulation? To survive the pressures of global competition. Why low taxes and impoverished public services? Because the globalization of financial markets rules out tax increases. Why falling real wages and dwindling social protection? Because our unskilled workers now have to compete with millions of hungry Asiatics, happy to work for even less."[7]

If the globalization is incomplete, it's moving fast. In a totally global economy, all markets would be "perfect." That is, the price of anything—money, goods, services, workers—would be about the same anywhere in the world. We're already there for money: the price that holders of deutsche marks or yen must pay for $1,000 is about the same, whether the transaction takes place in New York or Tokyo or Frankfurt. The price of goods, too, is evening out. As tourists are learning, it's much harder these days to get a bargain abroad than it was in the era before global markets and world trade took over.

Wages still vary widely, but not as widely as they once did. According to a theory called factor price equalization, if an object can be made in a low-wage country as well as in a high-wage country, the wages will converge over time. This is happening now, as any steelworker knows. As steelmaking has moved overseas, the wages of steelworkers in India and Brazil are going up while the wages paid by mills in America are going down. They haven't met in the middle yet, but if the trend continues, they will.

How soon? How fast is this revolution moving? Very fast, according to one of its prophets, Lowell Bryan, a senior consultant at McKinsey & Company, Inc. "We *are* moving toward a single global economy, and very quickly, in fifty to one hundred years," Bryan told me.[8] In other words, this is going to happen in the next century, and possibly within the working lives of today's students.

It will happen, that is, if it is permitted to happen. And that is up to the people to whom it will happen, and their governments. Globalization is an economic and political event that, like other economic and political events, can be controlled. Nations, acting alone or together, make choices about the kind of society they want. Globalization presents the nations of the world—particularly the wealthy nations of America, Japan, and Western Europe—with the most crucial choice since they decided to contain communism fifty years ago.

The Possibility of Choice

Globalization offers benefits in abundance—a cornucopia of new and cheaper goods and services from around the world, the boons of space-age technology, princely salaries for highly trained workers who can manipulate the information economy, and especially the chance for a decent life for millions of workers in poorer nations. No wealthy nation that claims any moral foundation at all can refuse to give these Third World workers an opportunity to share what we already enjoy.

But all this carries a high price, much of it being paid by the people and societies of the rich industrialized nations, the so-called First World. The force itself may be economic, but it is having powerful social and political effect. Generosity abroad must begin with generosity at home, or else the backlash of political resentment will deform the promise of an open world into a maze of moats and barriers.

This book will show how these wealthy nations, America and its allies, view this force and how they plan to seize its opportunities while minimizing its threats. Each is struggling with the same force but with different symptoms—the United States with falling wages, Europe with rising unemployment, Japan with stagnation. The United States tends to understate its own problems and exaggerate those of Europe and Japan. Americans give thanks that they do not have Europe's unemployment, even as the stability of their own work lives unravels and their living standards fall. "A priori, it is not clear whether the United States or the European model is preferable," writes Rebecca Blank, a Northwestern University economist. "They are simply different."[9]

A persistent theme here will be the fact that each nation can *choose* the answer to the question that begins this book: What is an economy for? The global economy is affecting the major nations in different ways, because they have made different choices. Americans tend to treat globalization as an impersonal force and feel that its effects—downsizing, wage disparity, instability—are inevitable. This is not true. Americans have these traumas because they chose them.

These nations will be treated separately, because they are very different nations. Throughout the Cold War, we viewed the world in bipolar terms. It was communism versus capitalism, a face-off between two monoliths. Communism itself was more complicated than that, as the Sino-Soviet split showed. But capitalism also was much more varied than any Cold War ideologue could admit. The end of the Cold War has brought the realization that there is not one capitalism, descended directly from Adam Smith and modeled on the American template, but a variety of capitalisms with great disparities in the roles they give to government, banks, corporations, workers, retailers, and market.

If the major economies are laid along a spectrum, the United States would be at one end, most devoted to the free market and free trade, most suspicious of government, most willing to accept both the benefits and agonies of open competition. Japan lies at the other end, with business and government so united in a web of mutual guidance and obligations that they have created a unique economy—not socialist, certainly, but not quite capitalist either. Europe lies somewhere in the middle, with a larger welfare state than either America or Japan, with more bureacracy and regulation than America, and a more open economy than Japan.

Between these mighty nations, laws vary, and so do customs. Owning different histories, they have different cultures and, hence, different economies. Even assumptions vary, and so do the answers that these nations give to our basic questions: What is an economy for? For whom does it exist?

Different Nations, Different Goals

The quick answer, which any politician would give, is that a decent capitalist economy exists to support its people. But this is not true. No major industrial nation really puts its people's wealth as its first priority. Each has other priorities, rising from its own history and character, and these priorities are dictating its response today to globalization.

The United States has stressed the strength of its giant corporations and smaller businesses. The health of the *Fortune* 500 and the vigor of the Dow Jones average have been the thermometer with which Americans took their economic temperature. When "Engine Charlie" Wilson proclaimed, "What's good for General Motors is good for America," he took heat from the nation's sophisticates but not its workers; no GM employee disagreed.

For Japan, the strength and self-sufficiency of the nation itself is paramount. The greatest traumas in the history of this insecure and lonely nation have come from outside, from its clashes with stronger powers. It is determined to control its environment, to minimize its vulnerability to what it sees as a hostile world. Corporations and government cooperate, with the acquiescence of a disciplined people, to create a tightly knit economic machine. This is Japan Inc. in action.

For Germany, the emphasis is on social harmony. Big government, big business, and big labor have cooperated to create a Social Market Economy, enshrined both in law and in custom, that sacrifices efficiency for social stability. A powerful welfare state is an expression of this national sense of mutual responsibility. Much of this springs from the teachings of a Catholic church, reinforced by generations of socialist thought; in central Europe, church and socialism owe more to each other than either cares to admit. Since 1945, this Social Market Economy has been reinforced by the memories of the Hitler era and World War II, when social harmony collapsed in an explosion that destroyed Germany and much of Europe. For a country that has much to be ashamed of in its recent history, its market is more than an economy: it is a source of national pride.

For France, state guidance of the economy has come naturally. Enshrined by Jean Baptiste Colbert, a seventeenth-century finance minister, this principle of state direction—*dirigisme* is the French word for it—has underpinned French policy for three hundred years. Elite bureaucrats recruited from the nation's top schools oversee the giant ministries and state-owned companies. Protection and subsidies, epitomized by the nation's coddled farmers, have permitted competition from abroad and a healthy private sector at home, without letting either get out of hand. It has been the very model of a mixed and managed economy.

These nations—the United States, Germany, France, and Japan—have very different goals and pursued them vigorously in the postwar years, even as they pretended that all practiced the same sort of capitalism. For each, the pursuit of these goals was immensely successful. All four prospered beyond the dreams of any nations in the history of the world. And, as they prospered, so did their people. If the well-being of the populace was not the primary motive of these economies, it was a stunning by-product.

Standards of living in all four—and in Britain, Italy, Canada, Australia, and the rest of the First World—rose to unprecedented heights. In each, broad middle classes emerged and enjoyed levels of prosperity and comfort that once were reserved for elites. As the people flourished, so did their democracy.

This political and economic strength won the Cold War. Communism failed on its own terms, but also by comparison with the record of the many capitalisms.

And now, suddenly, communism is gone. In their moment of triumph, the capitalist nations face a challenge from globalization that, if less lethal than the Soviet threat, is much more complex.

Instability and Insecurity in America

There is no good collective name for these nations which prospered so spectacularly in the postwar years. During the Cold War, they often were called the West, but Japan, the most amazing success story of them all, is in no way Western. To call them the "rich countries" sounds snide and ignores the fact that some newcomers, such as Kuwait and Singapore, have per capita incomes nearly as high. Perhaps they are best summed up as the First World. The Second World—the communist countries—is gone, and the Third World, which once implied poverty and underdevelopment, has splintered into nations and regions of widely varying development. But the First World remains—the pioneers of postwar development, the senior democracies, the repositories of much of the world's wealth, and the trustees of its economic and political stability.

We will be looking at four of these countries—the United States, Germany, France, and Japan—in later chapters. Each is a mighty and modern market economy. But each has its own unique economy that is the outgrowth of its unique history and culture. Each (unlike, say, Britain, Canada, or Italy) can be called a paradigm, a model of the market economies that make up the industrialized world. There are, in essence, four basic forms of capitalism in the First World, and these four nations define them. All four feel the winds of globalization. But their economies are so different and their experiences with globalization are so diverse that it is worth summing them up briefly here.

Globalization hit the United States first, and it is in this country that the impact has been most severe. The full force of globalization struck in the early years of the Reagan administration, a time of faith in markets and distrust of government. If America was bleeding jobs, running trade deficits, losing whole industries like television manufacturing and great chunks of other industries like steelmaking—well, this had to be the fault of inefficient managers, expensive regulations, or overpaid workers protected by corrupt unions. It occurred to few people that something was going on other than the normal working of a normal market.

This ideology left the country essentially helpless to cope with what was really happening. Millions of good industrial jobs disappeared, to be replaced by lower-paid service jobs. Beginning in the mid-1970s, wages began to fall for the least skilled and least educated. By the 1980s, as technology boomed and service jobs began to disappear, wages declined for more-skilled and better-educated workers. Increasingly, these skilled workers competed with the unskilled for the worst jobs, in a glut of job seekers that drove wages ever lower. By the 1990s, wages for all workers below the top 20 percent had fallen or stagnated. Median family wages held steady, but only because millions of women returned to the workforce; increasingly, it took two persons to earn what one person used to make.

My desk dictionary, less than ten years old, has only one definition for downsizing—"to produce smaller models or styles" of goods, like cars. Downsizing now is an economic and social byword. It means layoffs for the middle class—except that "layoffs" used to be temporary spells of unemployment for blue-collar workers during downturns at their factories. Today, neither blue-collar workers who are laid off nor white-collar workers who are downsized have any expectation of getting their old job back.

This has introduced what Edward Luttwak calls an "unprecedented sense of personal economic insecurity that has suddenly become the central phenomenon of life in America."[10] So has the nation's growing inequality between incomes, between levels of security, between living standards, between expectations. As wages fell for most workers, they skyrocketed for executives and for the minority of well-educated and highly skilled workers who can manipulate the technology and codes of the information society—the people whom former Labor Secretary Robert Reich calls "symbolic analysts."[11] The same companies that fire thousands of workers at a time give million-dollar bonuses to the executives who order the firing. As private pension plans shrink and vanish, the same executives negotiate "golden parachutes" against the day when they, too, will be downsized.

Stephen Roach, the chief economist for Morgan Stanley Dean Witter who was an early champion of globalization, American-style, wrote a dramatic mea culpa admitting that the cost has probably been too high. "The American strain of restructuring worked largely for one reason—the body politic in the U.S. was willing to accept nothing less than a dismantling of the social contract between government, corporate managements and labor. Elsewhere, the harsh extremes of the American experience simply may not be acceptable as a means to boost competitiveness."[12]

This analysis explains the great enigma of modern American life: if the economy is doing so well, why do so many Americans feel so bad? Profits have not been higher since World War II. Wall Street rejoices, and its traders rejoice along with it. American companies bestride the world, which marvels at the vigor of the U.S. economy.

But these profits and vigor rise from the ability of these mighty firms to tap the global economy, to invest wherever they want, to produce what they want with the cheapest workers they can find, to sell on the most lucrative markets and pay taxes where the rates are lowest. Back home, their workers, less mobile, wonder what happened to their lives.

There are other puzzles. Things that used to go together have become unlinked. Once, the fate of workers rose and fell with the fortunes of their employers. Not so long ago, rising productivity meant better jobs. If unemployment was low, wages would go up. None of these links holds today. In their place is a kind of economic schizophrenia, symbolized by the spurt in stock prices that greets every round of downsizing, as though bad news for employees is automatically good news for their employers.

This surrealistic inequality, the abiding sense of unfairness, and the erosion of the social compact that once bound Americans to each other menaces the balance of U.S. society. The menace can be seen in the way it has ripped apart the greatest source of strength of postwar American society, the nation's broad middle class.

This middle class was based on postwar prosperity, rising wages, confidence in personal progress, a sense of trust in both employers and government, and above all a feeling that each American had a stake in his or her country and community. That middle class has split now into three middle classes: the older middle class, which emerged from the Depression and World War II to enjoy the prosperity and security of the postwar years; the baby boomers, raised to expect prosperity but struck instead with the downsizing and insecurity of late-century America; and a younger middle class, just now coming of age, which accepts instability, embraces insecurity, and seems to expect nothing else.

This youngest middle class is the first American generation to doubt that it will enjoy a higher standard of living than its parents. Many commentators scoff that this expectation of ever-rising living standards is strictly a postwar phenomenon, a blip in a longer history of ups and downs. Not so. As Peter Drucker says, "In the developed free-market countries over the past 100 or 150 years, every generation has been able to expect to do substantially better than the generation preceding it."[13] Immigrants fled Europe for new opportunities in America. Farmers left the land for better jobs in factories.

Domestic servants left servitude for a better life in mills and stores. At each step they improved themselves economically. And each step was voluntary. The new insecurity rises from something new in the American experience—an involuntary step down.

Despite this, the American economy is often held up around the world as a model of success. Where Americans see instability, corporations and governments abroad see dynamism. The 13.5 million jobs created in the United States during the Clinton administration contrasts glaringly with double-digit unemployment in much of Europe and widespread underemployment in Japan. American companies are prospering; so are many Americans involved in the global economy, who are the Americans that foreigners most often see. In many countries, there is a feeling that the American model is inevitably the one to copy.

It may be the inevitable choice, but it's not a happy choice. Throughout Europe, the phrase *the American hire-and-fire economy* has become a cliché. Many Europeans say they realize that they must cope with globalization but want a kinder, gentler way that avoids the insecurity and destruction of the American experience.

Angst and Unraveling in Germany

"Globalization has come hand in hand with rising joblessness, job insecurity, and poverty," French President Jacques Chirac said in a widely quoted speech that summed up the European angst. "There are two faces to the threat, depending on which side of the Atlantic you look at it. Here [in Europe], the status of work is protected, but the unemployment rate stands high. There [in America], unemployment is lower but the precariousness of work is growing.

"Are we condemned to choose between the two?"

In Germany, the prized Social Market Economy has begun to unravel. Competition from low-cost, low-wage countries is gnawing at Germany's hugely popular but expensive welfare state. The same pressures are unbalancing the cooperation between big government, big labor, and big business. German companies, once committed to the German economy and German workers, are shipping production and jobs abroad, often to Central and Eastern Europe but also to the United States, which is seen there as a low-wage country.

German companies, which once focused on their obligations to workers and other "stakeholders," talk now about "shareholder value" and give their executives stock options. The same companies ignore the German tradition of cumbersome but consensual negotiations between trade unions and employers' federations, and force their workers to make concessions, including agreement to work weekends or lose their jobs. The cause: the global market.

Pressure generated both by these companies and by Germany's budget deficit is beginning to trim the welfare state for the first time since World War II. The first cuts reduced the frequency of government-paid visits to spas and authorized companies to cut sick pay from full wages, as it has been until now, to 80 percent of full wages.

To Americans, these hardships—weekend work and limited trips to the mineral baths—seem like pretty mild afflictions. Even in Europe, Germany's welfare rules and the abuse of benefits have become a continental joke. But this pampering is part and parcel of the overall social structure, the Social Market Economy, that guarantees German stability. Its philosophy is even written into Article 14 of the German constitution: "Property entails obligations. Its use should also serve the public interests."

It is one thing to bring Germany and its workers into the competitive world of the twenty-first century. It is something else to do this unilaterally, as German companies have been doing. The Social Market Economy depends on this close, often cumbersome collaboration among government, business, and labor. If any one of the three pulls out, the structure could collapse. For anyone familiar with German history in the twentieth century, this is no frivolous matter.

Flaws in France

Both France and Germany have come late to the globalization debate. Both, like the other members of the European Union, have been inward-looking, preoccupied with the creation of a single market within the EU. Germany in particular focused its money and its attention after 1989 on its reunification with the former East Germany. In both France and Germany, workers have aimed their fear and anger at visible outsiders—East Germans in Germany, Algerians in France—rather than on broader global forces that are causing the real problems.

In France, though, one issue has been decided. After three centuries, the French government has abandoned its tradition of directing a national economy that was only partly open to the outside world. The mandarins of Paris have accepted that, in an era of globalization, a middle-size country like France can no longer even try to run its own economy. They have turned instead to the European Union—fifteen nations with a total economy bigger than America's—and are trying to exercise influence and protect French interests through this bigger, more powerful body.

But this means that the EU must be ever stronger and ever more capable of acting like the national governments of old. This is the pressure behind the creation of a single currency, the Euro. The French government is determined to meet the criteria for membership in this currency union, but that requires drastic cuts in its budget deficit. As in Germany, this means a reduction in welfare benefits, including health coverage and pensions, that the French people always took for granted. It probably also means a cutback in the power and personnel of a national government that, in France, is a source of pride and admiration.

No French government, and few French citizens, want to give up France's role at the heart of Europe. But even fewer are prepared for the changes to come.

"The key question is what kind of state we want," Denis Kessler, the vice president of the Patronat, the French employers' association, told me in his Paris office. "We once had an efficient state in a closed economy. But as the economy opened, the efficiency of the state declined. Now it's not adapted to Europe."[14]

French workers have traditionally accepted relatively low wages in return for high benefits. This trade-off implies a strong and generous government. To many on the left, any change is a betrayal of this national compact.

Marc Blondel is the combative general secretary of the Force Ouvrière, the most unreconstructed of the large French unions. Blondel often sounds as if he wants to stop the world, but a substantial number of his compatriots would get off with him. In an interview, he said:

> There is a contradiction between this liberal society and people's acquired rights. Traditionally, a large part of the French way of life is collectivist. The

American approach is much more individualistic. If we go too far with this idea of competition and leave our acquired rights behind, Europe would become like China.[15]

Survival in Japan

Japan is both the most insular and the most international of economies. Intent on self-sufficiency, it invests lavishly abroad while blocking all but minimal foreign investment at home. It has run trade surpluses for decades, particularly with the United States, and has used this income not only to build its world-class industries but to subsidize inefficient companies and retailers at home. This is the key to its ability to keep unemployment at close to 3 percent and its people busy and content.

Japan calls itself a democratic country and has an elected parliament, but real power resides in the bureaucracy, especially the mighty Ministry of Finance, which controls virtually all financial life. It calls itself a capitalist country, and its companies are privately owned, but they take "advice" from the bureaucrats and exist more to strengthen Japan than to make a profit.

If globalization means the power of global markets to trump national rules and customs and invade the turf where governments reign, then Japan has more to lose than any other major nation. Indeed, its officials and businesspeople talk constantly now about Japan's recent five-year recession, about the impending death of its tradition of lifetime employment, about the growth of imports, about the way that high labor costs are forcing it to export its manufacturing base to Southeast Asia, much as American companies exported manufacturing jobs over the past twenty years. Japan, they say, is a country that must reform, must deregulate its economy, must moderate its banking and financial system. Japan, they say, "is at a crossroads."

But Japan over the years has come to more crossroads than a rural mail carrier. At each stage, its government and corporations have predicted disaster and promised reform. Each time, it has emerged stronger than ever. Each time, its "reforms" have left it looking more like Japan and less like America than before.

Japan is indisputably the winner in the emerging global economy of the last twenty years and seems unlikely to stumble now.

The reality is that, for all its hand-wringing, it isn't doing badly at all. The "recession" was no real recession—that is, not a downturn in national output—but a run of slow growth. National savings remain high, giving Japan an ocean of money, some $6 trillion, which amounts to 52 percent of all the savings in the industrialized world.

Some industry has indeed gone overseas, mostly to Southeast Asia. But overseas manufacturing by Japanese companies accounts for 8.4 percent of the nation's gross domestic product, compared to more than 22 percent for U.S. companies. More important, this exported industry is mostly in relatively low-skill, low-tech, low-profit areas, such as television sets and cheaper cars. The high-price, high-value, highest-technology production—high-speed printers, high-end flat panel displays, futuristic medical equipment, luxury cars—has stayed at home. "Japan didn't die after all," said Edward J. Lincoln, a Brookings Institution scholar who spent three years as an economic officer at the American embassy in Tokyo. I spoke with Lincoln at the end of his Tokyo assignment. Like many foreign experts in Japan, he was more ready to believe the evidence of his eyes than the cries of doom and forecasts of reform coming from the ministries and boardrooms.

"Can Japan survive now in a global economy?" Lincoln asked. "My guess is, it will. It will evolve, and it will loosen its government controls moderately, but not so far that the government loses most of its ability to manipulate and influence the economy. And this will work, for the same reason it has in the past."[16]

To Japan, globalization is a one-way street. It wants to exploit the new freedom to act on a global stage but intends to give the rest of the world no bigger share of its own economy than necessary. Will this work? As Lincoln said, why not? It always has.

The Power of the Market

How much of this global upheaval can be attributed to the global economy itself? Not all, of course, but a lot. The computer and its capabilities would change our lives—destroying old jobs, creating new ones, altering virtually every workplace—whether the rest of the world existed or not. Trade has always been with us, and imports from Third-World nations amount to barely 2 percent of the U.S. gross national product. Not all jobs will go abroad, and of those that can, not all will. American, Japanese, and European workers still have skills, knowledge, and habits that cannot be found in the newly industrializing nations of the Third World.

But globalization is already a powerful force, and as it develops, that power will only grow. Already, the virtually complete global financial market is driving changes that seem far removed from normal global competition.

It seems obvious that manufacturers of cars and steel, purchasers of computer software, and makers of running shoes will seek workers where the wages are lowest and the work quality is adequate. But the global financial market has given opportunities for efficiencies, scale, and profit to any company big enough to take advantage of them.

Wal-Mart, for instance, can go anywhere to borrow, and will borrow at rates unavailable to smaller companies because it can promise efficiencies that are beyond these companies. It can promise these efficiencies because it can scour the world for suppliers and, through its sheer size, dictate terms to those suppliers. Wal-Mart in fact is less a company than an economy. It is not only the twelfth biggest corporation in the world but the forty-second biggest economy, with sales greater than the annual gross domestic product of Poland, Israel, Greece, or Singapore.[17] Its technology gives it the best warehouses and distribution that money can buy. Communications keep its stores in instant and constant contact with headquarters in Arkansas and with suppliers around the world. In the process, of course, Wal-Mart wipes out local mom-and-pop stores and their suppliers wherever it sets up shop. But this is of no interest to the global financial markets, which care only about the profits that Wal-Mart delivers so reliably.

The same is true for Starbucks Coffee, Domino's Pizza, and Toys "Я" Us. It is true for companies that make goods or companies that sell goods. It is true for service companies, for wholesalers and retailers, for media companies, for companies that make the world's pharmaceuticals, and companies that collect and process society's waste.

All get their financing from global financial markets and globalizing stock markets that demand maximum return and relentless efficiency. Often, technology produces this efficiency. Too often, employees are considered a drag on efficiency, and hence a drag on profits. So the once-comfortable nations of America, Europe, and Japan ring with the cries of the downsized or quake with the fears of workers who, after a lifetime on the job, realize that they are seen not as members of a corporate family but as problems to be solved. McKinsey's Lowell Bryan, in a book written with Diana Farrell and called *Market Unbound*, put it enthusiastically if bluntly:

> An unfettered, unrelenting search for global profits is now well launched. At the core of global capitalism is the equity shareholder and the investor market that owns equities. Equity investors will demand globally competitive returns to capital. . . . Sleepy companies and sleepy industries, worldwide, will become a thing of the past.[18]

But a totally efficient world would be a world without string quartets, idle thought, or generosity. It would be a world of all Starbucks and no dusty corner coffee shops run for no other reason than the pleasure of the proprietor and his or her guests. It would be a world like the one envisaged in 1819 by the Swiss critic Simonde de Sismondi. When David Ricardo, the British economist, asserted that employment was unimportant so long as profits flowed, de Sismondi replied wryly, "There is nothing more to wish for than that the king, remaining alone on the island, by constantly turning a crank, might produce, through automata, all the output of England."[19]

The automata have multiplied since 1819. So has the demand for profits. Neither will disappear, nor should they. But they must be put to the service of people and their societies, not the other way around. The lead must be taken by the United States and its allies. They must act together because global markets, by definition, are beyond the control, if not the influence, of any national government, even one as powerful as the American one.

The World Is a Business, Mr. Beale!

The movie *Network* has entered the history of pop culture through the cry of its hero, television anchorman Howard Beale, that "I'm mad as hell and I'm not going to take it anymore." Few people remember another speech from that movie, a tirade by a tycoon named Arthur Jensen, whose company is Howard Beale's sponsor.

Paddy Chayefsky wrote *Network* in 1976, when the global economy was just beginning to take shape, but the powerful, prescient words he put in Arthur Jensen's mouth still dramatize both the dream and the menace of this economy:

> Mr. Beale, you are an old man who thinks in terms of nations and peoples. There are no nations! There are no peoples! There are no Russians! There are no Arabs! There are no Third Worlds! There is no West! There is only one holistic system of systems, one vast and immane, interwoven, interacting, multivariate, multinational dominion of dollars! Petro-dollars, electro-dollars, multi-dollars, Reichmarks, rubles, rin, pounds and shekels! It is the international system of currency that determines the totality of life on this planet! That is the natural order of things today! It is the atomic, subatomic and galactic structure of things today!
>
> You get up on your little 21-inch screen, Mr. Beale, and howl about America and democracy. There is no America. There is no democracy. There is only IBM and ITT and AT&T and du Pont, Dow, Union Carbide and Exxon. Those are the nations of the world today.
>
> We no longer live in a world of nations and ideologies, Mr. Beale. The world is a college of corporations, inexorably determined by the immutable bylaws of business. The world is a business, Mr. Beale! It has been that way since man crawled out of the slime and our children, Mr. Beale, will live to see that perfect world without war and famine, oppression and brutality—one vast and ecumenical holding company, for whom all men will work to serve a common profit, in which all men will hold a share of stock, all necessities provided, all anxieties tranquilized, all boredom amused.[20]

The present world order is breaking up, and a new order, celebrated by Arthur Jensen, is taking shape. The old order had its shortcomings and inequities, but it served the great majority of its people better than any order in history. What is coming is another, but not necessarily better, order. This is not the normal evolution of companies and industries, but a revolution whose outlines, dimly seen by Paddy Chayefsky in 1976, are becoming clearer now.

The erosion of the old order and the struggle of nations to shape its replacement are the subjects of this book.

2. STALKING WOOLLY MAMMOTHS

WHILE YOU ARE reading this, a German businessman in a Swiss airliner somewhere over France will pick up the airplane's telephone and buy American dollars with Japanese yen on the London financial markets. At a factory in China, Chinese workers will make parts for Airbus and Boeing airliners that used to be made in Bremen or Seattle. In a guarded industrial zone in western Java, hundreds of Indonesian women in a plant owned by South Koreans will make Nike shoes; the women earn about $10 per week. Posters on the wall proclaim the Nike slogan: "Just Do It."

On the edge of a village in the remote central hills of Cyprus, a motorist will buy gas from a twenty-four-hour, totally self-service station that takes only Eurocards or Visa cards and employs no one. In tense and busy offices in New York, Tokyo, and London, the lavishly paid employees of some fifty global investment and commercial banks will trade no less than $1.3 trillion on this day. Mostly young, very smart, as clannish as Kurds, they are the masters of this universe. In Brussels, European Union officials know that the biggest barrier to the introduction of a single European currency, which will complete their single market, is not political opposition from Europeans but the skepticism of these traders that Europe can pull it off.

27

In Bangalore, India, computer programmers will write state-of-the-art computer software for American firms like Motorola and Intel, but for wages only one-tenth as high as those prevailing in Silicon Valley. In the dusty mountains of El Salvador's Morazán Province, where winter never comes, dozens of former refugees, resettled by the U.N. after the country's civil war ended, work in a long brick shed sewing quilted panels for parkas to be worn in the snows of New England by American children. In a luxury restaurant in Hamburg, two German businessmen in red sport coats and pink shirts try to sell machine tools to two Japanese businessmen impeccably dressed in dark suits. All four speak the lingua franca of the global economy: bad English.

"What's the difference between the American, Japanese, and Korean brands?" I asked the salesman in Chicago trying to sell me a new television set. He laughed. "The Korean sets are made in Malaysia, the Japanese sets are made in the United States, and the American brands, which are owned by the Japanese and Koreans, are made in Mexico."

These are glimpses of the global economy at work. They are only glimpses because this economy is too big and complex to be seen whole. More important, it is growing and changing by the day as the process known as globalization sweeps the world before it.

The previous chapter gave an overview of globalization and the way the major nations of America, Europe, and Japan are reacting to it. In later chapters, we will explore these national reactions in greater depth. This chapter will take a closer look at globalization itself, its components, and how it is shaping the global economy.

A Truly Different Economy

Some economists and historians say that the global economy really is nothing new. We've been here before, they say. Paul Krugman, an economist at the Massachusetts Institute of Technology, notes the expansion in world trade and investment that occurred in the nineteenth century. With the British Empire leading the way, this internationalization flourished through the belle epoque, only to collapse beneath the shattering effects of two world wars and the Depression.

After World War II, this new international economy began to grow again, behind American leadership this time. "But it wasn't until 1970 that the world got back to its 1913 level," Krugman said.[1] The oil crisis derailed this process briefly in the mid-1970s. The latest and by far the strongest wave of globalization dates from the 1980s and is powered by technology.

Krugman is right that international trade and investment have been with us for centuries. Marco Polo's family first went to Cathay in the thirteenth century as traders. The great empires were based on trade. The United States borrowed heavily from European banks in the nineteenth century to develop its interior. Many of the great international banks that lead today's global markets have their roots in the international markets of another era. Renaissance Europe was largely financed by the Lombard banks of Italy.

Yet it's possible to have too much perspective. This long view obscures the fact that what is happening today is truly different and is creating a world economy that is as different from that of the belle epoque as the Information Revolution is from the Industrial Revolution. We have always had the shifting of the economic tides, with the rise of some industries and the fall of others. This goes on constantly in a dynamic economy and is to be wished, not opposed. What is happening now is a revolution, a totally new economy, the sort of upheaval that happens once a century but never so fast as it is happening now.

What existed before was an international economy—that is, commerce between nations, in which national governments set the rules. Usually, one government was the undisputed leader—Britain in the nineteenth century, the United States after World War II. What exists now is increasingly a global economy, with merchants and financiers treating the world as one big market. If national frontiers are not as irrelevant yet as state borders, the ability of governments to set and enforce the rules is severely weakened. There is no one guiding power, not even the United States. Global markets rule, not governments.

There are many reasons for this, including changing trade, spreading investment, developing technology, the growth of powerful corporations, the new dominance of global finance. The following sections discuss them separately, but only for the sake of simplicity. In practice, they interlock, reinforce, and strengthen each other to create globalization, a force that is greater than the sum of its parts.

The Myth of Free Trade

Free trade gets good press, and no wonder. Who could oppose something that sounds so good? Like "free markets," the idea of "free trade" is a no-lose motherhood issue for any politician or editorial writer. But the best things in life aren't always "free." Free love is destructive. A free lunch sounds good, but as we all know, there ain't no such thing. Freebasing can kill. So can a free fall. A freeloader is a pest. A freelancer is often a downsized wage slave. And a freebooter is nothing but a pirate.

In short, beware terminology. Especially when it deals with trade.

World trade is based on the idea that each nation should make what it makes best and most cheaply, and then trade those wares to another nation for what that nation makes best and most cheaply. In the process, both nations will prosper and will have access to better goods than if they tried to do it all themselves. This is the principle of "comparative advantage." It underlies the theory of free trade. It powered fifty years of international trade negotiations that produced first the General Agreement on Tariffs and Trade (GATT) and its successor, the World Trade Organization (WTO).

It also has very little to do with trade in the real world of the global economy.

Trade is a powerful force in this world, and often a positive one. It creates millions of jobs and great industries. It brings the best of the world's products to the shelves of stores around the globe. It expands both choice and competition. When goods travel, so do the ideas that created them and the skills that made them. A world without trade would literally be a poorer place. The Soviet Union tried to live without trade, which was one reason foreign visitors always described it as "drab."

But trade as it exists today bears little resemblance to the textbook image dear to the hearts of free traders, for several reasons. One reason deals with the ability of giant firms to create comparative advantage and move it around the globe. If world trade used to take place between companies in different countries, it goes on as often now between branches of the same company operating in many countries. International investment is crucial to this process. A single company will set up plants or subsidiaries in six or eight or ten countries, or form ad hoc partnerships with companies around the globe, to produce parts and components wherever the costs are lowest and conditions best. The products then are shipped to yet another country for assembly. With global communications, the costs and complications of being thousands of miles away from headquarters vanish. With global shipping, the costs of transportation don't begin to outweigh the savings in wages, raw materials, and taxes that can be gained from global manufacturing.

The result is that 40 to 50 percent of world trade is not between countries but between different parts of global companies. I visited a Caterpillar factory near Toronto that took in parts from other Caterpillar factories around the world—winches from Brazil, engines from Japan, axles from Belgium, transmissions from the United States—and put them all into equipment that was to be exported to countries around the world, including Brazil, Japan, Belgium, and the United States.

This is but one example; virtually every major corporation today could tell the same story. 3M makes tapes in Bangalore. BMW has shifted the production of cloth for auto seats from Bavaria to the Czech Republic, where wages are one-eighth the German level, and then ships the cloth back to Germany, where the seats are still assembled. Ford, NEC, and Thomson make auto parts, computer chips, and consumer electronics, as they always did, but they make them all over the globe, often collaborating in one country with firms that are hot competitors elsewhere. For example, NEC of Japan and Samsung of Korea make DRAM computer chips in collaboration in Europe. Between 1973 and 1976, there were only 86 such international collaborations; between 1985 and 1988, there were 988.

These are not cases of countries taking advantage of their natural comparative advantages to make goods that can be sold freely to less-favored countries. They are cases of companies using technology to create comparative advantage where none existed before, to build enclosed and controlled trading systems.

If most of this global investment has been in manufacturing, services are not far behind, much of it inevitably in information industries. Motorola has set up computer-programming and equipment design centers in China, India, Singapore, Hong Kong, Taiwan, and Australia. In Kingston, Jamaicans process reservations and tickets for major international airlines. In county Cork, 150 Irish employees analyze medical insurance claims for Metropolitan Life to determine

Exhibit 2.1

World's Top 100 Economies, 1995

Corporations in italics

Country/Corporation	GDP/Sales ($mil)		Country/Corporation	GDP/Sales ($mil)
1 United States	6,648,013		24 Indonesia	174,640
2 Japan	4,590,971		25 *Itochu*	*169,300*
3 Germany	2,045,991		26 *General Motors*	*168,829*
4 France	1,330,381		27 *Sumitomo*	*167,662*
5 Italy	1,024,634		28 *Marubeni*	*161,184*
6 United Kingdom	1,017,306		29 Denmark	146,076
7 Brazil	554,306		30 Thailand	143,209
8 Canada	542,954		31 *Ford Motors*	*137,137*
9 China	522,172		32 Hong Kong	131,881
10 Spain	482,841		33 Turkey	131,014
11 Mexico	377,115		34 South Africa	121,888
12 Russian Federation	376,555		35 Saudi Arabia	117,236
13 Korea, Rep.	376,505		36 *Toyota Motor*	*111,139*
14 Australia	331,505		37 *Royal Dutch/Shell*	*109,853*
15 Netherlands	329,768		38 Norway	109,568
16 India	293,606		39 *Exxon*	*107,893*
17 Argentina	281,922		40 *Nissho Iwai*	*97,963*
18 Switzerland	260,352		41 Finland	97,961
19 Belgium	227,550		42 *Wal-Mart*	*93,627*
20 Austria	196,546		43 Poland	92,580
21 Sweden	196,441		44 Ukraine	91,307
22 *Mitsubishi Trading Co.*	*184,510*		45 Portugal	87,257
23 *Mitsui and Co. Trading*	*181,661*		46 *Hitachi*	*84,233*

eligibility for reimbursement. "This is not grunt work," *Fortune* magazine said in an article on these workers. "It demands considerable knowledge of medicine, the American medical system, and the insurance business."

Wal-Mart Is Bigger than Poland

Many of these companies are literally bigger than the countries where they operate, according to a fascinating report by the Institute for Policy Studies in Washington, D.C. The study compared the gross domestic products of the world's countries with the annual sales of its biggest firms. By this standard, the report said, only forty-nine

Exhibit 2.1 (continued)

Country/Corporation	GDP/Sales ($mil)	Country/Corporation	GDP/Sales ($mil)
47 Nippon Tel. and Tel.	82,002	74 Nichimen	50,882
48 AT&T	79,609	75 New Zealand	50,777
49 Israel	77,777	76 Tokyo Electric Power	50,343
50 Greece	77,721	77 Peru	50,077
51 Daimler-Benz	72,253	78 Kanematsu	49,878
52 IBM	71,940	79 Unilever	49,638
53 Malaysia	70,626	80 Nestlé	47,767
54 Matsushita Electric	70,454	81 Sony	47,619
55 General Electric	70,028	82 Fiat Group	46,467
56 Singapore	68,949	83 VEBA Group	46,278
57 Tomen	67,809	84 NEC	45,593
58 Colombia	67,266	85 Honda Motor	44,090
59 Mobil	64,767	86 UAP–Union des Assurances	43,929
60 Philippines	64,162	87 Allianz Worldwide	43,486
61 Iran	63,716	88 Egypt	42,923
62 Nissan Motor	62,618	89 Algeria	41,941
63 Volkswagen Group	61,487	90 Elf Aquitaine Group	41,729
64 Siemens Group	60,673	91 Hungary	41,374
65 Venezuela	58,257	92 Philips Group	40,146
66 British Petroleum	56,992	93 Fujitsu	39,007
67 Bank of Tokyo–Mitsubishi	55,243	94 Indust. Bank of Japan	38,694
68 Chrysler	53,195	95 Deutsche Bank Group	38,418
69 Philip Morris	53,139	96 Renault Group	36,876
70 Toshiba	53,089	97 Mitsubishi Motors	36,674
71 Ireland	52,060	98 du Pont de Nemours	36,508
72 Pakistan	52,011	99 Mitsubishi Electric	36,408
73 Chile	51,957	100 Hoechst Group	36,407

of the world's one hundred biggest economies are nation states. The other fifty-one, a majority, are corporations (see Exhibit 2.1).

The twenty-one biggest economies, of course, are still countries, including the United States, Japan, and other First-World nations. Sweden is number twenty-one. From then on, corporations dominate the list. Two giant Japanese trading companies, Mitsubishi and Mitsui, are the twenty-second and twenty-third biggest economic powers in the world, bigger than Indonesia. General Motors Corporation, with $168 billion in sales in 1995, ranked twenty-sixth, bigger than Denmark or Thailand. Ford Motor Company is bigger than Turkey or South Africa. Wal-Mart is bigger than Poland, Ukraine, Portugal, Israel, or Greece. Altogether, the world's 200 biggest corporations control no less than 28 percent of the globe's economic activity, the report said.[2]

The institute's listing has been criticized for overestimating the corporations' power, by basing it on their annual sales instead of net earnings, which would have subtracted their substantial payments to suppliers and employees. In fact, the listing probably underestimated this power. The corporations' sheer size gives them a day-by-day dominance over both suppliers and employees that even governments, except the most tyrannical, would be hard put to match.

As these giant firms become global, they shake off their ties to any one country, even the one of their birth. Japanese firms, with the possible exception of Sony, retain a powerful attachment to Japan. But is Ford or Coca-Cola still American, or Siemens still German, or Philips still Dutch? Their headquarters remain where they have always been, but their boards and management are becoming increasingly international. A British citizen, Alex Trotman, is CEO of Ford. How long before a non-German becomes CEO of Siemens or a non-Japanese head of Sony? And how long before these nonnative executives decide to move their headquarters somewhere closer to their homes, just as so many American CEOs moved home offices of firms away from the cities where they were born and closer to their own suburban or Sun Belt homes? The *D* in Dasa, which is the aerospace arm of Daimler-Benz, Germany's biggest firm, used to stand for *Deutsche*; it's been changed to *Daimler-Benz*, a conscious step away from Dasa's German identity. As global telecommunications are liberalized, how long will the national telephone companies—Deutsche Telekom, British Telecom, Nippon Telegraph & Telephone—retain their national identities? Will the *A* in AT&T always stand for *American*?

One other facet of this multinational investment has created a problem that no nation has solved. Being footloose, these companies can arrange their pricing to achieve their profits in the countries where tax rates are lowest and tax inspectors most accommodating. Many of the world's biggest firms are global tax dodgers. In the short run, the losers are the societies everywhere they do business. In the long run, these global tax dodgers may be undermining the very global economy that has made them so prosperous. The reason is explained later in this chapter.

Japan Rigs the Market

Nations can also create comparative advantage within their borders. If they are single-minded enough, they can skew the terms of world trade to their advantage and prosper at the expense of their trading partners. In its ideal, trade is supposed to be a positive-sum game, in which both sides gain. But it becomes a zero-sum game, with a winner and a loser, if one side makes up its own rules and plays by them. This is what happened in the West's trade relationship with Japan, and it has forced a rethinking of trade policy, especially in the United States.

America has run record trade deficits for years, because Japan rigged the market. According to classic trade theory, persistent trade deficits cause an outflow of the deficit country's currency, as it spends more abroad than it earns at home. This outflow weakens the currency—in this case, the U.S. dollar—and lowers its value on world money markets. This cheaper currency in turn makes that country's goods cheaper on world markets, while other countries' goods become more expensive. As the prices shift, so does the trade balance; the deficit country buys fewer expensive goods abroad and sells more of its own, cheaper exports. The deficit shrinks and the problem is solved.

This theory works in the trade relationship between the United States and the developed nations of Western Europe. Over the years, these transatlantic partners have fought plenty of small trade battles, mostly over Europe's relatively protected farm market and the U.S. penchant for acting unilaterally outside world trade rules when it feels it has been damaged. But the battles have been settled peacefully. When the United States is in deficit to Europe, a weaker dollar usually sets the balance right, and vice versa. Over the past twenty years, transatlantic trade has been roughly in balance.

This just isn't true with Japan. Since 1980, Japan has run steady and growing trade surpluses with the United States and equally steady, if smaller, surpluses with the European nations. Since the mid-1980s, these surpluses with the United States have usually been between $40 billion and $60 billion per year. The contrast with Europe is startling. Between 1980 and 1992, America's total trade cumulative deficit with Europe was about $10 billion. During the same thirteen years, America's total trade deficit with Asia was $882 billion, most of it with Japan.

Over the same time, the yen has fallen from 260 to the dollar to only 80, before rising again to 120. Theoretically, this stronger yen and weaker dollar should have shrunk the U.S. trade deficit with Japan to nothing. Instead, it has had almost no effect at all. Something is going on that the textbooks haven't told us about.

A generation of study by American scholars, led by the University of California's Chalmers Johnson and Clyde Prestowitz of the Economic Strategy Institute, has uncovered a pattern of mercantilism that has tilted the playing field sharply to Japan's advantage. A pattern of protectionism and aggressive trade, built into Japan's history and culture, will be explored more deeply in Chapter 5, but can be summarized here.

How Japan Does It

Basically Japan, an island nation that has never been on easy terms with its neighbors, has always tried to be as self-sufficient as possible, to reduce its dependence on and vulnerability to that world. This attitude, and the world's reaction to it, led to Pearl Harbor. The militarism of World War II stirs only a faint echo in Japan today, but the attitude behind it lives on in Japan's trade policy.

After the war and with the blessing of the American Occupation, Japan rebuilt its economy behind a screen of high tariffs and quotas. Mighty conglomerates and cartels, called *keiretsu*, emerged from the ashes of the prewar *zaibatsu* and grew up to dominate the economy. The traditional cooperative relations between government and business reemerged, and government bureaucrats resumed their practice of "guiding" industry to produce results that strengthened the nation as a whole. Again with the Occupation's permission, American and other foreign companies were all but forbidden from majority ownership of important Japanese firms, and foreign manufacturers were barred from building factories. Huge pools of savings, overseen by the all-powerful Ministry of Finance, gave Japanese companies access to cheap and easy finance.

All this enabled Japanese companies, such as automakers, to develop and improve their products through fierce competition at home, protected from imports from more advanced industries abroad. This competition focused on quality, not price; because cheaper imports were all but banned, Japanese companies could charge as much as they wanted. In the 1960s, the Japanese companies, led by television producers and automakers, attacked foreign markets, particularly in the United States. *Attacked*, in fact, is the only word for this campaign. Armed with war chests built up through high profits at home, the Japanese exporters undercut the prices of their American competitors ruthlessly. Determined to dominate, they seized whole industries in consumer electronics, auto parts, and, later, in manufacturing computers and computer chip components.

When foreigners complained, the Japanese lowered tariffs until they were, on average, as low as any in the world. But in a world of floating currencies, tariffs are little more than symbolic, usually 5 percent or less. Whenever a nation's currency rises or falls by 5 percent on world currency markets, its exports become that much more expensive or cheaper, and the tariff becomes meaningless. This is not theoretical. In 1995 the dollar dropped by more than 5 percent against the yen for three months running, then rose by 50 percent over the next year.

As tariffs disappeared, quotas remained and a network of "non-tariff barriers"—so-called health and safety standards, quality standards, and the like—grew up to block any import that Japan wanted to keep out. Much of Japan's imports are controlled by mammoth trading houses linked to both manufacturers and retailers through the *keiretsu*. As noted, the trading houses of two of these *keiretsu*, Mitsubishi and Mitsui, are by themselves the two biggest corporations in the world. Thus, one part of the *keiretsu* had the power to keep Japanese shelves free of foreign goods that might compete with the products of another part of the *keiretsu*. Government bureaucrats steered contracts to Japanese companies. A strong farm lobby kept out any farm product, especially rice, that might compete with Japanese farmers.

This protectionism raised prices for Japanese consumers, as American propagandists are forever telling the Japanese. There is no indication that the Japanese even care. If living standards in Japan are marginally lower than those in the West, this is more than compensated in Japanese eyes by the strength of the nation and the security of Japanese lives—assets more prized there than in the United States.

A Different System

Japan has been able to pursue this policy for several reasons. First, it succeeded. For years, Japan has had the biggest trade surpluses, lowest unemployment, lowest inflation, and highest savings of any major nation. Second, this policy seems to enjoy overwhelming support at home. Third, the profits of this policy have bought regiments of lobbyists and political power abroad, plus a major industrial presence in the United States and Europe through direct investment there.

Finally, it took a long time for Americans to figure out what was going on, and some American economists and editorial writers still deny the evidence of their own eyes. Americans have always assumed that free markets were a prerequisite for success; if Japan was successful, it must be as devoted as America to free markets. The ability of Japanese exporters to drive American companies to the wall must be the fault of the Americans, grown fat and lazy through years of industrial dominance. The fact that American companies *had* become complacent and that Japanese goods often *did* show superior quality reinforced this belief, although it did not explain why American exports were doing so well elsewhere in the world. In due time, Americans improved quality and raised efficiency to Japanese standards. But this made no dent in the Japanese trade surplus. Neither did the rising yen and falling dollar.

Something else was causing that surplus. By now, all but the most unreconstructed free marketeers understand the structure of the Japanese economy, which still attacks foreign markets behind a shield of government cooperation and huge profits gleaned from protected markets at home.

Japan, in short, focuses on its producers, the United States on its consumers. Japan sees virtue in cartels, managed trade, and high prices, the United States in antitrust, free trade, and low prices. Neither is right nor wrong, but the difference gives Japan a built-in advantage in trade. This is more than economic theory. This is a difference in culture. Americans raised in one culture have had a terrible time understanding the imperatives of Japan.

When foreign governments have tried to change this Japanese structure, they usually have failed. Decades of U.S.-Japanese negotiations have produced more hard feelings than progress. The main reason, again, is the unique structure of the Japanese economy. The line between private business and government in Japan is so fuzzy that it is hard for foreigners to pinpoint responsibility for specific trade barriers. Many of the barriers are administered by the *keiretsu* and so lie beyond the government's ability to change.

But a major factor in the successful Japanese resistence to foreign pressure is that the Japanese system, while antithetical to Western ideals, is perfectly legal by the trade rules written by the Western governments themselves. Under the principle of "most favored nation," governments promise to treat all trading partners alike and to give no special advantage to one country without giving it to others. This principle underlies the ideal of free trade. The problem is that Japan does treat all its trading partners alike: none gets free access. But the United States or any Western nation would violate this principle of equal treatment if it singled out Japan for retaliation. This was a Catch-22 so thorny that any attempt to circumvent it could bring down the whole trading system.

China: The Next Power

But the trading system is in peril anyway, because the Japanese system of managed trade has become a model for other, fast-industrializing Asian nations, especially China. These nations are powerfully influenced by Japan, which is often the leading investor in their economies. They are attracted by the Japanese success. Often, they see little of value in Western civilization and its principles, including the principle of free trade.

This spread of the Japanese system would cause trouble under any circumstances to a world trading system based on Western ideas. Throw China into this mix, and the problems become explosive. Japan, for all its mercantilist ways, is basically a market economy based on private ownership. China is a nonmarket economy with a state sector that will remain central for the foreseeable future. Japan is a medium-sized nation with a limited workforce that has shared in its nation's prosperity. China is a vast nation with the biggest potential workforce in the world, some 600 or 700 million persons, most of them still outside the mainstream economy. It will be decades before China runs out of unused workers and is forced to begin raising wages.

How will the world trading system, as presently structured, cope with the sudden addition of hundreds of millions of Chinese—or of Indians, for that matter—working at minimum wages, whose goods will flood global markets to compete with products produced in Japan, Europe, or America by workers earning vastly higher wages? The answer is that it probably can't cope. If Western and Japanese wages fall to Chinese levels, the backlash from workers will destroy the system.

About 1.2 billion Third-World workers are about to enter the world economy, Yale historian Paul Kennedy has said. "How on earth does one reconcile their interests—their quite legitimate interests—with those of the 250 million North American and European workers who earn 30 times as much?"[3] The alternative is a worldwide system of managed trade, closer to the Japanese than the American model, to keep this flood of Chinese goods from inundating First-World civilization.

"The free trade system has lasted this long so far only because China and India are not in it," said Richard Koo, the highly regarded senior economist for Nomura Research Institute Ltd. in Tokyo:

> The United States started this system after the war and other countries joined in. Japan is not a full member even yet, but it played the game, through its exports—just as Korea and Taiwan have done since and China is beginning to do. Japan is certainly not a free trader. But if the problem is just Japan, it's tolerable. It's not devastating to the whole system. But if China plays the game like the Japanese have done, the system is not going to last without safeguards. We can get even with the Japanese, by driving the yen high enough. But with the Third World—there's no end to it.[4]

Many Westerners comfort themselves with the belief that it will be many years before China's relatively primitive economy will be able to cope with sophisticated, high-profit Western goods such as airliners, automobiles, electronics, and pharmaceuticals. To these Pollyannas, I can only say, Read on.

China Calls the Tune

As we have seen, much of the real action in trade lies in the investment policies of governments and global corporations. Sometimes corporations may be bigger and more powerful than the governments themselves. In these cases, they can demand concessions as the price for the investment. These concessions, too, often are at the expense of workers—a union-free environment, low wages, lax health and safety standards. Governments, which should be defending their own work-ers, give in to these demands because they want the foreign investment so badly. When Western governments tried to get the World Trade Organization to adopt a code of minimum labor standards, the indus-trializing nations of Southeast Asia refused, fearing these standards would raise their labor costs and frighten off foreign investment. In the end, the Southeast Asians prevailed, and the code died.

Sometimes the government is strong enough to demand conces-sions. The prime example is China, which insists that almost all pro-duction by foreign-owned factories there be exported. Exports of foreign-owned firms in China have risen from 1 percent of Chinese exports in 1985 to more than 33 percent now. Already, China's trade surplus with the United States has passed that of Japan. But so far, these Chinese exports have been mostly low-end goods, such as clothing and toys, that do not compete directly with American-made goods or, unlike the Japanese exports, take away American jobs.

That comforting fact is about to change. China is a developing country in every sense of the word. It has every intention of upgrad-ing its exports from clothing and toys to high-end, high-tech, high-profit goods such as cars, electronics, and pharmaceuticals. Already, it is exporting radio receivers and transmitters, scientific equipment, and electronics equipment. And it is using its trade and investment policies to force Western companies to help it achieve this mastery, which it clearly intends to employ to compete with these countries in the future.[5]

Western and Japanese companies that want to invest in China are forced to bring in modern technology and teach the Chinese how to use it. The foreign companies gain from the work of the low-paid but well-educated Chinese workforce and from the promise of even-tual access to the unimaginably huge future Chinese market. This access, in fact, is the bait that China uses to get this technology. West-ern aircraft makers and other exporters have learned that they can make sales to China only if they build parts factories there and teach the Chinese their business. But the Westerners know perfectly well that they are giving away their trade secrets and techniques and that this gift will come back to haunt them when a stronger, more pro-ficient China becomes a competitor in its own right. The scramble for global markets is such that they can't help themselves.

There is one other aspect to this foreign investment that, like so much of globalization, is good for the company that does it but no help to that company's employees back home. As Third-World companies develop, so does their people's taste for the consumer goods that the industrial countries produce in such abundance. Once, Western countries expected these growing markets, like India, to be great sponges for their exports. These markets are indeed growing, and Western companies are indeed selling consumer goods there. But for the most part, these companies have invested in factories in the countries themselves. Companies like Procter & Gamble have found a rich market in India, but this market is being fed not by exports from P&G plants in the United States, but from their new plants in India.

The Toughness of Trade

All this makes world trade a more complex and—until now—a stronger creature than is usually believed. In good times and bad, trade grows steadily by about 4 to 8 percent per year (see Exhibit 2.2). In other words, it usually grows two to four times faster than the international economy itself. From time to time, unions or companies have urged their governments to get tough with another nation over some real or perceived sin in trade policy. Such demands arise frequently in the United States over Japanese protectionism or Europe's protected farm market. These demands usually are countered by warnings that a get-tough policy will lead to a trade war that could threaten the entire structure of the world trading system. The warnings are supported by diplomats, who dislike unpleasantness, and by free traders, who distrust any government interference in trade. They are supported, naturally, by lobbyists for those, like the Japanese, who would be on the receiving end of any get-tough approach. Their joint theme is that trade is a tender flower that must be carefully protected from the rough-and-tumble of international politics.

Over the years, I became a battle-hardened war correspondent in any number of trade skirmishes between the United States and the European Union. My memory recalls the Brandy War, the Chicken War, the Cheese War, even the awful Offal War. All received their transient headlines and were settled in due time by diplomats earn-

Exhibit 2.2

Total World Trade
(in trillions of dollars)

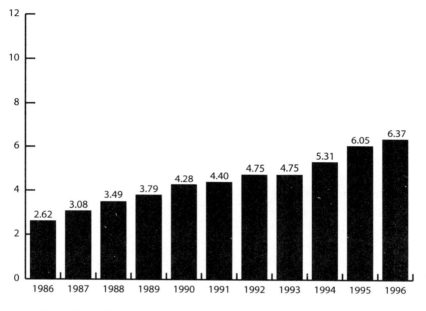

Source: World Trade Organization.

ing their pay, leaving the world trade system not only standing but strengthened through compromises that managed to increase the sales and prosperity of both sides.

I came to feel that world trade is hardier than many of its defenders think. The free traders see every trade squabble and proposed restriction as a return to the 1930s and the Smoot-Hawley Tariff Act of 1930, which is blamed for deepening the Depression. In fact, Smoot-Hawley was a blunt instrument—it sent tariffs soaring on about half of all U.S. imports—and it came at a time when the world's economic integration had already been undermined by World War I and the Wall Street crash.

By 1970, as Paul Krugman noted, the world economy had returned to its peak levels of integration of the belle epoque. Since then, it has become more integrated and more global by the day—immeasurably more tightly woven than it was in 1910 or 1930. Governments already are deeply involved in trade, and so are powerful corporations. Together they form a thick web of vested interests that cannot possibly be ripped apart by any dispute over auto parts or labor standards.

It is hard to think of anything that could seriously damage this structure of trade and investment. Hard, but not impossible. Another round of world wars and depressions would do it, but these happily are remote fears. The undigestible competition of China and other Third World economies will strain this trade structure severely. But the real threat comes from a refusal to recognize that global markets, if allowed to spin on unchecked and uncontrolled, will destroy themselves in the long run.

Trade and investment are crucial elements in the global economy and affect the lives of billions of workers. Governments that ignore this fact, because of free-trade ideology or fear of international disputes, serve their citizens badly.

The March of Technology

Like much else in the global market, trade is growing because technology enables it to grow. This trade is not only in goods but, as we have seen, in services and especially in finance. The computer and the computer chip stand at the heart of the global economy. The ability to send information instantly and cheaply makes everything else possible. It is the reason why the Information Revolution of today differs in kind from the Industrial Revolution of Queen Victoria's era.

"Before, the major link between countries was the ocean," Israeli economist Jacob Frenkel, now the governor of the Bank of Israel, told me. "This meant ports and manufactured goods. Today it's the satellite. This means information and trading in portfolios. This is fundamental."[6]

With the computer and the satellite, currency and stock traders can do business virtually anywhere at any hour of the day and night. With the computer and the satellite, specifications for manufactured goods can be sent from a home office to a factory halfway around the world, and the finished product tested by headquarters while it is still on the factory floor. With the computer and the satellite, software written in Bangalore can be "shipped" instantaneously to Palo Alto, Schaumburg, or Austin. Women in sweatshops from Bangladesh to New York City can sew clothes from designs drawn by computers and flashed around the world via satellites: a marriage of high tech and primitive exploitation.

Peter Huber, a senior fellow of the Manhattan Institute, is an enthusiast for the power of these electronically linked markets and has written rapturously of their potential, including their potential to override the rules of government. The power of technology, Huber said, permits companies to move manufacturing, and hence jobs, beyond the reach of the unions, labor laws, and government regulations of their home countries. Now services are following:

> American companies outsource data entry to countries in the Caribbean. Manufacturers outsource product design, logistics management, R&D and customer service across national borders, too. U.S. insurance, tax consulting and accounting companies send claims and forces overseas for processing. Software, films, music, finance, advertising and even health care and education all move as well. Haircuts? Not yet, but there's already serious talk of telemedicine. . . . Many services, especially financial and anything involving software, consist of nothing but information and can be moved by wire alone.[7]

Gordon Moore, the cofounder of Intel, proclaimed "Moore's law," which says that the capacity of a microchip doubles every eighteen months. So far, he's been right—although Intel says this pace is about to be halved, to nine months. Since the chip drives globalization, this means that the global economy is spreading at a speed immeasurably faster than the economic revolutions of earlier eras. As two consultants write:

> Potatoes were cultivated for 4,000 years in the Andes before diffusing to Europe in the 16th century, where it took another 200 years before they were widely eaten. Today, new strains of rice and wheat diffuse around the world within a decade as part of the ongoing "green revolution." In the integrated Triad [First World] economy, core innovations diffuse almost simultaneously. For example, it took an average of only 2.5 years for all the major semiconductor innovations to spread throughout the Triad.

Powered by this technology, they said, globalization will spread fast from "the 20 to 30 percent of the economy accounted for by manufacturing . . . to much of the 50 to 60 percent represented by services."[8]

Workers who look to government to shelter them from this revolution are finding that governments—especially democratic governments—cannot begin to move as fast as the world is changing.

The Birth of Global Money

While technology has vastly expanded the possibilities of trade and foreign investment, it did not create them. But the global financial market would not exist without the technology that makes instantaneous worldwide trading possible. It is this global financial market that drives the global economy, that makes it truly global instead of just international, and that has loosened the ability of democratic governments to control their own affairs. I have deliberately saved it for last, because it is the most important factor of all.

Small-scale trading in currencies and precious metals has existed for centuries. But the vast, powerful global capital market of today was born in 1973 when President Nixon destroyed the Bretton Woods system. The Western powers had invented this system in a meeting in 1944 at Bretton Woods, a New Hampshire resort hotel. The United States and its allies, determined to avoid the prewar financial instability that wrecked their economies and led to World War II, devised a framework of fixed exchange rates. The dollar was pegged to gold, at $35 per ounce, and all other major currencies were pegged to the dollar.

This meant that the dollar was a universal currency and the United States was the hegemon, the one great power, whose currency guaranteed the value of all other currencies. The dollar literally was good as gold—thirty-five dollars bought an ounce of gold—and the other currencies were worth exactly what they would bring in dollars. Currencies could be, and were, adjusted up or down from time to time when local conditions or government policies made the pegged rates unrealistic. But the international money market was small, because there was no point in speculating on prices that, for the most part, never changed.

Apart from guaranteeing the world's financial system, the United States adopted an open market toward the goods of other countries. This helped Europe and Japan to recover from World War II by giving them a market for their exports. At the same time, it enabled them to earn all-important dollars. Trade was the key to this system, and it worked brilliantly. American industries, having thrived during the war, prospered as trade grew. So did the economies of friends and former foes, first in Europe, then in Japan. The belief in the virtues of free trade, which has since become dogma to generations of American politicians, economists, and editorial writers, was born at that time; throughout history, free trade has always looked best to the strongest nation with the most competitive export industries.*

The postwar trading system depended on the willingness of the United States to run small trade and fiscal deficits, to enable other countries to earn dollars to finance their own expansion. This willingness, which was the strength of the system, also doomed it. No country, even a hegemon, can run deficits forever. Gradually, other nations piled up more dollars than they needed. A surplus of anything, even dollars, erodes its value. America's creditors began to doubt whether its currency was still as good as gold and whether the United States would continue to defend it.

The Vietnam War finished off the Bretton Woods system. President Johnson, by refusing to raise taxes to pay for the war, guaranteed an era of deficit spending that overheated the economy, created inflation, and led to more deficits. In 1971, Nixon bowed to reality and devalued the dollar. Eighteen months later, in January 1973, he abandoned Bretton Woods, unhinged the dollar from the gold standard, and ushered in the era of floating currencies.

---

*Lord Keynes, the British economist who virtually invented this postwar economy, would have looked on its offspring, the global capital markets and the theology of free trade, with a very cold eye. In an oft-quoted passage, Keynes wrote: "I sympathize, therefore, with those who would minimize, rather than those who would maximize, economic entanglement between nations. Ideas, knowledge, art, hospitality, travel—these are things which should of their nature be international. But let goods be homespun whenever it is reasonable and conveniently possible: and, above all, let finance be primarily national."[9]" No globalist, he.

Since that day, the world's currencies have been freely traded on world money markets and are worth, at any given moment, only what money traders say they are. (The exception is the European Monetary System, which tries to promote monetary stability within the European Union by permitting the currencies of most of the EU's members to float against each other only within a very narrow band. Despite periodic breakdowns and crises, this has worked. The plan for a single European currency calls for some of these currencies to be brought closer and then firmly pegged against each other, as a prelude to becoming one unit, the Euro.[10])

This combination of events gave birth to the global capital market. When the Bretton Woods system died, there suddenly was big money to be made in guessing correctly whether the dollar or the deutsche mark or the pound sterling would rise or fall against each other. By the late 1970s, the growing deficits and the downward pressure on the dollar forced the United States to raise interest rates. This sent the dollar soaring to new heights, leading to greater trade deficits. At the same time, President Reagan ran record budget deficits and relied on the global markets to finance them. The phony Reagan boom, financed by this borrowing, sent Americans on a global shopping spree that only worsened the trade deficits.

Enter technology. The world already was awash in dollars. Currencies, unshackled from gold and the hegemonic dollar, seesawed against each other, creating a demand for options and other means of hedging against loss. Computerized trading and instant communications took this chaotic, lucrative maelstrom and turned it into a global capital market.

At the start, this foreign exchange trading was relatively modest, about $10 billion per day—the amount traded every three minutes now. The development of information technology vastly expanded the ability to trade. So did the development of new instruments, such as derivatives, and the end of foreign exchange controls in Japan, France, and other countries.

Now, every day, these global money markets handle trades worth $1.3 trillion. This is an unimaginable sum. A year's trading would produce a stack of $100 bills reaching to the moon. This trading, in its purest form, is meant to fuel the world's economy. Yet most of it is speculation, as far removed from the "real economy" as a poker game, and has taken on a life of its own.

Money traders pioneered the global financial markets. Next came the bond traders, taking advantage of differences in prices of bonds, both corporate and government, in different countries. The huge U.S. budget and trade deficits that appeared during the Reagan administration propelled this market, because the government used the global bond markets to finance these deficits. In 1983 total U.S. bonds sold abroad were $50 billion; by 1993 these sales had grown by 1,000 percent, to $500 billion per year. Trading of these and other unmatured bonds—the so-called secondary market—has turned this market into a truly global bazaar, like the money markets. At the moment, the global bond market trades about $200 billion each day.

The global stock market is still relatively small, about $25 billion per day, because most investors prefer to buy stocks in their own countries. But international markets are growing and so are funds invested in shares around the globe. The global equity market is growing by some 25 percent per year and, as we shall see, will have an impact on the lives and jobs of men and women around the globe at least equal to that of the money markets.[11]

Global Opportunity

Money is made in these markets, particularly in the money markets, when a trader sees the possibility to buy an asset in one place for a lower price and sell it immediately in another for a higher price. In other words, the trader takes advantage of a "market anomaly" that he or she was the first to see. This is called arbitrage and is pure trading, without thought to the underlying value of the asset itself. Arbitrage depends on minute fluctuations in prices and the belief that, somewhere, someone else is making a mistake. The person who makes the mistake, who sells too low, loses money. The person who spots it, buys low and sells high, makes money. Winners in this game are those who move fastest and have the best technology.

These traders, by definition, are willing to take risks, sometimes appalling ones. But the development of derivatives—complex instruments that "derive" their values from the value of the underlying asset—enables these traders to protect themselves against risk, to "hedge" their risks, much as agricultural traders have done with their options on future purchases of corn or pork bellies. These derivatives, skillfully used, can limit risk. But, as we shall see, they are just one chip in a gambler's stack and, in the wrong hands, can multiply disaster.

With the growth in the global stock market and global investing, the traders are moving beyond money to companies, manufacturers, service providers, and jobholders around the world. The search is on for "best practice." This phrase, *best practice*, is a key concept in the global economy and will appear often in the chapters to come. Basically, it means the most economical, efficient, and profitable way to do or make something, no matter where that might be.

Just as the computer screens in trading houses scan the global market restlessly in search of a moment's profit on a foreign currency, so the global investor prowls the global economy seeking low costs, high productivity, and biggest margins. In this game, the winners will be those—countries, companies, workers—who can provide those profits. The losers will be those countries, companies, and workers with higher wages, bigger pensions, more expensive health systems, stronger unions, or other impediments to "best practice."

There is no geographic limit to this search. Equity markets seeking maximum return will reward companies that perform best. For some companies, this may mean a return from higher quality and worker education. For many others, it will mean greater profits from abandoning the high-cost First-World workers who have sustained them for decades and investing in low-cost Third-World countries where workers, given basic skills and splendid technology, can produce acceptable goods at one-tenth the cost.

The Power of Markets

Market Unbound, the book by McKinsey consultants Bryan and Farrell, explains global markets in great detail and clarity; I recommend it to anyone who wants a more thorough understanding of how these markets work. The two authors also are unrestrained rooters for these markets, and their enthusiastic predictions of where the markets are taking us can, for more skeptical readers, be hair-raising.

Bryan and Farrell write that these markets are growing so fast, and are so successful at leaping the barriers to growth, including government regulations, for one straightforward reason: "Because it is so profitable for the participants in the market to take actions that severely undermine the barriers."

Bryan and Farrell have a gift for unhappy similes and metaphors. At one point, they argue that governments are helpless to oppose this trend because "the global capital market, like nuclear weapons, has become a reality that is too big to ignore." At another, they compare traders to the early humans who roamed to America from Asia and, with their "new technology, an abundance of targets of opportunity and ambitious, hard-working people," slaughtered the woolly mammoths they found in their new home. Thousands of years later, the descendants of these first Americans were in turn slaughtered or rounded up by European immigrants, themselves new arrivals who "brought new technology and found unlimited opportunity."

"We are in the midst of a similar transformation in the global capital market," Bryan and Farrell write. "Only instead of hunting for woolly mammoths, fundraisers, financial intermediaries and investors are looking for opportunities to profit . . . in the market."

If the woolly mammoths and the Native Americans could have deflected the ambitious opportunity seekers who smote them, they would have been daft not to have tried. Bryan and Farrell expect some opposition on the market's march to the millennium, but they doubt it will do any more good than it did the mammoths.

Investors, many wage earners, and customers will benefit, they say, but even the rosiest scenario admits "great volatility and a high degree of uncertainty. Strong political and social tensions are likely to emerge." Investors, seeing "phenomenal economic incentives . . . are likely to be extremely aggressive in seeking resourceful and creative ways to push resistance aside and capture the opportunities. [But] all those who benefit or are protected under the status quo will resist these changes. Local labor interests that are threatened, either directly for the jobs or indirectly for their benefits such as extended vacations, short working hours, or greater coverage will oppose the threat. . . . Voters who want to maintain their growing entitlements to pensions or health care, or those who have come to feel that promoting the welfare state is a right and duty of any civilized, industrial nation, will reject many of the necessary changes. Producers who do not want to face up to the competitive threat, who have grown accustomed to stable, if not spectacular, returns and use of resources will fight to maintain their way of doing business and, in many cases, their ability to do business altogether."

To the true believers in the market, these objections are futile. The contest has ended. The markets are in control.

To this way of thinking, the answer to the question with which we began this book—for whom does an economy exist?—can be answered: the owners and the investors. "At the core of global capitalism, then, is the equity shareholder and the investor market that owns equities," Bryan and Farrell write.

Workers who believed that a life of toil entitled them to the respect of society and a comfortable old age are likely to be disappointed. "Cutting back on entitlements, such as pensions and health care, that individuals had always expected to receive, means that many will be severely unprepared when sickness or old age approaches." This rupture of the social contacts "can be truly devastating."

"On the other hand," they write, "the economic rent [returns] to those who are highly skilled, or to those who own the innovations and best practices across industries, has probably never been greater."[12]

No Mercy for Governments

Governments that try to maintain entitlements—be they social security systems, health care programs, unemployment pay, or welfare systems—will find themselves punished by the markets. In a way, the governments have only themselves to blame. From the 1980s, the American government, having cut taxes but not spending, used the global bond market to finance its deficits. In essence, the Reagan and Bush administrations, having cut taxes, spent more than they took in in tax revenues, and borrowed by issuing bonds. By the time President Clinton came to power as a modern but not wholly conservative Democrat, he discovered that his administration owed its soul to the bondholders, many of them in Tokyo. Continuing and growing deficits would simply be too expensive to finance. The markets demanded a program to cut budget deficits and control the national debt. Any backsliding would send the cost of debt even higher. One result has been the welfare "reform" that will cut off the means of life for millions of Americans, deserving and undeserving alike.

European governments, blessed with a higher public tolerance for taxes, have postponed this day of reckoning. But that day has come. Almost all the Europeans now have budget deficits higher than the American level. Taxation has reached its limit. So the bond markets, until now so accommodating, are in control and blowing the whistle.

"Rich people have always parked their money abroad when they didn't trust the political climate home," Huber of the Manhattan Institute writes in a paean to "modemization," or the ability of investors armed with a computer and a modem to send money around the globe at a keystroke:

> You can vote with your modem. Virtual establishments on the Web already offer incorporation in Belize, bank accounts in Switzerland, currency trading in Germany, brokerage accounts in New Zealand. . . . Millions of ordinary investors can move their wealth between currencies and countries as fast as they can click icons on a screen. . . .
>
> For any government that's seriously in debt, the globalization of financial markets puts a double squeeze on new discretionary spending. If global capitalists lose faith and drive up interest rates, it isn't just new spending that costs more, it's also the refinancing of old debt. The modemization of finance explains the federal government's mass conversion to more balanced budgets.[13]

Perhaps the first vivid demonstration of this power came in the early 1980s in France, when a new Socialist government under François Mitterrand tried to expand its economy, bucking a mood of austerity elsewhere in Europe. After two years of unexpected inflation and growing deficits, the French gave in.

Americans like to think that their economy is too big to be vulnerable to these forces. It's not. For instance, consider this scenario:

Japan, as is well known, holds hundreds of billions of dollars' worth of U.S. government bonds. The government badly needs this Japanese investment to pay the federal budget deficit. The Reagan administration could never have created this deficit without the Japanese willingness to finance it.

But what would happen if the Japanese, out of fear or spite, sold off these bonds? Then the government would have to raise interest rates to lure them back. But that would make investment in U.S. industry more expensive, threaten both inflation and a recession, and frighten American investors. The result would be a stock market collapse.

Fanciful? Not at all. That is precisely what caused the Black Monday crash on Wall Street on October 19, 1987, according to Nicholas Brady, who headed the presidential task force that studied the crash. "That, to me, is what really started the nineteenth—a worry by the Japanese about U.S. currency," said Brady, who later became secretary of the treasury. What he was saying is that the president and his government do not have the independent power to take steps to protect the dollar, stimulate the economy, or thwart inflation. They can do it, of course, but only at the risk that the reaction by other countries will make things even worse, as happened in France in 1983 and in the United States four years later.

The Squeeze on Companies

The equity markets will perform the same "service" for companies. Those with high wages, social costs—pensions, health plans, and other employee benefits—or other nonproductive expenses, such as community programs or philanthropy, will find their stock falling on markets devoted to "best practice" and maximum return. Companies that downsize their workforce, cut back their health programs, eliminate community outreach, cancel their pension plans, break their unions, or reduce wages will be rewarded.

This, of course, is exactly what has been happening in the American economy for the past twenty years. It is beginning to take place in Europe. So far, equity markets have been mostly national, so the competition for "best practice" has been largely a race to the bottom between companies doing business within the same countries.

As equity markets go global, the competition will increasingly be between First-World and Third-World companies. This competition has already received a great deal of attention from the workers of the First World and their champions.

But the process has just begun. A cold-eyed analysis by James Annable, chief economist of the First Chicago NBD Corporation, Chicago's largest bank, led him to the following conclusions:

> Senior managements in the United States are demonstrating a sharply increased willingness to make difficult decisions in order to improve profits, e.g., roiling corporate cultures by firing large numbers of employees, often when earnings are relatively robust. . . .

The toughened resolve to improve bottom-line performance is ultimately rooted in change in the capital markets. The enhanced capacity
to raise huge amounts of financing for hostile takeovers has transformed
attitudes in corporate boardrooms. In an increasingly hostile world, the
best defense is a strong equity price, which in turn requires strong earnings growth.

This means lower benefits, firing of higher-wage employees, and
abandoning automatic raises, including cost-of-living raises.

Once upon a time, Annable said, management could tend the needs
of workers, suppliers, and communities as well as shareholders and
could provide luxuries like rising wages and job security. Not anymore:

A CEO can no longer count on keeping his job just because he produces
generally good profits. Investors often believe earnings could be even
better, and insecure CEOs are working hard at redefining their relationships
with employees—as well as with vendors and communities—to the benefit of shareholders.

This is happening at a time of corporate profit levels unmatched since
the end of World War II, and it explains why low rates of unemployment, which theoretically should send wages up, haven't done so.

There may be political limits to this process, particularly to the
growing inequality it implies, Annable said. But what those limits are,
"we do not know." The limits in the United States, with its market-
oriented attitudes, are looser than in other nations. So, given "continued political tolerance, the best bet is that the process . . . will
continue throughout the 1990s."[14]

In other words, we haven't seen anything yet.

All of this is exacerbated by overcapacity, or global glut. In industry
after industry, for high-wage Europe to low-wage Asia, producers are
making more than customers can buy. This is true for chemicals, aircraft, consumer electronics, toys, steel, and clothes; in each, capacity
now outruns the market. The glut is greatest in computer chips and
cars: auto-industry analysts reckon that the world's auto companies
can produce about 80 million vehicles per year but can sell only 60
million of them—an overcapacity of about 25 percent. GM, Ford,
Chrysler, Toyota, and Honda alone have built or plan to build twenty-
seven new plants in Southeast Asia, for more than the staggering
economies there can consume. Hyundai, Honda, Kia, Daihatsu, and

Toyota all have or plan to have assembly plants in Turkey, churning out 1.2 million cars every year into a nation with an annual market of fewer than 300,000 cars.

All these nations plan to export the cars they don't buy themselves. But with ever more countries building their own auto plants, it's hard to see where these export markets will be. More likely, the law of supply and demand will take over. With too many goods chasing too few buyers, prices will fall: indeed, prices of both cars and computer chips already are falling. Lower prices sound like a boon and, for consumers, they are. But consumers are also producers, with jobs and salaries. As prices fall, so will corporate profits and, soon after, so will wages. Plants will close. Jobs will vanish. Bank loans will go unpaid. Bankruptcies will grow. Buyers will stop buying, making the overcapacity even worse.

The truth is that a modern economy relies on inflation—not too much, but a little—for its growth. Global glut menaces this growth by creating deflation.

This ludicrous and dangerous situation rises directly from globalization. As capital markets demand ever greater efficiencies and as technology makes manufacturing ever more mobile, the companies have gone global, cutting costs by locating in low-wage nations and cutting jobs by standardizing parts and models. Third World nations, anxious for the jobs and prestige that come with big car factories, have encouraged this process through tax holidays and relaxed labor laws. In the United States, car companies maintian production levels by outsourcing work to nonunion firms. In Europe, companies struggle to justify the cost of new labor-saving equipment by adding second and third shifts, which only increase the overcapacity. The result is a glut of cars that, sooner rather than later, will force the closing of assembly plants and the firing of hundreds of thousands of workers. These closings and firings, when they come, almost certainly will take place where costs and wages are highest: in the United States, Europe, and Japan.

This is the link between the growth of the global capital markets and the squeeze on First-World workers. The markets give companies an incentive to cut costs at home as much as possible and then, faced with continuing demands for "best practice," to move operations abroad. Technology, in turn, gives them the means to do this. It is simply easier than ever before to escape the unions, labor laws, regulations, and politicians of the United States, Europe, and Japan and to locate once-immobile factories anywhere the conditions are friendlier. Nations that insist on these laws, regulations, and standards—the components of a decent industrial civilization—will find their industry gone and their tax dollars, which support this civilization, dried up.

The Masters of Money

Who are these new masters of the universe, the traders whose instant decisions and lightning investments can drive markets, cut federal budgets, export jobs, transform companies, and override governments? By and large, they are very young, very quick, with the reflexes of a good third baseman and a long-range perspective of about fifteen minutes. There are about 500,000 bankers, traders, salespeople, and portfolio managers around the world, but the elite work for the fifty or so banks—J. P. Morgan, Nomura, Deutsche Bank, and the like—that dominate the markets. It's not a big industry; the ten biggest American investment banks employ 41,000 persons, or about the same number that AT&T announced it would downsize. But its practitioners are extraordinarily well paid, with annual salaries and bonuses in the millions of dollars. At the ten largest U.S. investment banks, the *average* annual pay is more than $200,000, and this includes secretaries and janitors. One firm, Donaldson Lufkin & Jenrette Inc., paid $261,000 per employee in 1996. The average pay for the professional staff is many times higher and has been rising by about 20 percent per year since 1990.[15]

These are, as Bryan and Farrell said, "some of the smartest, hardest working people in the world." Yet they spend their days scrambling for momentary advantage, producing nothing, but often putting people who do make things out of business or out of a job.

I have had the chance to sit on money-trading desks at banks in London and talk with the traders there. Most are in their twenties or early thirties; it's a high-burnout business. An amazing number left school at fifteen, when compulsory education ends in England, and had not entered a classroom since. They were engaging, smart, not given to reflection. Many were from poor homes. Their grandfathers sold old clothes from a cart, and their fathers drove a truck. By age twenty-five, they were dealing in billions of dollars and wanted only to get rich.

I recalled these traders in 1995 when Barings PLC, Britain's oldest merchant bank, collapsed after its twenty-eight-year-old chief trader in Singapore bet $29 billion by buying derivatives based on the Tokyo stock index. If the index had risen, he would have won big. It fell instead. Barings lost $1 billion on the gamble, the bank folded, and the young trader, Nick Leeson, went to jail.

Leeson was almost a caricature of the traders who rule the global market. He grew up in a public housing project in one of London's grimmer suburbs, left school at fifteen, went to work for Barings in London, and was transferred to Singapore in 1992, where he was put in charge of a bankroll bigger than the gross national product of many countries. His twenty-three-year-old wife, Lisa, incredibly enough, worked in the Barings office in Singapore that monitored her husband's activities. These activities enabled them to live like pashas in Singapore, one of Asia's money pots. When the couple took off on a weeklong flight before his arrest, their getaway car was a Porsche.

Senior bankers in London are notorious for their long lunches and gentlemanly attitude toward the markets. Not too sure what derivatives and other newfangled instruments are and totally baffled by technology, they are inclined to give their young traders their head, so long as they make money. It came out later that Leeson's bosses at Barings back in London learned, sometime during his big binge, that he was breaking their bank. But instead of trying to cut their losses, they actually threw good money after bad by sending him $70 million more to help him cover his bets.

It sounds ludicrous, this suggestion that one of the world's venerable banks would hire an uneducated lad from the slums, send him to the other side of the world, and let him gamble away its money on the Tokyo stock exchange. Ludicrous, perhaps, but all too common.

Kidder, Peabody & Co., the American securities firm, lost its independence after its chief government bond trader invented $350 million in phony profits. Salomon Brothers, one of the leaders of Wall Street, still suffers from the 1991 news that its chief bond trader faked customer bids. Traders for a German metals conglomerate, Metallgesellschaft, lost $1 billion in 1994 betting on the oil market. Kidder Peabody had given its errant trader a star employee award and $9 million in bonuses the year before he was caught. Salomon Brothers, in belatedly firing its three top executives, admitted they knew of the trader's scams for months.

American traders usually have more formal schooling than their British counterparts, but they have no less ambition and no more real knowledge of the world. Most know the difference between normal risk and betting the bank. But some don't. Most are honest. But some aren't. Barely prepared and innocent of ethics, these traders are pitched into stupendous sums of money. They often work for bosses who are simply ripe for the plucking. It is amazing that the scams and scandals don't happen more often than they do.

If the banks themselves aren't controlling these cowboys, it is up to governments to do the job. But as prophets of the global economy point out, this trading, being global, has escaped the jurisdiction of national regulators. If a government tries seriously to crack down, the market simply decamps to some other country. This, in fact, was why Leeson was in Singapore, not Tokyo. In 1992 the Japanese government tried to halt derivatives trading in Japanese stock exchange futures. The result was that the market for these derivatives moved from Tokyo to Singapore.

The global markets are already unimaginably vast. Liquid financial assets by the year 2000 are expected to be about $81 trillion, or three times as large as the total gross domestic product of the world's twenty-eight richest nations, the members of the Organization for Economic Cooperation and Development. These markets already have the power to override governments and their policies, and they're growing daily, almost hourly.

Never was this more evident than in late 1997, when the money markets swept through Asia, casting their baleful judgment on Thailand, Malaysia, Indonesia, and South Korea. By the time the contagion was stopped, these countries had seen their currencies devalued, their economies thrown into depression, and their economic policy sold to the mandarins of the International Monetary Fund, in return for the IMF's bailout of their banking systems. For the IMF, the cost of stanching the flow was $100 billion-plus, more than twice as much as it had cost to bail out Mexico in a similar crisis less than three years earlier. The impact of the crisis spread to Brazil, where the currency fell, to Estonia, where interest rates were doubled to protect the currency, and even Russia, where the stock market fell by 25 percent. (Six years earlier, when Mikhail Gorbachev was briefly deposed, world markets didn't even notice: Russia had not yet joined the global economy.)

The Asian typhoon was notable mostly for its speed and power. Since the Mexican crisis, the global money markets had become that much faster, that much bigger, that much more commanding. The information at their disposal had exploded, and their ability to react instantly to that information had multiplied. One other thing had multiplied, too: the number of green young bankers at the helm of the crisis. In the 1990s, Asia became the new frontier of the global economy. Big international banks rushed to get a piece of the action and shipped platoons of untried youngsters to work in outposts there. These cadets learned quickly how to make money, but the crisis of 1997 was their first experience at losing it. Many of them panicked, and the people of Thailand, Malaysia, Indonesia, and Korea paid the price.

Global Economy and the Fate of Nations

It is fashionable these days to scorn governments and their social programs. Americans, hostile to "big government," applaud the retreat of the welfare state. Europeans, reliant on big government, nevertheless fear this retreat is inevitable. Neither sees the real connection between big government, the welfare state, and the global economy, nor understands that, without the welfare state, the global economy will fail. Nor do they grasp that either the global economy or democracy will survive, but not both.

Yet these are the true issues of the twenty-first century, when the social and political implications of globalization will loom as large as the economic implications do now.

A number of scholars have pointed out that countries that are most open to imports from abroad also have the biggest welfare systems, including unemployment pay structures. The reason is obvious. Trade produces both winners and losers. Even trade that helps a society as a whole can hurt individual workers or whole industries. The long-term benefits may be real, but the short-term pain is acute, and usually politically explosive. Welfare eases the pain and helps workers and communities adapt to the new situation. In this way, it defuses the political time bomb, because even the losers will continue to endorse the system that caused their loss. In the process, both trade and democracy survive and thrive.

But welfare states are financed by taxes. The global economy, as we have seen, is permitting the biggest taxpayers—corporations and the wealthiest citizens—to escape taxes or to move their tax paying to countries where rates are lowest and evasion easiest. The results are dramatic. Before World War II, corporations paid one-third of all U.S. federal taxes; now they pay only 12 percent, as the government cuts corporate taxes to keep companies from fleeing. In Europe, the same pressures have cut the average tax rate on income from capital investments from 50 percent in 1981 to only 35 percent now.

But if the social contract is to be kept, the money must come from somewhere. Guess where? Taxes on wages—that is, taxes on workers—have taken up the slack. Income taxes now account for nearly 50 percent of all U.S. federal revenue, four times as much as corporate taxes. In the EU, as corporate taxes fell, average taxes on wages rose from 35 to 41 percent. Sales taxes went up, too, affecting mostly the poor and the middle class, who spend a bigger share of their income on consumption than the wealthy do.

Once the social contract expressed a deal between the wealthy and the poor, between businesses and their employees. Economic change has always brought both gain and pain. But in the short run, the wealthy were more likely to get the gain, and the poor more likely to feel the pain. The great stabilizer of postwar industrial society was the recognition by government and business that, if change creates both winners and losers, then the winners have an obligation to help and compensate the losers. This was more than simple fairness. It was good politics. It was the price that the winners paid to pacify the losers, who had the vote. If the pain became too great, the losers would stop supporting the system that caused this pain. So the Western nations created the safety net, a societal balm that soothed the pain and kept the losers nonmutinous.

This social contract has been broken. Footloose global corporations have stopped paying the taxes that financed it. The slack has been taken up, at least partly, by higher taxes on workers. In other words, workers are financing their own social contract. It's robbing Peter to pay Peter. The losers are comforting the losers, while the winners pay minimal taxes in Indonesia or buy bonds in cyberspace.

But there's only so much money to be made by soaking the poor. Even with higher taxes, governments just don't have the money they used to. For a while, they borrowed, but global bond markets have discouraged that. So now governments do the only thing they can.

They're cutting spending, reducing outlays, squeezing the nickel, and hoarding the franc to get their deficits down. Hence, the American welfare "reforms." Hence, the unraveling of the welfare state in Europe. On both sides of the Atlantic, the burden of globalization is shifted onto those least able to bear it.

All this means, as world trade grows, governments have less money to ease the pain of the losers. But more trade will create more losers, at least in the short run. Robbed of jobs and uncompensated for this loss, these damaged workers will withdraw their support for free trade. If there are enough of these damaged workers and if their pain is great enough, they become prey to protectionist politicians or hate mongers of the Buchanan–Le Pen variety.[16]

Globalization vs. Democracy

Can the global economy and democracy coexist? Not unless democratic governments can channel globalization to the benefit of their citizens. Even supporters of globalization, such as Peter Drucker, say it will create more losers than winners. Democracy, or majority rule, will become government of, by, and for the losers. This means the triumph of the politics of resentment and envy, which is no basis for a decent society.

The alternative is an economic dictatorship by all-powerful global corporations. People would still elect their governments, but these governments would have virtually no power beyond basic services, and their people would have no control over their own lives.

This process has begun. Ian Angell, a professor at the London School of Economics, wrote, "Corporations, unhindered by national barriers, will be truly global. . . . The global company no longer supports the aspirations of the country of its birth."[17]

Businesses, especially in the West, try to maximize their profits or, more accurately, the value of their equity. This is what they are supposed to do. In a healthy society, this legal and necessary pursuit of self-interest is balanced by the pursuit of society's self-interest through other institutions of power, especially government. It is this balance that is skewed now as business escapes the restraints of civil society. The mutual interest between business and government is broken. Governments, to be reelected, need to create and maintain healthy societies at home, but the money to pay for this healthy society is disappearing into a global void.

Even the functions that governments used to do are being taken over by the global market. With no global laws or regulations to discipline these global markets, a sort of a privatized form of justice has arisen. Around the globe, private arbitrators and arbitration centers are producing "a transnational legal profession and indeed a transnational private judiciary." These arbitrators, being private, compete for business and so depend on the goodwill of the corporations they judge. These corporations, in turn, use this private judicial system largely to escape the jurisdiction of national courts, and rarely resort to them for appeals. Many of these arbitrators are American international lawyers.[18]

This process is erasing the concept of space. Over half of all transactions on the fiber-optic cable network in Manhattan involve international deals. These deals, between persons or corporations legally based in two or more countries, take place entirely within Manhattan but lie outside the jurisdiction of American courts. Legal disputes are settled by international arbitrators, also often based in New York. The global economy is thus an economic state within a state, untouchable by the government that holds theoretical sovereignty over the soil where all this happens.

This is how the global economy is changing the very way we think about sovereignty and the law. Never before has any force this powerful operated beyond the reach of law and government. In the last chapter of this book, we will talk about steps that governments, acting individually or together, can take to make this force accountable to the people whose lives it is changing and ordering. In the very long run, nothing will do, short of new global institutions—not a world government, but wielding some of the powers now held by national governments. As these institutions develop, so will a sort of global democracy and a global citizenship.

But this day, if it ever comes, is still far off. In the meantime, Bryan and Farrell say, the global economy is inevitable and we would be smart to accept it. They deliberately echo Dr. Strangelove:

> The time has come to stop worrying and start to love the market. We believe the process will continue until there are no market anomalies worth pursuing.
>
> Until the last woolly mammoth is dead.
>
> Until we have a single, overwhelming, fully integrated, global capital market.[19]

3. THE NEW PROLETARIANS

EVERY MORNING IN the Zona Rosa, the heart of Mexico City, dozens of carpenters, plumbers, and electricians line up along the fence that surrounds the National Cathedral. Each puts his tool kit on the ground in front of him, with a small sign announcing his trade and his willingness to work. There he sits for as long as necessary, sometimes all day, until someone comes along and hires him. Sometimes he gets work, sometimes not. But he is patient. Life on the fringes of an economy is seldom easy, and there are no guarantees.

I am reminded of these Mexican workers whenever I interview a new breed of American artisan—the downsized middle manager, whose fate, if far from universal in the new global economy, has cast a thrill of terror through the rest of the workforce. These middle managers, once company men and women to the core, have been thrown onto the casual market to live by their wits. Each brings out a laptop, which is the manager's tool kit, and announces his or her willingness to work, probably as a "temp," by the year or the month or, if necessary, by the day or even the hour. These people call themselves consultants, but they are in truth unemployed workers, with no more stability nor guarantees in life than a Mexican plumber.

This is the proletarianization of the middle class, which once considered itself set for life in the cushioned cubicles of big corporations but now finds itself pitched onto the pavement, a loser in the global competition for jobs. If there is a focal point of the growing debate on the global economy, it is here, where people work. Whether you're middle class or working class, globalization's pressure on jobs has created anxieties and questions that seldom arose in the prosperous postwar years:

- Will there be enough jobs for everyone who wants to work, in the First World or the Third?

- Will computers kill more jobs than they create? If I lose my job, can I find a new one that pays as well?

- Am I really competing with an autoworker in Malaysia or a software designer in India?

- Can a machine take my job?

- Is trade to blame, or technology, or a combination of both?

- Or am I just one of history's castoffs, trained for the wrong economy, living in a country that is one of yesterday's giants?

The global emphasis on profits, the unrelenting pressure of the capital markets, and the search for best practice preclude comforting answers. The truth is that no one at this stage can give answers with assurance. The logic of global markets leads to more pressure on workers, not less. Millions of new workers appear on the world market every year, all hungry and ready to compete. The power of computer-driven automation makes it at least possible that, for the first time, new technology will be a job destroyer, not a job creator.

Are the Luddites Right?

The pessimists are clear: "The problem is starkly simple," writes Richard J. Barnet of the Institute for Policy Studies in Washington. "An astonishingly large and increasing number of human beings are not needed or wanted to make the goods or to provide the services that the paying customers of the world can afford."[1]

Even the optimists offer little comfort. Joseph Stanislaw, managing director of Cambridge Energy Research Associates' office in Paris, assured me that the new technology will create jobs in the long run, "but the time gap is going to be longer, because we're destroying old industries so much faster than we're creating new ones. We do have this social structure, the state, to deal with change, but it doesn't move fast enough."[2]

To mainstream economists, Cassandras like Barnet are little more than antitechnology descendants of the Luddites, the early-nineteenth-century textile workers in Leicestershire who smashed the labor-saving looms they feared would steal their jobs. Since then, Luddites have decried the electric motor, the assembly line, and the automobile. Each time, they have been wrong, as technology created millions more jobs than they destroyed.

This time, are the Luddites right? Is the computer different?

"Yes, I have this fear," Michel Hansenne, director general of the International Labor Office, said in Geneva. "Have we come to the end of industrial society? Our work concept is inherited from the eighteenth century. Now technology has run away with things. Do we now have to invent a new way to distribute our wealth?"[3]

The Organization for Economic Cooperation and Development (OECD), like the sixteenth arrondissement of Paris where it makes its home, is a conservative place, not given to alarms. It reflects the consensus of its members, who are the governments of the richest nations, and issues reports stressing that all is well, or that all will be well if the world lets the free market have its way. Officially, there's no job crisis now that higher productivity and fewer "rigidities" can't cure. But even here, concern intrudes.

A high-ranking OECD official, speaking on condition that I not quote him by name, said, "There is no reason to suppose that the Luddites are right. But this technology is much more pervasive than most new technologies. It's bigger even than the electric motor. It's all going so fast. You can lose your job in a steel mill, go to a travel agency, and then get hit by an automatic ticketing machine. If society can't adapt, then we're going to have serious social problems."

In Chicago, a friend named Roberta Woods, a longtime union activist, talked about how the steel mills in northwest Indiana are making as much steel as they ever did but with new technology and half as many workers. Now, she said, this firestorm is happening to the middle class, the downsized middle managers turned overnight into jobless "consultants." If you're working class, you're always one paycheck away from poverty," she said. "If you're working class, you've got to sell your labor. These 'consultants' are not middle class. They're just people who are getting cheated, too."

The Industrial Revolution took millions of farm workers from the farms, created new and better jobs, and in the long run, raised them to higher standards of living. But as a minority of farmers now produce all the food we need, so will a shrunken minority of industrial workers produce all the goods we need. The new global market is based on the power of the computer, which like any machine enables fewer people to do more work but, unlike most machines, shows no promise of creating more jobs than it kills.

"Few dispute that the world market, now that it is no longer a vision of the future but a global reality, produces fewer winners and more losers as each year passes," writes German author Hans Magnus Enzensberger. "The overarching, anonymous world market . . . condemns increasingly large sections of mankind to superfluousness. . . . In the language of economics that means: an enormously increasing supply of human beings is faced with a declining demand. Even in wealthy societies people are rendered superfluous daily. What should be done with them?"[4]

The Global Squeeze on Jobs

Economists talk about a "natural" rate of unemployment. By this, they mean that some unemployment is not only inevitable in a market economy but healthy. Some people are unemployed voluntarily, having quit their old jobs to look for better ones; this is a sign of optimism, not trouble. In any dynamic economy, companies die and new companies are born in an organic process that, like nature's cycle of birth and rebirth, nourishes the entire economy. This "natural" unemployment keeps wage inflation down by ensuring a steady surplus of workers. Normally, this kind of unemployment is short-term, with the hardship eased by unemployment pay. Workers in heavy industry, like steel and autos, knew there would be layoffs from time to time, when the market was soft and inventories high. Again, unemployment pay helped; so did the high wages that their unions had negotiated to enable them to save against this rainy day. Soon, they knew, the layoff would end and they'd be called back.

What's happening now across the mature and wealthy economies of Japan, North America, and Western Europe is different from this normal cycle. In the United States, whole communities are being laid waste. In Europe, a generation of young people finds the door closed to the world of work. On both continents, layoffs, once begun, never end. Industries die and old jobs don't come back. In Japan, where job security is part of the culture, companies are finding it is harder than ever to find places for the workers they don't really need.

On the Southeast Side of Chicago, in the Tenth Ward, where once steel was king, an entire civilization has vanished. This civilization was anchored to South Works, the giant U.S. Steel mill that died in the 1980s, taking 10,000 jobs with it, and Wisconsin Steel, which was mismanaged into bankruptcy and collapsed suddenly in 1980, killing another 3,400 jobs. The Southeast Side was an insular place, polluted but prosperous, where a United Nations of steelworkers—Poles, Slovaks, Croats, Mexicans, blacks—made America's steel. High wages shoved up costs but also supported a middle-class standard of living. These steelworkers owned their own homes, with a car and an RV in the driveway, children in college, and wives who didn't need to work. When companies discovered that steel could be made more cheaply abroad or by machines that replaced men, the steelmaking died and so did the area. Children were pulled out of college. Families collapsed. Homes were sold. Men drifted away to Texas or California in search of work. Stores and restaurants that depended on the steelworkers' paychecks went broke and closed. Today the area is empty of all but clean air and echoes.

In the prosperous suburbs west and north of the city, churches have begun to run job clubs or counseling services for their well-heeled members who are as jobless as the steelworkers on the Southeast Side. Downtown, in Chicago's Loop, organizations like Forty-Plus, which helps downsized executives over forty find new jobs, are thriving. So are temp agencies that specialize in accountants, lawyers, even doctors. "The days of 'the job' are over. People need to think of themselves now as a 'skill set,'" said Andrea Meltzer, whose company, Executive Options, places jobless executives as temporary workers in companies that don't want the expense or commitment of hiring them full-time.

Five thousand miles away, a winter wind off the North Sea blew through Bremen, a Hanseatic port city in the north of Germany, chilling the idle men loitering near the railway station. By the Weser River, gusts raised small eddies of litter along the half-deserted docks, where the shipbuilding industry has collapsed. Out near the airport, the cold penetrated the modern aerospace factory owned by Daimler-Benz Aerospace, or Dasa, which helps make the European Airbus. The shipbuilding has gone to Japan and other Asian nations. The aerospace industry is shifting to eastern Germany and abroad. As recently as 1993, Dasa employed 80,000 workers—mostly skilled, many white-collar—in Bremen and seven other cities around Germany. That workforce is down to 42,000 now. But all is not lost. The McDonald's near the railway station is hiring.

Around the world, in Tokyo, government and business combine to keep unemployment down. At 3.5 percent, it's as high now as it's ever been but is still beneath the U.S. rate and less than one-third the European rate. This low rate, though, hides a lot of *under*employment. Each Japanese company has what it calls "the window tribe," white-collar workers who sit by the window and while away their days writing essays on the meaning of work. One executive was assigned a desk in a basement lighted by a single bulb that was replaced periodically with bulbs of ever-declining voltage, until the man took the hint and quit. In the parks of Tokyo, you run across men sitting alone at dusk, drinking a can or two of beer before going home. When they were ambitious and valued members of Japan's clan of salarymen, they went out after work with other salarymen for the nightly drinking bouts that are part of Japanese business. Now cast out from this clan into the ranks of the window-sitters, they carefully get some booze on their breath before heading home, so their wives will think they still have real jobs.

Everywhere, the joblessness and instability have inched up from the working class into the middle class, and so into the view of journalists, academics, and politicians. Themselves members of the middle class, they see the job crisis affecting their neighbors, family, or colleagues, and so are reacting with a concern and sympathy that somehow they never extended to blue-collar workers.

This concern is not illogical. If American managers, German engineers, and Japanese salarymen are no longer safe, what has happened to their societies and economies?

Real Numbers and Real Costs

Unemployment rates vary widely from country to country. The underlying situations are not as different as the divergent rates would indicate, but the statistics, however flawed, tell something important about the different ways in which Americans, Japanese, and Europeans are coping with the jobs crisis.

Exhibit 3.1

Unemployment Rates in the First World
(in percent)

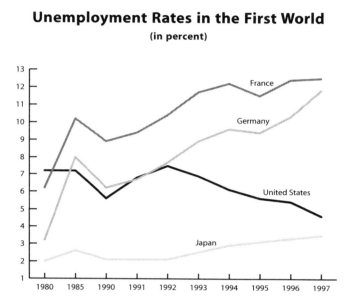

Source: Organization for Economic Cooperation and Development.

At this writing, the official unemployment rate in Japan is 3.5 percent, in America 4.6 percent, in Germany about 11.8 percent, and in France 12.5 percent (see Exhibit 3.1). All these numbers are suspect.

In Japan, that low unemployment rate mainly represents unemployed men. During hard times in that male-dominated society, women simply drop out of the workforce and are not counted as unemployed. (A Japanese saying has it that the average retirement age is fifty-five for men and twenty-five for women.) Students, too, stay in school longer or take training courses rather than try to crack the employment system, with its bias toward seniority.

Another key to the low official rate in Japan is the underemployment exemplified by the window tribe. Rather than fire male workers, companies often assign them to make-work jobs in subsidiaries. Large firms force their smaller suppliers to take on unwanted employees. Relatively inefficient firms, especially in retailing and distribution, employ millions more workers than they need. The retail economy is based on inefficient mom-and-pop stores, and even big department stores have three times more salespeople than equivalent American stores. Yutaka Kosai, president of the Japan Center for Economic Research, estimates that if this "disguised unemployment" were added in, Japan's real rate of joblessness would be about 9 percent, not much below Europe's.[5]

In the United States, government and business trumpet the nation's relatively low unemployment rate and dynamic job creation statistics as proof of a healthy economy. But here, too, statistics mislead. Unlike other countries, the United States has 1.5 to 2.0 percent of its potential workforce in jail; many of these potential workers are young, black, and male. Under rational counting, they would be added to the unemployment rolls. So would the millions who have exhausted their unemployment benefits and are no longer counted as unemployed. So would the hundreds of thousands of downsized middle managers who still collect severance pay and cannot register themselves as unemployed, but who are jobless just the same. So would the millions of idle Americans so discouraged that they have stopped looking for work. In Lawndale, one of Chicago's most decayed inner-city neighborhoods, the official unemployment rate is 18 percent. But a sociologist, Pierre Devise, calculated that only 40 percent of the potential workforce had jobs; most of the rest had dropped out of the economy, beyond the ken of the official statisticians.

Some 12 million Americans work at jobs that pay below the poverty line; many get no health coverage or other benefits, nor have any job security at all. Germany also has its "working poor," persons who hold what are called "590-deutsche-mark jobs." Under German law, a person earning 590 deutsche marks per month gets none of the benefits that can add an extra 80 percent to the average worker's paycheck. These jobs are often part-time jobs held by students or married women anxious to earn some extra money. But while the holders of these poorly paid jobs in Germany are officially included among the unemployed, in the United States the working poor are officially employed.

In Europe, as in the United States, official figures probably understate reality, if less dramatically. Most European governments also stop counting the unemployed after they exhaust their benefits. On both sides of the Atlantic, discouraged would-be workers have quit looking for jobs and have dropped out of the statistics. European countries sponsor widespread job training programs, especially for young people. Laudable in purpose, these programs have become parking lots for students being trained for jobs that don't exist. While they're in the programs, the youngsters are off the unemployment rolls. All too soon, they'll be casualty statistics in the job wars.

America the Flexible

A major theme of this book is that the First-World nations, although all capitalist, vary widely in their histories, attitudes, and cultures and that these variations lead to differences in their economies, which are the result of very different choices made in the past. Nowhere is this more true than in jobs.

Basically, the United States believes that any job is better than no job. It has created jobs but has let wages fall and benefits erode. American government officials and economists claim that these low wages and sparse benefits encourage companies to hire more people. Europe, preferring equality and more reliant on the welfare state, has kept wages up but has created fewer jobs and let unemployment rise. It says this unemployment is bad but the American-style wage disparity, poverty, and instability are worse. Japan, based on an ethos of mutual responsibility, claims the best balance, with both steady wages and low unemployment. But its consumers pay the cost through higher prices. The Japanese ethos says the strength and stability of Japanese society are worth the cost.

The Reagan, Bush, and Clinton administrations have taken pride in their job creation record. When Clinton says that 13.5 million jobs have been added to the American economy on his watch, he has a right to be proud. No other major country has put so many people to work. If the unemployment rate is understated, the number of Americans with jobs is accurate. And this job creation is no small thing. Seen as a whole, the American job picture is not healthy, and the long-run prognosis is grim. But work—even a desk by the window in Japan or a hamburger-flipping job in America—is better than no work. It gives purpose and focus to life. It lets workers feel that they are justifying their place on earth. It contributes to society.

A job, though, is not necessarily the same thing as a good job. In a landscape of peasants, each toiling long hours to subsist, there is no unemployment, but nor is there prosperity or growth. A complex modern nation like the United States depends on shared prosperity not only for its economic growth but for its social cohesion and democratic vigor. The Clinton administration claims that the

Exhibit 3.2

Cumulative Change in Real Wages of Lowest-Paid Workers
(in percent)

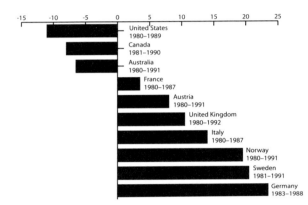

Source: World Bank, "The Employment Crisis in Industrial Countries: Is International Integration to Blame?" in *Regional Perspectives on World Development Report* (Washington, D.C.: IBRD, 1995).

majority of these new jobs are good ones, at wages higher than the average. Other signs undercut this claim.

The most damning evidence is the growth in inequality in the United States, which will be discussed in more detail in Chapter 7. No other major nation, not even Britain, shows as much inequality as the United States, nor in any is the trend toward greater inequality so strong. In the Reagan-Bush years and well into the Clinton administration, fully 98 percent of all income growth in the country went to the top 20 percent. In 1980, the best-paid 10 percent of American full-time male workers earned 3.2 times as much as the worst-paid 10 percent; by 1995 that gap grew to 4.4 percent. (Exhibit 3.2 shows the U.S. record compared with the rest of the industrialized world.)

During those fifteen years, the income of the top 10 percent rose 10.7 percent after taxes, while the earnings of the bottom one-tenth fell 9.6 percent. At the median, the fall was 3.6 percent. This fall stopped, at least for the moment, in mid-1996. Even then, wages only began to rise about 1 percent faster than inflation—better than a pay cut, certainly, but small consolation at a time when corporate profits, executive incomes, and the stock market all were going up at double-digit rates.

The turnaround in the late 1990s did nothing to alter the fact that the paychecks of the majority of American workers bought less in 1995 than they did in 1980—and this after one of the greatest and most sustained booms in American history, with corporate profits and stock prices at all-time highs.

Here are more statistics: The top 20 percent of American wage earners now earns more than the middle 60 percent. The poor are getting poorer, and there are more of them. In 1973, 11.4 percent of all families with children lived in poverty; by 1995, that figure was up to 18.5 percent, or nearly one-fifth of all the families in the country. Many of these poor had jobs; when we talk about the "working poor," they are the people we mean. Fewer Americans have health insurance or guaranteed pensions, and only about 35 percent of the unemployed are covered by unemployment insurance, a figure that also has fallen over the past two decades.[6]

There is a direct link between the growing number of jobs and the falling wages that most of these jobs command. Economists call that link "flexibility." It means that, in the bottom-line world in which most businesses live today, companies will not hire expensive workers, with high wages and benefits, or workers who are hard to fire. But if these wages and benefits are low enough and work rules loose enough—that is, if the labor market is "flexible" enough—then that's another matter. Many companies or stores that would balk at creating high-wage jobs will create low-wage ones. This happens when wages fall so low that it's cheaper for an employer to hire workers than to automate jobs or to send them overseas. Workers who have few demands or expectations, or who are desperate enough, can usually find these jobs.

This is the "race to the bottom," a process that drives incomes ever lower. It is also straightforward supply-and-demand economics at work. In economic theory, when the supply of any commodity is higher than the demand for it, then its price falls to the point at which customers are willing to buy it. This is the dehumanization of labor. No other major country treats its workers as commodities in this way, as raw materials or components that can be bargained to the lowest price.

This supply-and-demand system of labor works both ways. Some employees, like some materials, are so scarce or valuable that they command top dollar. Hence, the soaring income for investment bankers, international lawyers, well-connected consultants, executives skilled at raising stock prices—in short, anyone who can manipulate the new global economy. In an economy in which workers are treated like commodities, these relatively uncommon specimens can exact incomes higher than in more balanced economies.

For other, more common workers, the premium falls. Manufacturing jobs that once paid middle-class wages are replaced by jobs in stores that pay poverty wages. I have talked with sons of steelworkers who work in clean, safe offices behind word processors, wearing white collars and suits that remain clean at the end of the day, but who earn a fraction of what their fathers drew from their dirty, dangerous, carcinogenic jobs in the mills. College graduates work as stock boys or bag groceries. When the Class of 1985 at a highly rated high school in the Chicago suburb of Evanston held its tenth anniversary, a class poll showed that 30 percent of the alumni, most of them college graduates and well into their late twenties, were still working part-time or "freelance" jobs.

All these people are working. Many of them hold down some of the 13.5 million new jobs of which President Clinton boasts; in fact, some hold down two or three of them. These jobs pay a wage. They keep bread on the table and gas in the tank. But by virtue of their very "flexibility," they have little feeling of permanence or stability. Because of this, the Americans who hold them feel little stability themselves or have a sense of the social compact, the shared responsibility between employer and employee, that underlay the postwar economy and created an American community based on work.

Europe: Rigidity and Pain

The European job picture, in many ways, is a mirror image of the American scene. Wages have held steady. Some companies have downsized, but they pay a heavy price in severance pay and other benefits. Dasa, the German aerospace firm, took a $340 million charge in 1996 after it announced the layoff of 5,100 workers. Those who already have jobs feel a sense of security that has long since disappeared in the United States.

But unemployment, especially among the young, is twice the American level. Across the continent, a young generation is growing up without work and is prey to the xenophobic preachings of neofascists like France's Jean-Marie Le Pen. Even older Europeans work less, retire earlier, and rely more on welfare payments. The proportion of European men between fifteen and sixty-four who have jobs has fallen from 86.5 percent in 1973 to only 70 percent now; the American percentage was 81.5 percent in 1973 and about the same now.[7]

This unemployment is a blight on Europe's most prosperous nations. Leaders like German Chancellor Helmut Kohl have promised to cut it in half, but the truth is that no one knows how to do this without inviting the instability and inequalities of the American system, which no European wants. Kohl's aides say privately it just won't happen.

If flexibility has created the American phenomenon of plentiful jobs at low wages, inflexibility is blamed for the European phenomenon of scarce jobs at high wages. Economists dispute how much this difference in flexibility can account for either phenomenon. The consensus is that both continents have been hit by the twin impacts of globalization and technology but have responded in two different ways. Which side of the Atlantic has responded more realistically depends on the viewer.

"When we talk about globalization, we often mean what's happening in the United States," Klaus Friedrich, chief economist at the Dresdner Bank in Frankfurt, told me. "We like what you're doing. We like the flexible markets. We like the way that your economy has created jobs. Our wages have to go lower. Otherwise, we'll just be an old-age home."[8]

"There's an admiration in Europe for the way the American market is creating jobs," said Klaus Bünger, a director at the German Labor Ministry. "We always say we don't want the American hire-and-fire system. But we in Europe pay for our way with unemployment, while you in America pay for your way through the working poor. There must be a third way between these two paths."[9]

Until the mid-1970s, Europe kept low rates of unemployment, usually 3 percent or less. Then, as globalization began and traditional heavy industries declined, this rate went up. Many Europeans feared that unemployment above 5 percent would lead to revolution. But the rate passed that point and kept rising, and nothing happened. Today the unemployment rate for the entire European Union is 11 percent (see Exhibit 3.3). It's 12 percent in France and nearly 12 percent in Germany. In some German cities, like Bremen, it's 13 percent or worse. Bremen's sister city, Bremerhaven, a port where the Weser River meets the North Sea, has 18 percent unemployment.

Exhibit 3.3

Unemployment Features in European Union Countries, 1994

	Unemployment Rate	Youth Unemployment Rate	Long-Term Unemployment[a]	Low-Skilled Unemployment[b]
	(%)	(%)	(% share of total unemployment)	
Belgium	10.0	24.1	58	52
Denmark	8.2	10.7	32	31
France	12.3	29.1	38	46
Germany	8.4	8.6	44	22
Greece	8.9	27.7	51	40
Ireland	14.7	23.3	59[c]	64
Italy	11.4	32.3	62	59
Luxembourg	3.5	7.7	30	63
Netherlands	7.0	10.7	49	32
Portugal	7.0	15.1	43	79
Spain	24.3	45.3	53	68
United Kingdom	9.6	17.0	45	58
Austria				
Finland	18.4	33.6	21	
Sweden	9.8	22.6	10[c]	
European Union	**11.2**	**21.8**	**48**	**50**

Source: European Commission Annual Report 1996, Brussels, in Thygesen et al., *Globalizaion and Trilateral Labor Markets* (New York: The Trilateral Commission, 1996).
a Unemployed for more than 12 months
b Educational level lower than secondary among persons aged 15 to 59 years
c 1993 data

Those who still have jobs are doing well, and even those on unemployment pay aren't doing badly. "We have 18 million unemployed persons [within the European Union] while the United States has 6 million unemployed," said Hugo Paeman, the EU's ambassador to Washington. "But 12 million Americans with work live beneath the poverty line, while our unemployed are paid for doing nothing, but are paid above the poverty line."[10]

Paeman's comparison explained why high unemployment in Europe has not led to revolution. In both the United States and Western Europe, the average unemployed person can expect to get unemployment pay equal to about 50 percent of his or her salary in the first month of unemployment, and from 68 to 80 percent if the person is married and has two children. But for the long-term unemployed, conditions vary radically on the two sides of the Atlantic. After five years out of a job, the average American with two children gets about 17 percent of his or her old salary in various benefits. The figure is 65 percent in France, 71 percent in Germany, and more than 80 percent in Denmark and Finland.[11]

This means that a European who has been on the dole for five years can probably earn as much as he did on the job, assuming that he brings in something on the side through odd jobs on the gray market—the unofficial economy where workers work for cash, give no receipts, and pay no taxes. Social security at this level keeps the wolf from the door so effectively that a jobless worker has no economic reason to mount the barricades—or to look for work. This protection has also helped raise the share of long-term (more than one year) joblessness in Germany to a third of all unemployment.

It is harder for a European employer to fire workers in the first place. In Germany, workers by law get notice of firing two weeks to six months in advance, depending on their seniority. If a company wants to downsize across the board, in a blizzard of pink slips similar to those in American companies, it must negotiate these firings with workers' representatives and the government, which can delay them by up to two months. Severance pay varies, but amounts to about half a year's pay for an average blue-collar worker. In France, employers must give workers notice of one to two months, depending on seniority; for middle management, the period is three months. In most American states, employers can fire at will, with severance pay, if any, varying from company to company. Because of these restrictions and costs, short-term layoffs in Europe are rare.[12]

Sharing the Pain

American economists often cite these rules and regulations as the "rigidities" that keep official European unemployment rates so high. There is something in this: common sense says that an employer forced to cut costs is less likely to hire a worker if he or she thinks this worker is going to be hard to fire. But this isn't the whole story. A bigger part is the slow growth in many European Union nations, like France and Germany, caused largely by the tight budget and monetary policies these countries are following to qualify for the EU's single-currency program. Another part is the exodus of manufacturing and jobs from the EU nations to the cheap-labor ex-communist countries of Central Europe. As Ray Marshall, the former American secretary of labor, has noted, the "rigidities" didn't keep Germany from having a lower unemployment rate than the United States for almost every year between 1972 and 1993.

The fact is that every major economy has a "flexible" labor market, but each is flexible in its own way. Susan Houseman of the Upjohn Institute for Employment Research is one of the few American academics to ask seriously if other countries might be handling hard times more sanely than Americans do. Houseman has studied how American, European, and Japanese companies cope with downturns. In all three countries, companies try to cut costs and workers suffer some pain. But the cost cutting and pain differ significantly.

American companies, Houseman says, lay off workers temporarily or fire them outright. Downsizing is literally the American way. "In contrast, companies in . . . European countries and Japan tend to rely more on short-time work, attrition, early retirement, internal transfers, and layoffs among peripheral workers to achieve labor reductions." When American companies need to cut their overall staffing, about 70 percent of these cuts come from layoffs. In Europe, about 70 percent of the cuts are through short-time work.

At Opel, the German subsidiary of General Motors, management and labor agreed to an average workweek of thirty-five hours over the course of a year. But the hours worked within any given week could range from thirty to forty, depending on business. Volkswagen workers agreed to work a twenty-eight-hour week, at reduced pay. More commonly, hard-pressed companies make ad hoc arrangements with unions to put some workers on short hours. Under the law, companies and governments in both Germany and France make up 50 to 80 percent of the workers' lost pay and benefits.[13]

"U.S. and German companies faced with similar declines in sales make very similar labor cuts," Houseman wrote with Katharine G. Abraham, the U.S. commissioner of labor statistics, in the *Brookings Review*. "The difference is that U.S. firms lay off many workers immediately, while German companies reduce workers' hours."[14] The upshot is that German workers escape the instability of unemployment, the taxpayer avoids having to pay full unemployment benefits, and the company knows that, when business picks up again, its experienced workers are still there.

The Europeans, like the Japanese, also use part-time and temporary workers more than American companies do. But as we shall see in a moment, "part-time" and "temp," like "flexibility," mean different things in different countries.

Houseman's point is that there is no ironclad law of capitalism that forces companies to lay off workers in times of trouble. There are other ways to cope with downturns, she says. Countries and companies have a choice in the matter, and this choice will be dictated by culture and national goals—in short, by what kind of economy and society these countries want.

This mesh of protection around European and Japanese workers can help channel the forces of globalization, but it can't confer invulnerability. Daimler-Benz, Germany's biggest company, has eliminated 70,000 jobs since 1990. Deutsche Telekom, the German telephone company, worked out a deal with unions that will cut 70,000 out of 213,000 workers by the year 2000. In France companies have been slimming and trimming for years but less dramatically. The announcement in 1996 by an appliance maker, Moulinex, that it would cut 2,600 jobs was front-page news.

Most of these job losses will come gradually and through attrition. But a job loss is still a job loss. It means one less job for someone who wants to work, especially for young people who find themselves outside the economy, barred from inheriting their place in the world of work.

All blamed cost pressures caused by global markets and foreign competition. The pain is real in all First-World countries. The only difference is in how it is shared.

Weasel Words

If there's a growth industry in the new economy, it's in euphemisms. In a book called *The New Doublespeak*, Rutgers English professor William Lutz reports the delicate language that companies use to say they have fired someone. "Downsizing" isn't vague or comfy enough any more, Lutz said. When Procter & Gamble fired 13,000 employees, it said it was "strengthening global effectiveness." General Motors of Canada said it was adopting a "lean concept of Synchronous Organization Structures." Tandem Computers talked about "focused reductions," National Semiconductor went in for "reshaping," and Security Pacific Bank announced "a release of resources."

If Americans talk about downsizing with weasel words, Europeans aren't much better. Two current German euphemisms are *freisetzung*, which means to set free, and *Gesundschrumpfen*, or health through shrinkage.

Why Productivity Is Not the Answer

In the face of layoffs and cutbacks across the First World, economists and government officials have taken to whistling in the dark. Faster growth, they say, will mean more jobs. But both the United States and Western Europe have been growing. American workers are working more but for lower pay, while European workers are working less for more pay.

Within individual companies, growth doesn't necessarily generate more jobs. Often, in fact, growth comes through higher productivity generated by machines, not people. Sometimes, it just means fewer workers working harder. In Munich, Manfred Schoch, a union leader at BMW, told me, "We have to make more cars with the same workforce. This year we're doing about 30,000 cars more with the same number of people. This is more productivity, but it comes from technology and longer hours."

Dominique Meda, a French scholar, has pointed out the contradiction at the heart of the dictum that the goal of any economy is to increase productivity, because this is the only way to increase profits that are used for new investment and new jobs. Once upon a time, this worked. But productivity can mean either doing more with more, or doing more with less. Increasingly, employers are taking the latter road, making more with fewer people, and using machines, which don't take sick days or go on strike, to make up the difference. Even workers on Wall Street have noticed this phenomenon. During the stock market boom of the late 1960s, unemployment in New York City fell to 3.1 percent, partly because of the jobs this created. In the 1980s, another boom created hundreds of thousands of new jobs—many of them the kind of clerical and maintenance jobs that employed less-skilled workers. But in the mid-1990s, the greatest bull market in history created only 12,500 new jobs. Automation had stolen many jobs, such as the tasks of delivering, registering, and storing bonds and stock certificates.[15]

Productivity *does* create more and better jobs, but only if its gains are widely shared. Gains produced through exported jobs go to workers abroad, through salaries, or to executives, through bonuses and stock options, or to shareholders, through dividends or increased share prices. Gains produced through technology could be shared with workers but, as the stagnation of wages shows, are going instead to executives and shareholders. This linkage between higher productivity, more jobs, and higher wages is one of many that have been broken in the age of globalization.

Airbus is one of Europe's success stories. It is a consortium of aerospace companies from four European countries, Germany, France, Britain, and Spain. The Airbus airliners command 30 percent of the world's market, up from 5 percent twenty years ago, and rank second only to Boeing among the aircraft powerhouses of the world. If there's an example of an industry and a company that has made maximum use of education and technology to increase productivity and growth, this is it.

But the payoff in jobs isn't there. All four of the aerospace companies in the consortium have, like Dasa, been cutting jobs. Even at the Airbus headquarters in Toulouse, France, the boom in marketing and other administrative duties has produced virtually no new jobs. Richard Brown, the British human relations director, told me that the Toulouse workforce of 2,100 persons has been frozen for three years because "we don't need any more."

Brown, a reflective man, was deeply troubled by what he saw in the economy's inability to create jobs. For companies like Airbus, unemployment and actual job losses "are not the issue":

> The issue is whether we are reaching the level of automation that man has been striving for ever since he invented the wheel. Man can now sit on his butt and produce. But he hasn't been able to figure out how to share this. We've reached the point where unemployment is engendered by rising productivity. We're busting a gut not only to keep our jobs but to keep others from sharing these jobs.
>
> How long can you keep society going in this way? There's increasing productivity but a declining requirement for labor. How do we keep people busy?[16]

Japan: A Different Flexibility

Japan also has its own form of flexibility. Japan's famous system of "lifetime employment" is widely credited with keeping its unemployment rate low. In fact, this system never applied to more than 40 percent of the workforce and probably affects no more than 30 percent now. Even this percentage is concentrated in the giant, world-girdling corporations, not in the tiny shops and firms that make up much of the economy. In these smaller firms and in lower-ranking jobs in the big corporations, millions of workers are officially considered "temporary" or "part-time," even though they may work full workweeks and have been on the job for years.

This Japanese system of employment is called the "core versus peripheral" strategy, in which relatively insecure "part-time" employees orbit around a nucleus of extremely secure and well-paid permanent executives and managers.

This lifetime employment at the upper levels gives Japanese management a stability unknown among the job-hopping executives of the United States. In a visit to Fujitsu Laboratories Inc. in Akashi, a branch of the giant Fujitsu electronics firm, every executive with whom I talked had been with Fujitsu for his entire career, and expected to be there until he retired. This custom is enshrined in both tradition and law. Japanese courts have ruled that these permanent, full-time employees have strong job rights that can't be violated unless the company can prove serious misconduct.

For the other 70 percent of the Japanese workforce, life is less certain. Generally, employees who would be fired in the United States are kept on the payroll, often in meaningless tasks. The giant *keiretsu*, or conglomerates, that dominate the economy frequently park unneeded employees in subsidiaries or with small suppliers, who survive at the whim of the *keiretsu* and so have no choice but to hire the castoffs. Many of these workers end up in make-work jobs in philanthropy or public relations, traditionally the caboose on the Japanese economic train. Major corporations have been known to set up amusement parks or market gardens solely to employ these castoffs.

Cutbacks themselves take place largely through attrition or early retirement, which is getting easier as Japan's workforce ages. When Nippon Telegraph and Telephone, the country's largest corporate employer, announced in 1995 that it would cut 45,000 jobs over the next five years, it knew that at least half of these would come through retirements, often accompanied by extra lump sum payments.[17]

Many companies urge workers to retire at age fifty-five. Others keep older workers on but reduce recruitment of young workers. Young Japanese aged fifteen to twenty-four have an unemployment rate of 7.2 percent, more than double the national average. Most live with their parents, go to graduate school, or take part-time jobs.

Japanese companies have other ways of saving money. Bonuses and overtime pay, a relatively large part of total pay, can be cut back faster and more easily than basic salaries. During downturns, companies give workers one or two days of "holiday," with three-fourths of their salary paid by unemployment insurance.[18]

Cutbacks fall disproportionately on women, who traditionally hold the insecure or part-time jobs. Japanese companies boast that they never lay off a male head of household, but this praiseworthy goal is achieved at the cost of widespread discrimination against women. Westerners may find this appalling, but there is no indication of any widespread resentment among Japanese women, who seem to accept that their role is to rule the home, which they do vigorously, not the workplace. There is no real feminist movement in Japan, where relations between the sexes seem to be about where they were in the United States forty or fifty years ago. Women workers earn about half as much as men, a ratio that hasn't changed in twenty-five years.[19]

The pressures on Japanese companies from competition from the lower-wage nations of Southeast Asia is real, and has had an impact, but nothing like the mass layoffs common in the United States. Employment at Fujitsu, for instance, was 50,768 employees in 1991, peaked at 54,442 in 1993, and was down to 48,225 in mid-1996.[20]

A World of Temps

Nowhere is the sense of instability in the American workplace greater than in "temping"—the temporary or contract work that has become a major force in this new dynamic American economy. For that reason, it surprises Americans to learn that temps occupy a bigger share of the workforce in both Japan and Europe, and always have. But once again, the rules differ.

Until the 1980s, American temps were usually receptionists or secretaries, filling low-paid clerical jobs in offices needing a little help at busy times or over vacations. Now, in those same offices, almost anyone you meet below the level of the CEO could be a temp.

Temp jobs are only 2 percent of all American jobs, but they account for fully 20 percent of all new jobs, according to the Economic Policy Institute in Washington.[21] In the last twelve years, the number of all temp workers in the United States has quintupled, to more than 2 million persons. Many of these new temps are still in lower-skilled or lower-paid jobs. This is what the Teamsters' strike at UPS was all about: of the 46,000 unionized jobs that UPS added in the mid-1990s, 38,000 are part-timers earning an average of $9 per hour, half the full-time rate. Manpower Temporary Services, the giant temp firm, has replaced General Motors as the nation's biggest employer. The entire temp industry, in fact, employs two and a half times as many people as the auto industry.[22]

Executive Options is one of more than 140 executive temp agencies in the country. It has 6,000 professionals and executives on its database, according to its head, Andrea Meltzer. They are "middle-management people on up," she said, people who have been directors of marketing or human resources, company treasurers, lawyers, accountants, traders. Most used to work full-time. Now they are farmed out to companies on contract, some for months, others for hours or days. Stock traders may be sent out to work the peak morning hours only. An accountant may spend a few days at the end of a month doing the books for a small company or a nonprofit group.[23]

Co-Counsel, another national temp firm, finds temporary jobs for lawyers. In Chicago, the firm's database contains 1,200 lawyers, culled from 3,000 applicants, including many recent law school graduates who go straight from graduation to unemployment.

"Every six months, when there's a new swearing-in ceremony, we get a raft of new applications," said Frank Troppe, Co-Counsel's national sales director. But these beginners almost always get turned down because employers want lawyers with at least two years of experience. There's no shortage of such experienced lawyers, according to people in the field, because corporations, facing the need to trim costs and increase profits, are firing in-house lawyers. Law firms, under cost pressure from their corporate clients, are taking on temp lawyers as needed, rather than hiring them on a full-time basis.

None of these temp lawyers, needless to say, will ever make partner. Most are well paid. Many earn as much as they would in a normal full-time job. But there's no pension, seldom health insurance, no bonuses, and, of course, no permanence. "In law," Troppe said, "there's no such thing as security anymore."[24]

For many workers, temp work is the same—sometimes literally the same—as permanent work, only more unstable. I talked with a young Chicagoan, Peter Craig, who spent ten years working his way up in the Chicago advertising world until he became an art director at Leo Burnett, a leading firm. Then, just before Christmas of 1993, when his wife was seven months pregnant, Burnett fired him. He began freelancing and ended up with a temp agency, which sent him to one of Burnett's suppliers, which in turn seconded him back to Burnett, where he did the same work, as an art director, as he did when he was fired. He got paid by the hour, and the hours were long, so the pay was good. Still, he lacked benefits and paid his own Social Security contribution. To save money, he scaled back the full-service health insurance policy that Burnett once provided to a bare-bones plan, costing one-fourth as much, and hoped that no serious illness struck.

"From what I understand, I'm the wave of the future," Craig said when I talked with him. Like many young Americans, he seemed to accept this instability as a fact of life. "This project I'm on [at Burnett] could last as long as a couple of years. But I'm already looking ahead to see what I'll do next."

Temping, by its nature, also encourages weasel words. No one likes to talk about "temps." These new freelancers call themselves "self-employed" or "consultants." Temp lawyers say they are "lawyering on a contract basis." A help-wanted sign in a Starbucks coffee bar advertised for "hourly partners."

Temping is nothing less than the just-in-time principle applied to people. Just-in-time (JIT) was pioneered by Japanese companies to reduce inventory and storage costs. Instead of keeping large supplies of parts on hand, the Japanese companies organized manufacturing schedules so tightly that they could order up the parts as needed, to be delivered "just in time," passing almost directly from the loading dock to the assembly line. Properly run, this saves a lot of money. But even the Japanese stop short of expanding this principle to workers.

In the United States, the JIT employment principle is known as the core-ring strategy, according to Meltzer, who told me, "Companies . . . want to keep a core of full-time people, keeping just enough [supervisory staff] to get by, and augmenting them with a ring of temporary professionals." This sounds a lot like Japan's "core versus peripheral" employment system, but there are differences. Even for the outer ring, life in Japanese corporations is still more secure than in American companies. Inside the Japanese core, jobs are all but guaranteed. Inside the American core, they can disappear at the drop of a pink slip.

Part-time and temp work, though, are keys to Japanese flexibility. Part-timers and temps are no less than 16 percent of the Japanese workforce, eight times the American rate. The trend is up; in 1982 only 11 percent of Japanese workers were part-timers. The reason seems to be the pressures of globalization: "Japanese businesses have come under greater pressure to reduce labor costs and increase employment flexibility. Businesses have increased their use of part-time workers, who earn lower wages, receive fewer benefits and enjoy less job security than regular workers, in response to these pressures."[25]

But these part-timers are not necessarily either part-time or temporary. More than 20 percent of them work as many hours as full-timers. Many have held their jobs for years. But they fall into a workplace limbo beyond the reach of lifetime employment or unions. They have no job guarantees and don't share in the seniority-based wages enjoyed by permanent workers. Their pay is lower, they get fewer benefits, and they can be fired more easily than permanent workers.

Not surprisingly, most Japanese temps are women. In a country where women are only 35 percent of the workforce, they account for 83 percent of the part-time employment. Many of the industries that make heavy use of part-timers—such as construction, manufacturing, communications, and real estate—are the same industries where women's pay lags furthest behind that of men.[26]

The average pay for a Japanese part-time worker is only 95,000 yen, or $790, per month. An average full-time worker makes 409,000 yen, or $3,400, per month (or $4,100 for male workers only).[27]

Temp work has been a fixture on the European industrial scene for years. About 10 percent of all German workers are temps, the same as in 1983. Temps were barely 4 percent of the French workforce in 1983, peaked at 11 percent in 1990, and have kept that level ever since. In both countries, women and young workers are most likely to be temps. All have job guarantees; in fact, it's as hard to fire a temp as a full-time worker.

In Germany, employers can keep temps only eighteen months, or for two years in small companies. After that, they have to let them go or hire them as full employees with full benefits.[28] In France, special Regulations for Precarious Employment say that firms can hire temps only to replace a missing employee or to help out during peak periods. A temp's contract is limited to eighteen months, and the employer must pay full benefits. When the contract ends, the temp gets a bonus to compensate for the life of instability.[29]

Is Technology to Blame? . . .

These comparisons describe the different reactions of Japan, America, and Europe to the global pressures on jobs. But they don't answer the two big questions: Exactly what parts of the global economy are killing jobs and pushing wages down? And why have experiences differed so much from country to country?

Amid the footnotes and formulae of the scholarly economic journals, a terrific debate is going on over the causes of the First-World job crisis. On one side are the majority of economists, who say that trade may be causing part of the problem, particularly for low-skilled and low-wage workers, but only a small part. Imports from Third-World countries don't dominate First-World trade, they say. For instance, they amount to only 30 percent of American manufactured imports, which themselves amounted to only 2.1 percent of American gross national product. This, they say, is just too small a percentage to have such a major impact. It might have cost some jobs at the bottom of the labor market, but that's all.

As for the growing inequality in wages, they say, that is mostly due to the domestic impact of technology, which has wiped out most of the jobs in American industry that called for weak minds and strong backs. According to this way of thinking, technology has created an ocean of unneeded unskilled labor, driving down wages. At the same time, this technology has driven up the demand for smart, skilled workers who know how to handle it. Their wages go up, while the pay of the less skilled goes down, creating the wage gap.

Technology can't be clearly separated from globalization. Instant communications, robots, computers, and modern transportation make most foreign investment and Third-World manufacturing possible. But these economists argue that it is a stretch to blame trade and the global economy for unemployment and wage disparities, when most of it is the fault of machines used at home.[30]

Technology's impact has been huge. From factory robots to office computers to automated teller machines, technology has changed the way everyone works—or doesn't work. More is to come. Machines soon will be able to diagnose illnesses, prepare tax returns, enter data through visual scanning—even invest on capital markets, taking advantage of instantly perceived opportunities, without the help of human traders.

Technology, of course, creates jobs, too. It has created 18,000 jobs at Microsoft, the most successful information technology company of them all. But it would take three Microsofts to replace the 50,000 jobs lost at Sears, Roebuck, or two to replace the 40,000 workers that AT&T plans to cut, or another three to make up for the job losses at General Motors, or another two to make up for the 33,000 eliminated since 1990 by United Technologies (which created 15,000 new jobs outside the United States at the same time; the other 18,000 jobs are gone forever).

Peter Drucker, the management expert, coined the phrase *knowledge workers* and celebrates the revolution that is creating the knowledge society. But even Drucker doesn't think that most people will benefit from it. He has warned, in fact, of "a new class conflict, between the large minority of knowledge workers and the majority of people, who will make their living traditionally, either by manual work, whether skilled or unskilled, or by work in services, whether skilled or unskilled."[31]

"People are now becoming the most expensive optional component of the productive process and technology is becoming the cheapest," writes Michael Dunkerley, a British software specialist. "People are now specifically targeted for replacement just as soon as the relevant technology is developed that can replace them."[32]

. . . Or Is It Trade?

So much evidence piling up points at globalization and trade as the major forces that it is impossible to accept technology as the sole culprit. A smaller group of economists, led by British economist Adrian Wood, argues that trade with low-wage Third-World countries has played a greater role in increasing unemployment among low-skilled workers. Overall, he says, trade has lowered the demand for unskilled workers by about 20 percent. This impact will grow as these countries—some of them, such as South Korea and the former Soviet Union, with well-educated workforces—become more competitive in more-skilled manufacturing.[33]

In fact, no economist has enough information yet to rule out anything. Even Robert Z. Lawrence, the Harvard economist who has hotly denied that trade is a big part of the problem, has pleaded the problem of "data limitations." Lawrence and most of his mainstream colleagues are devoted free traders, literally trained from their under-

Exhibit 3.4

Change in Unemployment Rate of Low-Skilled Workers
(in percent)

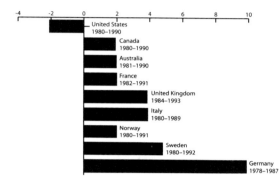

Source: World Bank, "The Employment Crisis in Industrial Countries: Is International Integration to Blame?" in *Regional Perspectives on World Development Report* (Washington, D.C.: IBRD, 1995).

graduate days to reject the thought that trade can cause more harm than good. Lawrence has even warned against letting such ideas get around: "The very perception that a link exists [between trade and labor problems] could put the continuing evolution of trade and investment flows at risk."[34]

No one actually accuses these economists of faking their evidence to protect the sanctity of free trade. But it's clear that many economists have carefully limited their research to produce the results they wanted. The growing evidence that free trade can indeed cause severe damage, and that this damage may even outweigh the gains, is producing nothing less than a religious crisis among the true believers in the economics departments of American universities. (See Exhibit 3.4 for unemployment changes in major countries.)

One of Lawrence's Harvard colleagues, Dani Rodrik, has published a thoughtful booklet acknowledging that "the process that has come to be called 'globalization' is exposing a deep fault line between groups who have the skills and mobility to flourish in global markets and those who either don't have these advantages or perceive the expansion of unregulated markets as inimical to social stability." Rodrik says he still believes free trade is best in the long run but admits that it can cause severe problems. He wishes his fellow economists would show a little less statistical rigor and a little more willingness to figure out how ordinary human beings can be protected from these problems.[35]

The debate over the global economy is still so new that no one has really tried to tie together the three aspects of globalization—the global capital markets, the growth of trade and competition from low-wage countries, and the revolution in technology and communications—and apply them to the jobs crisis. The truth, as those in the front lines already know, is that capital, trade, and technology are combining and reinforcing each other to take jobs and drive down wages. Alan Ehrenhalt, a Washington editor and author, expressed this frustration at being told by experts "that the plain evidence of the senses is wrong":

> Ordinary Americans look at their country and note the disappearance of 40 million jobs in the past two decades and conclude that something terribly disruptive has been going on. They see that many of the nation's biggest corporations now do most of their manufacturing in Third World countries, and infer that precious livelihoods are fleeing to Thailand and Sri Lanka. The response of many economists is to insist that no such thing is happening.[36]

The anecdotal evidence is piling up. As Rodrik said, the economists must recognize it.

The Root of the Problem

This link between trade, technology, and global capital markets is the key to the global economy's impact on the First World. It is to this process that we now turn.

As we saw in the first two chapters, global capital markets and their insistence on "best practice" and highest returns have been pushing companies for twenty years to lower their costs by moving jobs overseas, cutting jobs at home, increasing the use of labor-saving technology, and, if possible, reducing wages and benefits. These capital markets, which are by far the most advanced segment of the global economy, are the root cause of all else.

A study by David Howell of the Jerome Levy Economics Institute at Bard College casts serious doubt on technology as a prime mover. The real decline in low-wage, low-skilled jobs occurred in the 1970s, he said. But this happened before technology—computers, robots, and other forms of computer-aided manufacturing—truly transformed the American workplace. All statistics show that wages began to fall about 1973, beginning with the lowest-paid workers and moving up to better-paid workers. But if technology didn't make its real impact until ten years later, then something other than technology caused this collapse.[37]

There are some tantalizing suspects. The year 1973 was the year that the United States unlinked the dollar from gold, the Bretton Woods system died, and the global capital market, in effect, was born. This global capital market, as we saw in the last chapter, is the engine of globalization.

The same year, 1973, also was the year of the first oil crisis, in which the members of OPEC began to multiply the price of oil, forcing First-World countries to cut other costs by automating and holding down wages. Frank Levy of the Massachusetts Institute of Technology, one of the nation's leading labor economists, notes that the oil crisis led to high inflation. The Federal Reserve increased interest rates to cool off the economy and bring inflation down. These higher rates brought investment money flooding into the United States, which sent the dollar up on the nascent world money markets. The strong dollar, in turn, made foreign goods, especially from Japan and Germany, cheaper than American-made goods. Imports flowed in, and for the first time, American companies and American workers had to compete with relatively low-wage, low-cost foreign companies. Many workers lost their jobs as manufacturers moved overseas or laid off workers at home.

The 1970s also was the time when a free-market fever began to sweep America. Deregulation of airlines and other industries was a mantra of the Carter administration of the late 1970s, well before Ronald Reagan went to Washington.

In short, the first rising of the global tide coincided with and nurtured the growing gospel of the free market. Businesses were encouraged to get lean and get tough. Many closed plants in the high-wage North and moved to the low-wage Sun Belt, only recently made habitable by the arrival of air conditioning. The Sun Belt also was not only nonunion but often aggressively antiunion, and the newly hired unskilled workers there lacked the collective bargaining power of the newly unemployed workers of New England and the Rust Belt.

Technology *did* take over the workplace in the 1980s, and the problems of jobs and wage disparities got worse. Secure, high-wage, well-skilled workers, both blue-collar and white-collar, found themselves replaced by computers and robots. A second round of OPEC price increases in 1979 intensified the pressure on companies to lower costs. The global capital markets grew exponentially, demanding ever lower costs and ever higher profits from companies. To business managers, the message was: Make maximum return or be swallowed up in the wave of mergers, acquisitions, and buyouts that the markets, now up and roaring, made possible. Companies that had gone south to the Sun Belt moved again, to the Third World. Outsourcing became the buzzword, as big companies took many of the jobs they used to do in-house—from maintenance to design to accounting—and shipped them out to specialized and lower-wage firms that grew up in their shadow. Imports from Japan and the Asian Tigers destroyed entire American industries.

Ronald Reagan became president and the free market found its champion. Deregulation expanded in transportation, communications, energy, financial services, and other industries. When Reagan broke the air traffic controllers' strike, corporations everywhere knew that open season had been declared on unions. They launched their assault on organized labor, benefits, pensions, and the minimum wage. The unions, themselves grown fat and corrupt, were no match for this new corporate vigor.

The impact on labor was devastating. First, in the 1970s, low-skilled workers had lost the good jobs that manufacturing once provided and were forced to scrap for lower-paying jobs. Then, in the 1980s, they were joined by higher-skilled workers displaced by technology and the downsizing of growing globalization. Suddenly, once-prosperous employees, many of them members of the middle class, found themselves competing for low-wage jobs with unskilled workers.

Steelworkers ended up collecting tolls on tollways. Bank tellers became telemarketers. Stock handlers in unionized factories became stock clerks in nonunion grocery stores. Some never found jobs. Many of those who did made a fraction of their former pay. With a surplus of labor and a shortage of jobs, the law of supply and demand drove wages down. Weak unions, low minimum wages, and emasculated government agencies could not stop the fall. With no floor beneath them, wages fell into the basement.

A few workers at the top, well educated and able to cope with the global economy, saw their wages soar. And so the United States plunged into an era of job insecurity, falling wages for most workers, and the most unequal wage and wealth structure in the industrialized world.

All this happened, remember, at a time when the stock market was booming, corporate profits were rising, national wealth was growing, and America was becoming the world's sole superpower. For the first time in the postwar years, the economy and the people who lived within it had become unlinked. "There's no longer an automatic connection between a growing economy and rising prospects for ordinary workers," Robert Reich said. "Millions of white-collar supervisors and midlevel managers are joining blue-collar production workers in a common category: frayed-collar workers in gold-plated times."[38]

What Globalization Does to Wages

Workers who still had jobs discovered they were caught in a vise that the economists call factor price equalization. This theory says that, if goods can be made as well in a cheap-wage place as a high-wage place, then the wages in the two places will tend to converge over time. In other words, the wages of American and Brazilian steelworkers should end up being about the same.

This creates a decent life for the Brazilian steelworker and for other Third-World workers who can compete with workers in the First World. But their American counterparts find their wages cut, with disastrous effects both on their living standards and on the purchasing power of the American economy. If this can happen in steel, it also can happen in automaking, pharmaceuticals, data entry, computer programming, or stockbroking—any job that can be done anywhere in the world, given the proper technology.

Factor price equalization was conceived by Paul Samuelson, the dean of American economists, but most mainstream economists hate the idea, because it says that free trade can destroy First-World incomes. This puts economists in the position of renouncing their faith in free trade or writing off the well-being of their fellow citizens. Dani Rodrik's book was nothing more than a plea that economists recognize this dilemma.

So far, most First-World workers have higher skills than most Third-World workers, and skills still count for something. But both these worlds have equal access now to global capital markets. Increasingly, modern technology augmented by training are leveling out the differences between Third-World and First-World skills. Wages of workers in many Third-World countries are indeed rising. As we have

Exhibit 3.5

The Global Labor Pool, 1989

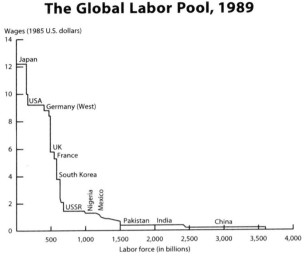

Note: Widths of segments represent population.
Source: Trilateral Commission.

seen, wages of workers, at least in the United States, are falling. Gary
Burtless has this to say about the implications:

> If these assumptions hold, free trade between the United States and Mex-
> ico will equalize U.S. and Mexican wages for equivalent labor. . . . If one
> accepts the assumptions of the [factor price equalization] theorem, the
> North American Free Trade Agreement represents good news for most
> Mexican workers and bad news for U.S. workers whose skills are equiva-
> lent to those of average workers in Mexico.[39]

This pressure will grow as hundreds of millions of new, young
workers enter the global workforce in countries that, until now, took
little part in the world economy (see Exhibit 3.5). The world's labor
force amounted to 1.5 billion workers in 1950. Some forty-five years
later, it had grown by 2 billion workers. Over the next thirty years,
it will grow by another 2 billion workers, as the Third-World countries—especially China and India—become full participants in the
global economy. Fully 90 percent of all these new workers will live
in these Third-World nations. By the year 2025, no less than 83 percent of the world's workers will be Third Worlders; the workers in
America, Japan, and Europe will be a minority, only 17 percent,
skilled, pampered, and beleaguered.[40]

The prophets of globalization celebrate this trend, assuming it will create new markets. But the truth is that no one knows if there will be jobs to employ these billions of new workers, or what their entry into the economy will mean to their richer rivals in the older industrial nations. They will earn $5 per day at the most, but they will work under skilled management, with modern technology and the blessing of global capital markets. There is no reason to assume that their productivity will be any less than that of workers in Minnesota or Mannheim who earn twenty times as much. If economists want a laboratory test of the factor price equalization theory, they are about to get it.

Workers vs. Workers

One of the most tortured areas in this debate concerns labor standards. Basically, this means that First-World workers are in competition for jobs with workers in countries that condone not only low pay but child and prison labor, bans on unions, long hours, dangerous conditions, and other abuses that have been outlawed for years in the wealthier nations. In effect, First-World companies are profiting from practices that are against the law in the country where they are headquartered.

Movements have begun to establish at least minimum standards: a ban on child labor, for instance. But no one imagines that Third-World conditions can be raised significantly any time soon. For one thing, many of these abuses are better than the alternative. Many victims of child labor practices are the sole support of their families. Real reform must be coupled with the kind of economic progress that make it more advantageous for children to study than to work.

Union officials who talk about international labor solidarity are kidding themselves. There can be no common ground between workers at such different levels, whose only relationship is competitive. Just as Third-World countries refuse to adopt minimum labor standards, fearing they will only send investment elsewhere, so their workers have a vested interest in opposing any "solidarity that protects high wages for rich countries, preferring to undercut them by at least a bit," said Benjamin I. Page, a Northwestern University professor:

> It may be in the interest of the world's poor to go ahead and outcompete the rich; to work for the 20 or 25 cents an hour that seems like a pittance

to us but is an improvement over past conditions for them; to take over
world markets for manufactured goods and (more slowly) services; to
accumulate profits, attract investment, and gradually build up their wages
as their productivity increases and the reserve army of cheap labor around
the world gradually gets called up. In other words, international labor solidarity may not be in the interest of workers in poor countries.[41]

How Trade Kills Jobs

Those who say that trade has little effect on jobs are taking too narrow a view of the effects trade can have, for four reasons. First, companies in First-World nations don't have to invest abroad to kill jobs
at home; this is done whenever these companies adopt labor-saving
technology to meet competition from Third-World imports. Second,
it is a truism among industrial developers that each factory job creates four or more "spin-off" jobs in the restaurants, banks, construction firms, and other businesses that serve the factory worker
and his or her family. This means that every job that dies takes four
more jobs with it. Doubters should drive through the old steelmaking neighborhoods of Chicago and other Rust Belt cities and see the
boarded-up diners, bars, dry cleaners, clothing stores, and gas stations. The employees of these establishments never worked for the
steel mill, but they relied on that mill every bit as much as the workers on the blast furnace. Third, even the threat of foreign competition is often enough to frighten employees and keep wages down.

Finally, even businesses far removed from the world of trade—
bookstores and city governments, hospitals and grocery stores—cannot escape this trend. As wages fall and jobs disappear for industrial
and office workers, these workers flock to other businesses to find
work. As we have seen, they are desperate, and there is no floor under
their wage. Willing to work for anything, they drive down the wages
of everyone, including the hospital orderly and grocery store clerk
who never set foot in a factory in their lives. The city of Chicago,
which once used $8-per-hour city workers to clean up after street
festivals, now hires freelance cleaners at the minimum wage.

Gary Burtless, who works at the Brookings Institution in Washington, is a mainstream economist not known for protectionist thinking. But he wrote that the evidence is growing that, while laid-off
workers can be helped by training or subsidies,

they might also benefit from trade protection. These studies imply that liberal trade can affect adversely the real earnings of a wide class of workers, and not just those workers employed in a handful of hard-hit industries.

Even if the new evidence does not affect the policy preferences of most economists, we should acknowledge that the evidence, if valid, offers powerful ammunition to the opponents of free trade.[42]

Institutions to the Rescue

There is no mystery why the American, European, and Japanese reactions to this global assault on jobs vary so greatly. The source of the difference lies in what the economists call "institutions." The institutions that protect workers—labor unions, wage floors, free collective bargaining, minimum wages, laws that restrict firing, strong social security structures—are still intact in Europe. Forty percent of German workers still belong to labor unions, as against about 11 percent of private-sector workers in the United States. The Teamsters' victory in the 1997 strike against UPS, coupled with a new vigor in signing up low-wage and minority workers, has encouraged American unions. Commentators called it a "shot across the bow" of American business. But the union's revival so far is more a faint hope than a reality. In France, only 10 percent of workers are union members, but the national scope of collective bargaining means that unions help set wages for 80 percent of the workforce. High minimum wages and strong social security systems set a floor under wages, keeping workers out of the poverty trap familiar to nearly one-fifth of American families. The same institutions still reign in Japan, except for the high social security benefits; unemployment pay there is lower than in the United States. But Japanese companies see themselves as part of the Japanese cultural barrier against unemployment. If women are quickly cast aside in a downturn, the emphasis on maintaining jobs for men guarantees a steady family income in a country where the nuclear family is still the norm.

Of course, the same institutions that keep wages high and poverty low in Europe have helped produce the high unemployment there. Neither Europe nor Japan has repealed the laws of globalization. The triple threat of capital, trade, and technology has hit these countries, too, and has cut into the supply of work to be done. Because wages cannot fall, marginal jobs remain unfilled in Europe. In Japan, barriers to trade solve some of the problems. High prices enable companies to keep jobs for workers who would be fired in other countries.

As Ray Marshall noted, the European institutions that are blamed now for high unemployment were in place in the palmier years of low unemployment, and caused no problems then. What has changed, then, is the situation, not the institutions. Globalization has cut into European growth, as it has cut into American growth. Economic systems in both countries that helped share the wealth in growing economies have magnified the problems of sharing the hardship in more stagnant economies.

The problems are not going to go away, as Rebecca Blank of Northwestern University wrote:

> To the extent that part of the problem is due to growing global economic competition (particularly from rapidly developing nations), this competition will only continue and even accelerate. To the extent that part of the problem is due to the growth of "smart" technologies that privilege more skilled workers, these technological shifts are still under way in most industries.[43]

There are rich ironies in all this. It took a century of agitation and politics to get the workweek down to forty hours. Now it may go to twenty hours, involuntarily. The same people who wanted to cut work hours traditionally decried the foul conditions and hard labor of industrial life. Now they are finding that only one thing is worse—no labor at all.

In the United States, the competition for jobs, constant temping, career shifting, and need for constant innovation will create a civilization of rootless hustlers existing, like Willie Loman, on a smile and a shoeshine. In Europe, young people going straight from school to the dole queue will create a permanent underclass, a lost generation that doesn't know what work is.

For workers across the First World who must deal with this global jobs crisis, the bad news is that the people who should be coming up with the cure are still debating the diagnosis. No solution is in sight.

PART II

Trouble in
the Triad

4. AMERICA: MIDDLE-CLASS BLUES

NOT SO LONG AGO, to be an American was to be, almost by birthright, middle class. At one point, 80 percent of all Americans called themselves members of the middle class. Americans, traditionally uncomfortable with European notions of an upper class, working class, or lower class, found both solidarity and identity in this middle class. The whole concept never seemed to have much to do with wealth; the waitress, the factory hand, the teacher, the executive, the stockbroker all called themselves middle class without irony. More truly, the concept embraced shared values, shared dreams, a shared civilization. The middle class meant Norman Rockwell and Ozzie and Harriet, and never mind that those icons had more to do with our image of ourselves than with reality. They summed up what we wanted to be and what, in our best moments, we were. The American Century may only have spanned 20 or 30 years, but while it lasted, the middle class defined and ruled it.

The middle-class ethos embraced attitudes toward social stability, religious acceptance, family cohesion, especially politics. In a nation made up of so many other nations, other creeds, other histories, the middle class provided the goals on which these diverse fragments could agree, a focus for their common striving. This broad middle class provided the ballast of American politics, leveling the ideological swings that roiled other, more class-ridden nations. With

103

80 percent of the population sharing a common class, political equilibrium was all but guaranteed.

If the middle class was social in form and political in practice, its underpinnings were economic. America was a country where people came to work, earned a decent living, bought a home, owned a car. If you weren't wealthy, you could be. Your son or your daughter certainly would be. Equality was the ideal, if not the fact. The American idea meant getting ahead, promotions, moving on and moving up. American optimism was at root an economic optimism. If the middle class was commercial and a little grasping, well, what was wrong with that? If you're so smart, why aren't you rich?

The Three Middle Classes

Somewhere in the gale of globalization, the winds of economic change eroded this great American middle class and split it, not into two parts but into three.

One part is the now-aging traditional middle class, which lived the American dream. The members of the middle class came out of the Depression and World War II, grew up in the greatest boom in American history, married and bought homes early, raised kids safely, held jobs for life. They saw life as a passenger train passing through town; all they had to do was get on and ride, and they'd get where they wanted to go. For many of them, this is just what happened. These middle-classmates radiated security, confidence, and generosity. They had affluence. They may have been an historical aberration, the inheritors of a golden moment in American life, but their middle-class values shaped the way America looked at itself and still thinks it ought to be.

The second middle class is their children, a cheated class. The members of this class grew up in comfort and came of age in the sixties, against a background of Vietnam and Aquarius. Some rejected the old middle-class values, but most did not. Raised to expect the stability and growth of an expanding economy, they inherited instead downsizing, global competition, and fear. Many of them had good jobs in middle management and now, having been laid off, know they probably won't get back on the ladder at the same rung. Having known affluence, they now stand to lose it.

The third middle class, just coming of age, is an anxious class.

Its members have more trouble finding a good job and keeping it than did earlier generations. If employed, they can't afford to buy a house, get married, start a family, at least as early as their parents did. In fact, they realize they probably will be the first American generation to remain poorer than their parents. To a surprising degree, they accept instability, embrace insecurity, and seem to expect nothing else. They have the toys of affluence—a vcr, a health club membership, gourmet coffee—but not the real affluence of a house or savings or a stake in their communities.

If the original middle class rode the train to a safe destination, the new middle class seems stuck on a bus plying the same old route. Or, to change the metaphor, the old middle class inherited an escalator economy: anyone who got on seemed to rise. Members of the new middle classes still can rise, but they're on a ladder now, with stationary rungs. Some people climb, some fall off, and some are in the middle, just holding on.

The traditional middle class was broad, stable, a little stuffy, slow to change, optimistic, patriotic, and a touch prudish, focused on family and community, committed to education and the old verities. Pay as you go. A penny saved is a penny earned. With this went conformity and not a little hypocrisy, but it underlay the most successful era in the country's history.

The Middle Class Stalls and Shrinks

Like the global economy, the middle class is a fuzzy entity that means something real to people who can't quite describe it. Some economists define it as narrowly as the 20 percent smack in the middle of American wage earners. That means 80 percent of Americans are either upper class or working class, and even in these times, that won't do. Others say it's the middle 60 percent, and that's probably more like it, since it lumps the rich at one end and the poor at the other. Then you realize that the top 20 percent starts with people who are making about $50,000 a year, and that just isn't rich.

A frequent definition is anybody making between $25,000 and $70,000 a year. But this means that a married truck driver and a teacher each making a little more than $35,000 a year are too rich to be middle class. This is a ludicrous idea in an era when a $35,000 salary can be swallowed in two gulps by a rather modest new car and a child's year at a state university.

Perhaps the best definition of middle-class life has more to do with comfort. In essence, it's a secure middle ground, neither rich nor poor, shared by people with the means to live a decent life, pay their bills, and have some money left over for optional pleasures. Cynics would define a middle-class family as one too rich to qualify for college financial aid but too poor to pay the tuition themselves. One of my colleagues, Lisa Anderson, says it simply: "Being middle class simply meant that if you worked hard, stayed sober, and stayed the course, you were promised the chance to get ahead and make a good life—not rich, not poor, but prosperously content." By this measure, the dues for membership in the middle class have been rising by the year.

Other chapters in this book have chronicled the impact that the demanding global capital markets have had on American job stability and salaries. These markets reward the investment bankers, traders, CEOs, consultants, journalists, corporate lawyers—the men and women whom Felix Rohatyn called the "technological aristocracy."[1] But they punish everyone else outside this exalted stratum. Trade steals jobs at the bottom. Technology takes over jobs in the middle, and the people who used to do them find themselves fighting with the former working class for the badly paid jobs that are left.

So median wages fall. The gap between the rich and the poor grows. It is greater now than in any other industrial nation, even Britain. More people, in fact, are rich and more are poor, meaning that there are fewer than ever before in the middle. The great expanding middle class, in short, has stopped expanding and is shrinking.

Not so long ago, millions of Americans who carried lunch pails in calloused hands lived middle-class lives at home. This surely was one of the great glories of postwar America. Truck drivers and assembly line workers owned their own homes, took decent vacations, and sent their kids to college. The majority of those jobs are gone now, and those that are left no longer support this kind of life. I talked with a woman on Chicago's Southeast Side, Danuschka Borsuk, who grew up in the shadow of U.S. Steel's mighty South Works, where her father, a Belorussian immigrant, worked on the open-hearth furnace. Six years after the Borsuks arrived in Chicago, they bought their own home. There were polka parties in the yard, with enough sausages and cheese to feed the neighborhood. Especially Danuschka remembers the cello lessons. She and her brothers and sisters all took music lessons. She played the cello and still glows with the memory of it.

South Works is closed now and its workers are scattered. U.S. Steel, which had 120,000 workers in 1980, makes just as much steel today with only 20,000. Borsuk still lives in the neighborhood and works as a school security officer, bringing home about $14,000 a year after taxes. That's more than her father ever earned at the mill but, forty years later, it doesn't go nearly as far. There's no money left over for cello lessons, and besides, the schools on the Southeast Side don't have music classes anymore.

One in ten Americans, or an estimated 26 million people, get all or part of their food in charitable food agencies, according to Second Harvest, the nation's biggest food bank.[2] Some of these people have always been poor, but a fair number of former middle-class Americans are lined up in these soup kitchens. Go into one of these kitchens in the morning, and you'll see well-dressed young women standing there with their children, waiting for breakfast before they go to work. They have jobs, but these jobs don't pay enough to feed their families.

The statistics show a persistent withering in the middle of U.S. society. Until the 1970s, a middle-class American had about an equal chance of moving up into high income or falling down into low income. More important, those who moved out of the middle class, either up or down, were more than replaced by low-income Americans, both blue-collar and white-collar, who began making enough money to call themselves middle class. Thus the middle class grew.

About 1980, that stopped. Middle-class Americans now have a slightly greater chance of falling down into the lower classes than they have of moving up into the upper classes. More dramatically, statistics show they aren't being replaced. There are more rich Americans and more poor Americans than before, but there are fewer in the middle. In the early 1970s, about 75 percent of all Americans had middle-class incomes; by the late 1980s, this was down to 67 percent.[3] (Exhibit 4.1 shows this withering of U.S. family incomes.)

Exhibit 4.1

Median Family Income,* 1947–93
(in 1993 dollars)

Year	Median Family Income*
1947	$ 18,099
1967	31,579
1973	36,893
1979	38,248
1989r**	39,696
1992r**	37,668
1993	36,959
Total Increases	
1947–1967	$ 13,480
1967–1973	5,314
1973–1979	1,354
1979–1989	1,448
1989–1992	− 2,028
1989–1993	− 2,737

* Income includes all wage and salary, self-employment, pension, interest, rent, government cash assistance, and other money incomes.
** r indicates revision using 1990 census weights.

Source: U.S. Bureau of the Census (1993) and unpublished census data. From Mishel and Bernstein, "The State of Working America," M. E. Sharpe, Armonk, N.Y., 1994.

A lot of this withering is happening to young Americans. Men who turned twenty-one before 1980 had an easier time making middle-class status by the time they were thirty than did the next generation, which came of age after 1980. This hit hardest at those with only a high school education. Only 32 percent of those of the post-1980 generation made it into the middle class by age thirty, compared with nearly 50 percent of those before 1980, when the country still had a wealth of factory jobs and other blue-collar work. But college-educated men had the same trouble. Of those who came of age before 1980, fully 69 percent were into the middle class by the time they turned thirty. Of those who came of age after 1980, that figure was only 55 percent.[4]

Downsizing has wiped out millions of middle-class jobs in the last decade, and if the vibrant economy has created millions more, they are often not as good nor as stable. Government figures show that men aged twenty-five to fifty-four who lost their jobs made 20 percent less when they found a new one; for women, the drop was even worse, 25 percent.[5] Economist Robert C. Topel says this bites deeper into more experienced workers. According to his figures, downsized workers who got new jobs earned, on average, 14 percent less than before. But for those with more than ten years on the old job, the new job paid 28 percent less. Those who lost a job after twenty-one years or more got 44 percent less if and when they worked again.[6]

The Conference Board, an industrial research organization, surveyed a broad swatch of American companies and found that 72 percent of them admitted to having fewer middle managers than five years earlier.[7] The Lutheran Brotherhood, a financial services company for Lutherans, commissioned a poll that showed that the fear of unemployment was the highest among those in the prime of life and at the top of their professions—employees in their thirties and forties, college-educated and making more than $50,000 a year.[8] At that salary, they're in the top 20 percent, which, statistically, is doing great. Maybe so, but they're scared.

The Avenging Scythe

They're right to be scared. If you've read this far, you've seen that the new economy is a model of efficiency and profit, jettisoning waste and excess baggage, trimming business to its core, delivering ever more goods at ever lower prices, creating a sinewy nation devoted to maximum return. You've heard gurus, like McKinsey's Bryan and Farrell, report that this process is only beginning, that the equity markets have just started to swing their unforgiving searchlights across the companies of the world, singling out best practice where they find it, creating rich earnings for investors and a new, efficient world for us all. No fat, just lean. And who can argue with that?

But no one can ever be sure if they're part of the fat or part of the lean. Even the best know, in their heart of hearts, that they aren't *that* good. It was OK for the company men when the avenging economic scythe cut across factory floors, mowing down potbellied union guys and their padded benefits. It was a little scarier when entire industries, like the one that used to make television sets, fell to the Japanese, but, hey, they'd have been all right if they had just worked harder or innovated more. But it became truly frightening when companies on the cutting edge, like AT&T, or wildly profitable, like major banks, laid off thousands of employees, most of them indisputably middle class.

The justification for the market's search for best practice, at the cost of these jobs and lives, was spelled out in blunt candor by a Chicago trader named Robert Sanborn, in an interview with John Callaway, the dean of the city's television interviewers. The more that a clearly appalled Callaway probed, the more Sanborn revealed the mind of the market:

SANBORN: As more and more markets are run by professionals like ourselves, they put pressures on companies to run businesses for the owners.

CALLAWAY: Do shareholders worry about fairness and loyalty?

SANBORN: Investors want to maximize their investment. What is the obligation of a company? In our economy, the obligation of a company is to maximize the value to its owners. That means that the considerations of managers and owners trump the interests of workers sometimes. People have to learn to take control of their own lives in this economy. You have to be entrepreneurial. You are not going to be coddled like people are in Japan.

CALLAWAY: Corporate responsibility—benefits, loyalty. Is that day over?

SANBORN: I think that day is over. Large companies are competing on a global basis, against companies with different wage structures, different standards of living, different expectations. The days where a large company could say, this is a lifetime job, those days are over. It is very important for people to realize that and conduct their lives with that assumption.

CALLAWAY: Should the worker herself or himself say, "I'm going to be loyal to this company, I'm going to work my butt off for this company, and this company, if it's smart, will not be loyal to me, it'll dispose of me the first chance it can, if that is done in the name of efficiency"? Is this the new handshake?

SANBORN: I think it is. I think people have to be understanding about that and realistic about that. It's really a trade-off.

CALLAWAY: So I should say, "God, thank you for economic insecurity because it'll make me a better person"?

SANBORN: Yes, as hard as that is to understand.[9]

New Loyalties

I have interviewed many middle management executives in their thirties or forties who have taken Sanborn's lesson to heart and, as a result, display remarkably similar attitudes. These men and women say they like their jobs but don't expect to keep them. Even those who work for companies with stable employment records have friends who have been downsized, and they assume the same will happen to them. So their loyalty is to themselves, not to their employer. They work hard and well, but they are working for themselves and their résumés, not for the employer who signs their paycheck.

These are the 1990s version of Tom Rath, the loyal and hardworking hero of Sloan Wilson's 1955 novel, *The Man in the Grey Flannel Suit*. When Rath chose family obligations over a promotion, his employer smiled and gave him an even better job, which he would clearly keep until he retired. The hero of today's corporate fiction is Sherman McCoy, the bond salesman in Tom Wolfe's *The Bonfire of the Vanities*. Rath, lucky man, retired ten years ago. If he were still working today, McCoy would put him out of a job.

G. J. Meyer, once a public relations executive for companies like McDonnell Douglas Corporation and J. I. Case Company, endured round after round of downsizing and restructuring and wrote a funny, bitter book about it. He summed up his experience in a passage that sounds like a requiem for the middle class:

> A good many self-proclaimed organizational gurus have been writing and lecturing about how the corporation of the not-very-distant future will have only a tiny, almost vestigial permanent staff. This corporation will meet most of its needs for white-collar work by hiring outsiders temporarily, project by project, inviting them to come aboard long enough to complete some specific, limited task and then inviting them to go away again. Most of the kinds of people who until now have had conventional salaried jobs will become a new class of migratory brain workers, moving into and out of assignments as opportunities ebb and flow. Their lives— *our* lives—will become a jumble of brief encounters.
>
> But the people who describe this future never seem to wonder what kind of society it's going to be when many of us are skittering not merely from assignment to assignment but from job to job and company to company and, presumably, city to city. I haven't yet heard any of the gurus

explain what we're supposed to do, where we're supposed to go, *between* our wonderfully exciting assignments.

Is that a fit society for the mass of human beings? Are most people *made* for that kind of society? Is it going to be wonderful—or constant misery on a global scale? Peel away the uplifting rhetoric about the exciting workplace of the future and what you're left with is an America in which stability, continuity, and security—the basic elements of a coherent life—are going to be beyond the grasp of all but an increasingly small, increasingly isolated minority.

Does anyone expect that the people in this kind of world are going to be capable of building or sustaining communities? Of even knowing what community is? Of raising families?[10]

Peter Drucker, the management guru, says that the old communities are a thing of the past, and not necessarily to be mourned:

The old communities—family, village, parish and so on—have all but disappeared in the knowledge society. Their place has largely been taken by the new unit of social integration, the organization. Where community was fate, organization is voluntary membership. Where community claimed the entire person, organization is a means to a person's ends, a tool.[11]

But the old communities implied safety and stability that the new corporate communities cannot offer. They provided continuity and relationships across the generations, rules that didn't change no matter how often we broke them, and leaders, trusted men and women, who had the interests of the community at heart. The continuity is gone, the rules keep changing, and somehow the downsizing captains of today's corporations are no one's idea of trusted community elders.

The Scariness of Middle-Class Life

This fragmentation has many causes, many of them as local as they are global. Economic cycles dictate good times and bad times. The turmoils of the 1960s and the civil rights revolution guaranteed that young Americans would live in a different country than their parents. Air conditioning and television eliminated the communal lives of earlier times, conducted from front stoops and over back fences, and turned American families in on themselves.

But these social changes cannot, by themselves, create the disequilibrium that afflicts so much of America. What has happened is new and has its base in economics, in the ability of people to make their own ways in the world. Local self-sufficiency is replaced by distant forces. Self-reliance—the knowledge that honesty and hard work will be rewarded—is replaced by the whim of an impersonal market. Self-respect can be shattered in an instant by economic decisions taken on the other side of the globe.

G. J. Meyer asked if people in this new world will be capable of creating communities, or even raising families. On that one, the results are in. The third middle class, the young and the anxious, haven't stopped making homes, communities, or families, of course. But they are doing it later, with more hesitation, than earlier generations. In 1950, the average age for a first marriage was twenty-two for men, twenty for women. By the time she was 21.8 years old, the average woman had had her first baby. By 1990, all this was being postponed. The average age for a first marriage was twenty-six for men, twenty-four for women, and young mothers were closer to twenty-five years old when their first child was born.

These delays no doubt owe a lot to the Pill and the end of the draft, which prompted many young men to escape the army by embracing marriage and fatherhood. But people are buying homes later, too. In 1976, the average age for buying a first home was twenty-eight. By 1993, it was thirty-two. In the 1960s, a young family could pay the principal, interest, and taxes on a new home with 15 percent of its income. It's more than 30 percent now. In 1996 median wages, which had been falling for years, finally went up 1 percent, but median housing prices rose 5 percent. Not surprisingly, home ownership in America is falling for the first time in nearly a half century. This fall is most dramatic among the young. Twenty-five years ago, nearly 40 percent of young married couples with children owned their own homes; now it's barely 24 percent. (Exhibit 4.2 shows the decline in home ownership among all but older Americans.)

These major steps—getting married, having a baby, buying a home—are more than milestones in life. They are statements of confidence in the future. We take on these responsibilities not when we're

Exhibit 4.2

Home Ownership Rates, by Age
(in percent)

Age of Householder	1982	1985	1988	1991	1993
Under 25	19.3	17.2	15.8	15.3	15.0
25 to 29	38.6	37.7	35.9	33.8	34.0
30 to 34	57.1	54.0	53.2	51.2	51.0
35 to 39	67.6	65.4	63.6	62.2	62.1
40 to 44	73.0	71.4	70.7	69.5	69.0
45 to 49	76.0	74.3	74.4	73.7	73.9
50 to 54	78.8	77.5	77.1	76.1	77.1
55 to 59	80.0	79.2	79.3	79.5	78.8
60 to 64	80.1	79.9	79.8	80.5	80.9
65 to 69	77.9	79.5	80.0	81.4	80.6
70 to 74	75.2	76.8	77.7	78.8	79.9
75 and over	71.0	69.8	70.8	73.1	73.3

rich or settled but when we're "starting out," a phrase that implies progress down a road and steps up a ladder. We do it when we're confident that we'll be able to live up to these responsibilities. No newlyweds ever had enough money to put the baby through college or pay off the mortgage. But that didn't matter, because they were sure that, when the time came, they *would* have enough.

That confidence is missing now. In Oak Park, the Chicago suburb where Ernest Hemingway was born and Frank Lloyd Wright created architectural masterworks, I spent an evening with a pleasant couple named Judy Presta and Mark Geraci. He was thirty-seven, a doctor of pharmacy and a manager at a university cancer center in Chicago. She was thirty, an administrator for a Catholic charity. Between them, they earned in the high five figures. They had been married for two years and went to Italy on their honeymoon. They own their own home, two four-year-old Hondas, two color TVs, a microwave, a VCR, a cordless phone, and a personal computer. The word they used often was *scary*.

"I thought I'd have a family when I was twenty-five," said Judy, who was raised in a good Catholic home with two older sisters; all three are in their thirties now and childless. "I couldn't understand how some liberal career women could say they wouldn't bring a child into this world. Now look—there's the cost of day care, of health care. There's crime, sex, drugs. In my heart of hearts, I think I will have children, but it's really scary."

Mark said, "My parents were able to buy a new three-bedroom home on one income when my father was twenty-eight. We've got a three-bedroom old house on two salaries. At thirty-six, until last year, I was still paying off my student loans. At the same age, my father had four children."

To a Third World peasant or to Mark's and Judy's grandparents, struggling through the Depression, this fear and dissatisfaction would sound ungrateful, even frivolous. But they were not frivolous people. They were an intelligent, articulate, serious couple who have their credit card debt well in hand, who give to their church, who hope to have children but want to bring those children into a secure world. And that world, as of today, doesn't look the way they thought it would.

On the day after they returned from that Italian honeymoon, Mark's cancer center, as cost-conscious these days as any private business, announced a "restructuring that has put everybody on the firing line. At any time, you could be laid off for nonperformance reasons. We've learned to live with this as a reality. Until recently, there definitely was a lot of loyalty there. But in the last two years, everything has taken on more of a corporate attitude and there's much less loyalty. I'd rather not live with this insecurity, but I don't think I have much choice."

Mark and Judy and many Americans like them do not live badly, not at all. But the erosion of the economic security of their lives has exacted a large cost, not only in confidence but in so much else that builds on that confidence. Scholars have found a decline in membership in community organizations.[12] Politics has become more unstable and more ideological. Voters, as though unhinged from the stable center, swing heavily to the Republicans in one election, back to the Democrats in the next, at a time when European politics, ironically, is becoming more centrist and less ideological.

Alan Ehrenhalt, an editor in Washington, wrote a lovely, elegiac book called *The Lost City* about the Chicago and the America of his youth and the changes since then, for better or for worse. In 1957, he recalled, *House Beautiful* magazine commented, "Our era, despite its imperfections, is the most widely and deeply enjoyed golden age of all time," and *Time* magazine reported that in the United States, "fear and fretting were made ridiculous by the facts of national life."

Ehrenhalt, who clearly recalls the corruption and inequities of that time, commented, "the most interesting thing about these statements is not their excess but that nobody would dare say anything similar today." Americans of the 1990s, who certainly have more and shinier things than Americans of the 1950s, somehow do not feel themselves so blessed, so secure, so confident:

> The major themes [then] were stability and confidence. They are themes
> that the baby-boom generation, middle-aged and younger, raised in afflu-
> ent expectation and now living amid stagnant reality, cannot instinctively
> understand.[13]

John Hoesley lives on the Southwest Side of Chicago, not far from Ehrenhalt's old neighborhood. He was born just after the war, one of the first baby boomers, and went to work for R. R. Donnelley & Sons Company, the biggest printer in the city, best known locally for printing the telephone book. In his twenty-five years and two weeks with Donnelley, he rose to become a supervisor at one of the company's suburban plants. He made $52,000 per year, which rose to a very comfortable $65,000 with bonuses, and felt as if he belonged to one big family.

On October 1, 1993, Hoesley and 122 others were told that Donnelley was downsizing and they would be out of a job on New Year's Day. Three weeks later, Hoesley and his wife, Jean, went to Donnelley's annual party, a Lake Michigan cruise, to honor him and other twenty-five-year workers. It must have been a surrealistic affair. "At our table, everyone, six couples, were going to be cut loose on January 1, after twenty-five years. There were a lot of jokes about the *Titanic*. A couple of the wives actually found out that night [that their husbands were losing their jobs]."

Hoesley sent out 400 résumés with no takers. Two months after he left Donnelley, he bought a small mail and business services office in the suburbs. When I talked with him, he and Jean were working twelve hours a day, including the commute, to build it up. He was enthusiastic about his work and not sore at Donnelley, which gave him forty-four weeks of severance pay and kept his medical insurance going for two years. But somehow I felt that, when he was working his way up through the Donnelley ranks, he never expected it to turn out this way. I also doubted he would ever again know the security of those years.

The "Standard of Living" Debate

Much of this goes to the issue of "standard of living," which is a phrase as vague as *middle class* or *global economy*. It is a phrase heard on the political stump and at cocktail parties, as Americans debate whether their lives are as good as they once were, or whether children will ever know the "standard of living" that their parents did. As blurred as it is, it sums up how Americans feel about themselves and their country and so is a potent determinant of the decisions—social, economic, political—that we make in life.

To many economists, "standard of living" means no more than a salary and the things—big things like houses, little things like microwaves—that a salary can buy. Americans these days, they say, own more things—more and better cars, TV sets, household appliances, European vacations, bigger houses, cleaner water, medical care—than at any time in their history. For part of the population, this is true and is not to be scorned. One-time luxuries, such as air conditioning, a second car, or a dishwasher, have become necessities. For some families, necessities like a personal computer were not only beyond the means but beyond the imagination of their parents.

"The sense of deprivation comes not because we have so little but because there is so much to have and we cannot 'have it all,' all the time," Robert J. Samuelson writes in his book, *The Good Life and Its Discontents*, debunking late-twentieth-century angst as the whining of a spoiled nation that expected perfection and cannot live with anything less:

> All problems ought to have solutions. We believe in happy endings and react sullenly when they don't arrive. . . . We feel entitled. Among other things, we expect secure jobs, rising living standards, enlightened corporations, generous government, high-quality health care, racial harmony, a clean environment, safe cities, satisfying work and personal fulfillment.

All this, he says, is a pipe dream, "the excessive optimism of the early postwar decades."[14]

This is a powerful argument, but a flawed one. Most of the expectations that Samuelson dismisses as excessive and unrealistic actually were fulfilled in an earlier era, and many now have been lost. People really did have secure jobs and rising living standards. By comparison with today's standards, corporations were enlightened and government was generous. Cities were safer, as those who grew up in them recall. Only the environment is indisputably better now than then.

Access to good medical care is a fascinating, confusing question. As recently as 1970, no fewer than 28,000 Americans died from measles, diphtheria, typhoid, polio, whooping cough, mumps, and rubella. In the 1990s, virtually no one will. The power of medicine to treat heart diseases and many cancers has exploded, and many Americans are alive today after suffering illnesses that would have killed them thirty years ago. No one facing brain surgery or a kidney transplant can be ungrateful for the skill and techniques of today's doctors, or the availability of the machinery at their command. But most Americans don't need brain surgery. Instead, they face more common calamities, like a broken arm, or commonplace procedures like childbirth, and it's hard to argue that the improvements in these areas justify the soaring costs. A four-day stay in a maternity ward cost $1,120 in 1975; today's new mothers pay $4,000 and get to stay only two days. It costs about $50, plus days of waiting, to see a doctor in his or her office; not so many years ago, it was $5 and the doctor came to see you. Health insurance covers much of the cost, but 41.7 million Americans don't have any. Of the rest, only 37 percent have health insurance totally paid by employers; fifteen years ago, twice as many did. And if conquered diseases like mumps and measles no longer kill anyone, a new disease, AIDS, unknown in 1970, now kills 55,000 persons every year.

Racial progress, if not racial harmony, is real. The past three decades in particular have seen once-closed doors open for the vast majority of blacks. Anyone who can recall the legal segregation of the immediate postwar years must marvel at the changes. But economic problems threaten much of this progress.

Already, the collapse of heavy industry in America's cities has caused much of the unemployment, economic disintegration, and social pathology in urban ghettos. As William Julius Wilson and Nicholas Lemann have written, these ghettos were largely settled by blacks who came north during and after World War II to work in the great northern factories. In the 1960s and 1970s, many of these factories collapsed, moved overseas, or, more likely, moved to the suburbs in pursuit of their white workers, who had taken advantage of the suburban housing boom to escape the city. Housing segregation, formal or informal, kept these black workers from following. For the least skilled of them, automation eliminated most available jobs.[15]

As manual labor for black men disappeared, new jobs in offices and services opened up for black women, who became the breadwinners for their families. Of all the causes of the breakdown of black family life, this is certainly the greatest. The civil rights revolution finished off this process by enabling skilled, educated, and ambitious blacks to move up and out into better jobs and neighborhoods. Those left behind were, by definition, the least skilled, least educated, and least ambitious. They and their children remain in the ghettos today, locked in a cycle of poverty, crime, and hopelessness that is the single greatest blight on America's national honor.

Nor is the black middle class immune to the threats of a tighter, tougher economy. In the past thirty years, this middle class has grown sharply and now includes 45 percent of employed blacks. Fifteen percent of blacks earned more than $50,000 per year in 1990, double the percentage (adjusted for inflation) in 1967. But blacks still earn less than whites, and while they hold about 10 percent of all jobs, they hold relatively few of the good ones—only 3 percent of all doctors and lawyers, for instance.[16] Now the wave of downsizing, restructuring, mergers, and cost cutting threatens the jobs of those blacks who have climbed the corporate ladder. Most are the first members of their families to rise into the middle class. If unemployment comes, they have fewer resources to tide them over. One survey showed that whites at the same income level as blacks own twelve times as much in savings and other assets.[17]

In an earlier era, government recognized that black Americans carried exceptional historical baggage, so it instituted affirmative-action programs to usher them into the American economy and help keep them there. But in tough economic times, generosity flags. The impulses that powered the great social experiments of the affluent 1960s—the civil rights movement, the Great Society, affirmative action—have disappeared in the 1990s. Congress is attacking welfare, and white voters, frightened for their own jobs, pass referendums calling for an end to affirmative action.

Vanishing Security

Samuelson's lecture misses this point. As Ehrenhalt says, there was a sense of security and confidence in earlier eras, when people actually had less, than there is now. More to the point of my argument, this sense of security and confidence still exists in many industrial nations, especially Japan, that must cope with the same economic pressures Americans feel.

The global economy is not an American phenomenon. It poses its problems and challenges to each nation. But only in the United States and, to a lesser degree, in Britain has it created the insecurity and the fragmentation of the middle class. The Europeans in particular know that their society is changing, from workplace to government, and must change more. But they and the Japanese still have the sense that the major institutions in their lives—the government, unions, even corporations—exist to protect jobs and standards of living. If change comes, it will be tempered by these institutions. Their societies, like the American society, have a choice in how they respond to economic forces. The choices they have made sacrifice some dynamism for stability.

It has been a long time since Americans could feel that. And so they collect toys, as talismans against the future. Americans seem to feel that if they have enough dirt bikes and vcrs, belong to enough health clubs, own the latest stereo, surf the 'Net and drink designer coffee, then they will have the geegaws of affluence, or at least enough to fool the economists who measure living standards by such accumulation.

But those who tend the American psyche and soul aren't fooled. They report disquieting changes in the way Americans view their lives and themselves. Dr. Harold Visotsky, a professor of psychiatry at Northwestern University, told me that he and his colleagues "are seeing more anxiety and depression than ever before. Technology is supposed to create leisure. There's no quality of life if the workforce thins out because of technology. So technology is becoming the enemy, the displacer."[18]

Technology is neutral and can help or harm anyone in its path. For Rohatyn's "technological aristocracy," the PC in the den opens the door to a cyberworld that is both financially and psychologically enriching. For the factory hand or bank teller, the computer is the machine that stole his or her job.

Nor are retailers fooled. The people who make their living selling things to America are clearly aware that both the rich and the poor are increasing and the middle class is shrinking, and they are rearranging the nation's shops and shelves accordingly. Giant stores are still being built along suburban blight strips, but increasingly they are high-end stores like Bloomingdale's or low-end stores like Kmart, with not a lot in between. The top 20 percent of America's wage earners now account for 54 percent of new-car sales volume; the other 80 percent mostly buy used cars. Nieman-Marcus stores are doing fine. So, appallingly, are shops selling second-hand clothing, which have doubled their sales in the past decade. Some retailers go both ways: The Gap owns Banana Republic stores, where blue jeans sell for $58, and Old Navy stores, where jeans sell for $22.[19]

It takes huge, computerized, highly efficient chains like the Gap or Wal-Mart to carry off this sort of sophisticated, market-driven retailing. Smaller and independent stores, lacking sophistication and economies of scale, are overwhelmed. Many traditionally catered to a middle class that, for retailers, isn't there anymore. As these smaller stores go out of business, the bigger stores move in and take over. For all the carnage in neighborhood shopping and suburban malls, there aren't all that many empty shops or vacant lots.

There are, however, fewer jobs. Each small store needed a manager, a buyer, a bookkeeper, stock handlers. The big stores do, too, but because they are so big and so centralized, they don't need as many. Ten stores needed ten managers, ten buyers, ten bookkeepers. The one Wal-Mart or Kmart or Marshalls that replaces them needs only one manager, one buyer, one bookkeeper. Before, a store buyer talked to a manufacturer's representative. Now a computer talks to a computer. In the process, retailing jobs are lost, and so is income, and so, of course, is purchasing power—which means fewer customers for the stores that remain.

The Elites Leave Home

Commentators often say that the American economy has been "hollowed out" by the departure of heavy and traditional industries. The information industries can replace some of the jobs and much of the economic power of these older industries. But a hole remains at the center of the economy, where things used to be made and are made no more.

It seems to me that the same sort of hollowing out has taken place in society as a whole, as the poor and the rich increase in numbers and the middle class shrinks. The upper 20 percent retreats to its gated communities in the suburbs, withdrawing not only physically but psychologically and socially from the country around it. They are not only the wealthy, the executives and traders, but also the economists, journalists, and others who tout the global economy largely because they are best equipped to cope with it and most insulated from its effects.

These fortunate few go by different names. Rohatyn calls them the "technological aristocracy." Robert Reich, the former secretary of labor, calls them "symbolic analysts," the sophisticated tribe that can manipulate the symbols and process the data of the information age.[20] I prefer to think of them as global citizens, having more in common with the elites in Tokyo and Frankfurt than with the other Americans who live beyond the gates, in the shantytowns on the outskirts of the global village.

Any country needs its elites. It needs their money, and more important, it needs their leadership. Now the United States is losing its elites.

This is neither fanciful nor unprecedented. What is happening in the United States as a whole happened over the past forty years in American cities—in New York, Chicago, Cleveland, Boston, Detroit, Philadelphia, and the other cities of the American north that never recovered from the great postwar industrial exodus.

Great factories—the steel mills, automakers, metal fabricators, pharmaceutical houses—underpinned the economies of these cities and, indeed, were the reason many of them existed in the first place. As these factories and foundries left, they took their payrolls and tax dollars with them to the suburbs, small towns, or Sun Belt, where wages were lower, costs cheaper, and unions nonexistent. Company headquarters and top executives often stayed put for a generation and continued to lead the communities and contribute to the civic civilization. But then they, too, moved, to the suburbs or to other states and took their allegiances with them. Cities that once counted on these corporations and on the civic spirit of the corporate titans—the men and women who literally created the skyscrapers, universities, symphonies, museums, and mansions of the American urban landscape—woke up one day to find that the payrolls and taxes had decamped to Mississippi and the civic spirit to suburban causes. Captains of industry who once endowed civic art galleries focus now on the artistic splendor of their corporate headquarters.

The cities left behind have coped in their own ways, by fostering services and finance industries and tourism. But in all of them, even the relatively successful ones, real incomes have fallen, stores have closed, schools have deteriorated, once grand neighborhoods have become ghettos, crime has risen, social pathology has grown, and the quality of life has eroded for all but the fortunate few.

Now these vast corporations and the allegiance of their leaders are on the move again, not within their native countries but beyond them, into the global economy where their future lies. Companies that see their future in Third-World workers will be interested in training those workers. They will be less interested in the education of American workers whom they deliberately left behind. A corporation that does business in fifty countries will not worry as much about its obligations to the one country it used to call home.

The Politics of Insecurity

If the broad middle class was the ballast in the American democratic system, its erosion has implications for the nation's politics that are only beginning to be seen. Of all the candidates running for president in 1996, only Pat Buchanan raised these issues of economic decay and social unfairness. He was awarded with a mini-boom from voters until they realized that his solution, basically, was "Stop the world, I want to get off." The swings from Democrats to Republicans and back again, with some support going to such unlikely Napoleons as Buchanan and Ross Perot, indicate considerable unease at the heart of the American body politic.

The key document in American political life begins with the thought that all men are created equal. This does not mean that all people are equal, but it does imply an ideal of equality, in which every person has an equal chance to pursue happiness as he or she sees it, or to rise and fall according to his or her talents and efforts. That promise has been broken. America not only is becoming more unequal than it used to be. It is more unequal than any other major industrial society in the return it gives for those talents and efforts.

The ability to rise through society, to be born poor and die rich, also has diminished. A study by the Organization for Economic Cooperation and Development (OECD) found that economic mobility in the United States was no greater than anywhere else. Low-paid workers moved up or down the economic ladder at about the same pace in most countries. The United States had by far the biggest share of its workforce in low-paid jobs, the OECD said, but didn't move them up into better jobs any faster than, say, the more egalitarian Scandinavians.[21]

The new, squeezed middle class is inclined to be more conservative, more suburban, more suspicious of cities and the darker-skinned people who live there, more hostile to immigrants, more opposed to taxes, more isolationist. This, of course, is a sweeping characterization and ignores the considerable differences within it; recent elections, for instance, have shown that middle-class women are more likely to vote Democratic than middle-class men. But these broad trends are hardly surprising in a class that feels cheated by a world that promised more than it delivered. The search for scapegoats is on, and the resulting politics could be ugly.

Edward N. Luttwak has warned of "the unprecedented sense of personal economic insecurity that has suddenly become the central phenomenon of life in America." Like many others, he has wondered how a stable, secure political system can persist in the midst of this insecurity.[22]

Stephen Roach, the chief economist of Morgan Stanley, was once a drumbeater for downsizing and restructuring but has publicly recanted:

> The so-called productivity resurgence has been built on slash-and-burn restructuring strategies that have put extraordinary pressure on the work force. This approach is not a permanent solution. Some form of worker backlash is an inevitable byproduct of an era that has squeezed labor and yet rewarded shareholders beyond their wildest dreams.[23]

By workers, Roach means not working-class factory hands in cloth caps, but the industrial elite and proud professionals who used to make up the American middle class. No stable, secure political system can persist in a nation in which this class is in revolt.

5. JAPAN: THE LONELY EMPIRE

WALK DOWN ANY street in Tokyo, and you'll see store after store carrying colorful, if often illogical, names in English. There's the Life of Easy clothing store, the Let's kiosk, the Goody grocery, and the Geronimo Shot Bar. Many of these stores have one additional English-language sign in their windows: Sale. But go inside, and you'll find stores that are totally Japanese, from wares to workers. No one speaks a word of English. And there's no particular "sale" going on. English is chic in Japan these days, but its use is both superficial and misleading, a Western wrapping on a Japanese core.

So it is with the Japanese reaction to the perils and pressures of globalization. Japan already reacts more consciously to the world economy than any other country, and is acutely aware of how that economy changes and develops. With this in mind, the Japanese government and Japanese companies are reacting to globalization with phrases that sound familiar to Western ears. There is much talk in Tokyo about deregulation and fiscal reform and more open markets. There also is much hand-wringing about the weaknesses of the Japanese economy, about government deficits, growing unemployment, banking crises, and the hollowing out of the nation's industry.

But take a closer look. Like the English-language signs, these phrases surround an extremely Japanese core. Japan is changing; indeed, a key to Japan's economic genius since World War II has been its ability to change and adapt. But most change in Japan is intended to control the rate of change.[1] The more Japan changes, the more Japanese it seems to be. Each change, ostensibly intended to make Japan's economy more like those of the West, actually adds another layer of armor in its battle with the Western world.

125

Exhibit 5.1

Import Penetration Rates for Manufactured Goods
(in percent of total consumption)

	1970	1975	1980	1985	1990	1991	1992
United States	5.3	6.7	8.9	12.2	14.8	14.6	16.0
Japan	3.8	4.1	5.3	5.3	6.4	5.9	5.7
Germany	13.4	15.4	19.6	23.8	25.0	27.1	27.2
France	15.8	17.5	21.3	25.6	29.6	30.4	30.2

Source: Organization for Economic Cooperation and Development.

Far from opening itself to the winds of global change, Japan is battening down the hatches. The bureaucracy, especially the powerful Ministry of Finance, retains control of the nation's budget and investment. Recent reforms haven't changed this. Some mass manufacturing is going overseas, mostly to Southeast Asia, but the high-value, high-profit manufacturing still stays at home. Unemployment, although at record levels, is only 3.5 percent and not rising.

Despite decades of protests by the United States and other governments, trade barriers still play a key role in keeping Japanese industry strong. Foreigners can penetrate the Japanese markets for Big Macs, clothes, or videos, but imports of high-value manufactured items like machine tools still are strictly controlled (see Exhibit 5.1). Foreign investment in Japanese manufacturing is prohibitively expensive, and majority foreign ownership of any strategic Japanese company—in computers, for instance—is flatly prohibited. Trade laws prohibit the use of foreign nails in Japanese wood, and courier services such as Federal Express cannot get national truck licenses. No large retailer can open a big new store until it gets permission from competitors, including the myriad of mom-and-pop stores it might put out of business.[2] An old-boy network of interlocking companies and suppliers—not cost or quality—still dictates purchasing and procurement.

Japan's bureaucrats and conglomerates still control access to the Japanese market and hold sway over the nation's economy and politics in a way unmatched among other industrial nations. The economy and its corporations still exist not for profits or shareholders but to preserve jobs and to keep Japan as independent as possible—

a new imperative now that globalization threatens the independence of all nations.

For this insular and very organized nation, globalization is a one-way street, with Japanese goods and investment flowing out but as little as possible coming back in.

Thinking About Japan

For most Westerners, thinking about Japan is hard because, behind a veneer of Westernization (those English-language signs and Big Macs), it is a very different and very non-Western place. Samuel P. Huntington, whose theory of the "clash of civilizations" has provided an important if controversial new way of viewing the post–Cold War world, says this world contains seven or eight major civilizations—Western, Sinic or Chinese, Hindu, Islamic, Orthodox, Latin American, possibly African, and Japanese. The Japanese civilization is by far the smallest and is the only civilization contained within one country:

> Japan is a civilization that is a state. No other country shares its distinct culture, and Japanese migrants are either not numerically significant in other countries or have assimilated to the cultures of those countries (e.g., Japanese-Americans). Japan's loneliness is further enhanced by the fact that its culture is highly particularistic and does not involve a potentially universal religion (Christianity, Islam) or ideology (liberalism, communism) that could be exported to other societies and thus establish a cultural connection with people in those societies.[3]

More pithily, Huntington told me, "Japan is a lonely country, a civilization unto itself."[4]

One of the problems of dealing with Japan is that the Japanese feel this isolation from the world and the uniqueness of their civilization acutely, but hotly deny it when dealing with the outside world. It is generally believed that foreigners (known as *gaijin*, a vaguely perjorative term like *gringos*) can never learn to speak good Japanese nor really understand Japan. Japan and Japanese culture—indeed, an entire concept of "Japaneseness"—is considered utterly different from the rest of the world, a given force that is so superior that any criticism can be brushed off as "Japan-bashing." Japan is seen as racially pure to the extent that minorities, such as the large ethnic Korean population, are virtually ignored or denied.[5]

Occasionally, this sense of uniqueness and superiority slips out. A Japanese minister justified bans on meat imports on grounds that Japanese intestines are a foot longer than gaijin intestines and so cannot digest foreign meat. A Japanese prime minister, Yasuhiro Nakasone, said the United States was less "intelligent" than Japan because of its black and Hispanic minorities. Officials periodically justify Japanese aggression in World War II as the right of a superior civilization toward lesser beings, usually other Asians. Such statements always cause an uproar, are always followed by an apology and occasionally a ritual resignation, and then, after a while, slip out again.

Japan's allies, especially the United States, have urged it for years to begin playing a political and diplomatic role in the world equivalent to its economic role. What they're saying is that Japan, having taken so much from the world, must begin to take some responsibility for that role, share the West's burdens, and become a leading nation in every field. But the idea that Japan, like Britain, could escape its sense of seagirt singularity to seek political and intellectual preeminence in the world, equal to its economic might, is "ultimately preposterous," writes R. Taggart Murphy, an American banker living in Tokyo:

> This was a country where an entire literary genre was devoted to proving that its inhabitants were fundamentally set apart from the rest of humanity, where an accredited scholar could maintain that the Japanese process language differently from everyone else and be given a serious hearing, where senior government officials could sit in international forums and announce that . . . American ski equipment [was] not appropriate for Japanese sports lovers because the snow was different in Japan. It was a place where landlords routinely listed "no gaijin" in the specifications given to agents, where the alma mater of the emperor could, after years of hemming and hawing, finally offer tenure to one non-Japanese professor, only to fire him in violation of Japan's own labor laws three years later, all the while raising a massive new building to house a massive new program of international studies.
>
> This was not a country ready to run the planet. . . . The Japanese elite settled for growing rich under American hegemony. But Japan would not be asked and would not seek to play hegemonic functions.[6]

Yet a vast propaganda machine exists to impress the rest of the world with the modern, capitalist, "Western" nature of a Japan that plays the positive role in the world economy that would be expected of a strong, normal nation. Japan has vigorous corporations, as the West does, and these corporations make profits, as Western corporations do. An indisputably democratic constitution exists. It provides that the emperor is the figurehead leader of the nation, like Queen Elizabeth II, while a prime minister, who leads the strongest party in parliament, leads the government. Private enterprise flourishes, a free press covers the news aggressively, and courts oversee the majesty of the law.

All of this is perfectly true, and perfectly misleading. Japan plays in the world economy by its own rules and has amassed great power and huge surpluses through an aggressive trade policy and mercantilism that has left its rivals both damaged and outraged. Vigorous corporations compete furiously and report profits; yet the competition within Japan is controlled and the profits are so secondary to the principle of power and market share that one American economist, Alan Blinder, later a Federal Reserve Board governor, wondered whether any country that paid so little attention to return on capital could be properly called "capitalist." Eisuke Sakakibara, Japan's most powerful monetary official, called the system "a non-capitalistic market economy."[7] The constitution, dictated by the American occupation after the war, reads like a model document and is all but ignored. The same party, the misnamed Liberal Democrats, has led the government since the end of the war, except for a ten-month hiatus in 1947–1948 and another ten months in 1993. Politics in Japan is democratic in the way that politics is democratic in Mexico or in Chicago, where the Machine, as flexible as it needs to be, is never really challenged for power, so long as it delivers the goods—the services and stability—that its citizens want.

Karel van Wolferen's *The Enigma of Japanese Power* is probably the most detailed and clear-eyed guide to the reality of Japan. This reality, he said, is seldom what it seems:

> The Japanese have laws, legislators, a parliament, political parties, labor unions, a prime minister, interest groups and stockholders. But one should not be misled by these familiar labels. . . . The Japanese prime minister is not expected to show much leadership; labor unions organize strikes to be held during lunch breaks; the legislature does not in fact legislate;

stockholders never demand dividends; consumer interest groups advocate protectionism; laws are enforced only if they don't conflict too much with the interests of the powerful; and the ruling Liberal Democratic Party is, if anything, conservative and authoritarian, is not really a party and does not in fact rule.[8]

The rich theatricality of Japanese life is understood by the Japanese but seldom by foreigners. The lunch hour strikes by company unions, the elaborate politeness, the promises of reform, the atonements for corporate wrongdoing—all are a ritual that substitutes for real action or effectiveness. The key to dealing with Japan is to figure out how much is theater and how much is real. The Japanese acknowledge all this. They even have names for it. *Tatemae* means the pretense, which polite people accept as the truth when they know it is not. *Honne* means the real thing, the truth that is known but not stated. In a complex and crowded country, these central concepts keep life flowing with a minimum of friction. In politics, the central concepts are *omote*, which is the above-board activities that foreigners see, and *ura*, which is the reality existing behind closed doors. Americans assume that Japan works as the United States does: When Morihiro Hosokawa became prime minister in 1993, American commentators rejoiced that Japan had a leader who was "a governor from a small southern state bent on reform." Hosokawa lasted eight months and reformed nothing.[9]

In Chicago, at least, the mayor has clout and exercises real power. In Japan, the government has relatively little power. Real power is diffuse, across a ruling class rather than vested in any office or party. Mostly, it rests with the bureaucracy, especially the Ministry of Finance (MOF), and is beyond the ability of any prime minister or politician to influence. This is why so many trade "agreements" between the U.S. and Japanese governments have yielded so little in practice; in Japan, governments simply cannot deliver the goods.[10]

Often, the giant corporations—organized in cartel-like *keiretsu* linking manufacturers, distributors, and banks—do have this power. Occasionally, they will use it, in cooperation with the bureaucracy, to fulfill an agreement the government has reached; Japan's agreements in 1986 and 1991 to let American semiconductors capture 20 percent of the Japanese market are an example. More often, these agreements—in fact, the normal exercise of the markets and the normal give-and-take of free trade—would cut into the monopoly of the *keiretsu*, force them to cut prices, reduce their profits, and compromise their power, so they are simply ignored.

The press is frenetic but, as critics have charged, never really questions the workings of the system.[11]

The courts exist and administer laws that are as comprehensive and democratic as those in any Western nation. But access to these courts is all but impossible for the average Japanese. Critics of the American system often point out that Japan produces more engineers than the United States while the U.S. produces more lawyers: 1 lawyer for every 360 Americans, in fact, compared to only 1 lawyer for every 9,294 Japanese. On the one hand, this means that America is absurdly overlawyered. On the other, it means that Japan is equally absurdly underlawyered. Japanese citizens have almost no access to their legal system and, therefore, no right of legal redress for any wrong done to them by the government, the bureaucracy, or the corporations.

The Revisionists and the Chrysanthemum Club

When I first went to Japan, a dozen or so years ago, I walked out on my first day in Tokyo into Hibiya Park, where a Japanese skiffle band was playing "I'm Gonna Sit Right Down and Write Myself a Letter," with lyrics in English. Men in blue suits strode along the sidewalks, Toyotas filled the busy streets, and strategically sited McDonald's restaurants did a booming business. "This place," I thought to myself, "looks just like Chicago." It was only a couple of days later that I became aware, as I never had in any other country, of strange undercurrents guiding this modern, seemingly Western nation, subterranean impulses that I sensed but couldn't begin to understand.

Generations of Western businesspeople, government negotiators, and traders have had the same feeling, mostly to their sorrow. They came to Japan in their straightforward Western way, expecting a country that accepted the same rules and laws as the rest of the world, and discovered later that Japan was following different laws and playing by different rules. The same forces that guided the rest of the world seemingly did not apply to Japan. It was like playing basketball with opponents who had repealed the law of gravity.

Over the past fifteen years, a furious debate has arisen, mostly in the United States, between two contending schools of thought on the true nature of Japan. On one side are the traditionalists, sometimes derided as the Chrysanthemum Club. These traditionalists insist that Japan is a normal, Western-oriented, thoroughly reformist nation, plucky and unarguably good at economic combat but otherwise no different than its Western rivals. Members of this club tend to be apologists for Japan. Some are no more than paid lobbyists or occupy university chairs partially funded by Japanese money. The theme of their song is that, if Japan is a normal nation playing by normal rules, its success is due in equal parts to its own virtues in beating the West at its own game and to Western, especially American, failures and shortcomings. All else is Japan-bashing.

The Chrysanthemum Club has received great help from many free-market economists. Some, like the Nobel Prize–winning economist Milton Friedman, argue that trade deficits are good because American consumers get access to cheap, well-made Japanese goods. This argument, often echoed by editorial writers, ignores the fact that these consumers are also producers who won't be able to buy those goods if the imports drive their employers out of business.

More insidious were the economists, schooled in the laissez-faire economics of Adam Smith, whom we met in Chapter 2. These economists believed so devoutly in free markets that they assumed only free-market economies could succeed. Therefore, if Japan were as successful as it seemed to be, it must be as devoted to the free market as any Western nation. If Japan's markets were as open as these economists assumed them to be, then any trade imbalance was due to the shabby nature of American goods. Later, these goods improved but the deficit continued. To the economists, this only proved that the dollar was overvalued and the yen undervalued; correct this imbalance, and the trade deficit would right itself. Freetraders, especially within the Institute for International Economics in Washington, championed this view.

The dollar was, in fact, overvalued, not only against the yen but against European currencies, causing severe U.S. trade deficits everywhere in the mid-1980s. When it eventually fell, after the Plaza Accord of 1985, so did the deficits with the Europeans. But the deficit with Japan continued to grow. Where Japan was concerned, the laws of economics, as defined by Adam Smith, did not apply.

Americans "had been taught to think of corporations as profit-
and utility-maximizing black boxes, responding rationally to a rational world of price signals," Taggart Murphy writes:

> That there were corporations somewhere in the world for whom profit
> making was an unimportant, if not positively unworthy, goal did not enter
> their considerations. They had never thought about the possibility that
> economic entities could be free of the fear of bankruptcy and still be
> competitive, or that there were successful economic systems where credit
> was allocated on a basis that had nothing to do with the capacity to gen-
> erate profits.[12]

By now, for many Americans economists, the facts have become
too clear to deny. Japan's economy is no model of free-market economics but a much more controlled device, dependent on rigged markets and managed trade. For the economists, four years of lagging
growth in Japan, accompanied by a falling stock market, weakened
banks, and a government deficit, have made this conversion easier to
take. A triumphant Japan had to be seen as a free-market Japan. A
Japan in trouble is a nation that violated the gospel according to St.
Adam and is being duly punished. One wonders how these economists
will react when the Japanese economy turns up again, as it must.

The *Economist* magazine bears much of the blame for the West's
failure to understand Japan and, hence, to deal with it in a mature
and effective way. The *Economist* has compared criticism of Japan
to "McCarthyism," still complains seriously about "Japan-bashing,"
and reported in 1990 on "the radical changes that are, in reality,
remaking Japan in a freer-market image." These "radical changes"
never took place, but this did not stop the magazine from reporting
in 1997 that "against all expectations, it looks as if Japan really is
reforming its economy."[13] The *Economist*'s ex cathedra tone and its
reputation as a leading international journal on politics and economics have made it required reading for the world's opinion makers. This influence means that its inaccurate, and often dishonest,
reporting on Japan and trade has caused exceptional damage.

The other side of the debate has been carried out by the "revisionists," who have insisted that Japan is a unique nation with a
unique economy that demands a different and deeper understanding
than Western economists, hobbled by their free-market preconceptions,
have been able to give it. These revisionists, unlike the economists,

are Japan experts who have lived in the country, speak the language, know its history and understand its culture.

The revisionists' godfather is Chalmers Johnson, a professor at the University of California, San Diego, whose 1982 book, *MITI and the Japanese Miracle*, first described the Japanese economy as it really works. Then came books by Clyde V. Prestowitz, Jr., Edward J. Lincoln, James Fallows, Eamonn Fingleton, R. Taggart Murphy, and especially van Wolferen's *The Enigma of Japanese Power*, a stunningly thorough dissection of Japanese society by a Dutch scholar and journalist who has lived in Japan for more than thirty years. Each author peeled away layers of the Japanese onion, penetrating ever closer to the heart of this complex, fascinating society.

The revisionists' ideas have triumphed, to the degree that many Japanese officials admit now that their analysis of the postwar Japanese economy was correct. The same officials insist that Japan now "has reached a crossroads" and is changing, reforming, becoming more Western, assuming its rightful place. Maybe. But maybe not.

A Personal Note

The foregoing should make it clear that writing about Japan is not a straightforward descriptive task but involves the reporter in an emotional tug-of-war, a "clash of civilizations," in Huntington's words, freighted with centuries of historical and cultural baggage. I should state my own attitude in this debate. I feel the free-market economists, and their journalistic and political bellboys, have greatly harmed the West's ability to cope with the Japanese challenge to its economy. I find the revisionists' analysis persuasive, since it has helped me make sense of my own observations there. I am too Western to find Japan—with its racism, xenophobia, discipline, conformity, repression of women, and frequent arrogance—a congenial place; I could never feel at home there.

But my comfort is beside the point. As a nation and as an economy, Japan is a winner. More than any postwar society, it has succeeded on its own terms. It has taken a hard look at the needs and priorities of its own society and has proceeded rigorously to meet those needs. If it has played by its own rules, it is the West's fault to misunderstand what it was doing and to mishandle its own response.

Throughout this book, I am trying to judge the reaction of the major industrial nations to globalization by their own lights. Their reaction should not be seen as a matter of "right" or "wrong," but should be judged by the degree to which they succeed on their own terms.

Sakakibara said the Japanese system stresses "management for the stakeholders rather than management for the shareholders." It is, he said, "a well organized but extremely competitive market economy with considerable egalitarian income distribution and high social mobility. Indeed, the system is . . . to the mind of individualistic Westerners, too well organized. To date, however, it has proved to be highly efficient and competitive."

The rest of Asia, in particular, has studied the Japanese economy and is adopting much of it. As Sakakibara wrote, "The real choice now facing the world seems to be not between capitalism or socialism, but between a capitalistic market economy or a noncapitalistic market economy."[14]

The competition between these two systems will be fought out in the new global economy. My contention is that Japan may be better prepared than any of its rivals for the challenges ahead.

The Opening of the Hermit Nation

Japan has always changed and adapted to external pressure, from its original "opening" by American warships in 1853 to the U.S. occupation after World War II, to the oil crises of 1973 and 1979. It is adapting again now, preparing itself for the global economy, often taking on the trappings of Western economies, but like the stores with English-language names, not changing much inside.

Japan's history is one of island isolation punctuated by dramatic, often traumatic, encounters with the world. An ancient civilization, never colonized, it first met the West in the shape of sixteenth-century Portuguese traders, followed by Spanish Jesuits. Although Japan then was an advanced society by Western standards, the shoguns who ruled it feared the impact of Christianity. First they banned the religion, then forebade any dealings with the outside world, even ordering the destruction of oceangoing ships.

For the next two centuries, Japan was a hermit nation. Its modicum of trade went through Dutch traders, who held a monopoly at a single post near Nagasaki. A small group of Japanese scholars learned the Dutch language so they could watch the outside world.

As historians have pointed out, this controlled and monopolized trade, plus the careful monitoring of the world while keeping the world from monitoring Japan, has echoes to this day.

The isolation ended in 1853 with the arrival of the "black ships," the American fleet commanded by Commodore Matthew Perry, who had been sent to Japan by President Fillmore to open Japan to American traders. From the American point of view, such trade would benefit both sides. But to the Japanese, the arrival of the black ships was not only one of the most important dates in its history but a symbol of the use of Western force and technology to force Western ways, including Western trade, on a Japan that, after two centuries of isolation, had become relatively backward.

Partially because of the Western incursion, the shogunate was overthrown in 1868 by the Meiji oligarchy. The purpose of the Meiji state was to catch up quickly with the West, so that Japan never again would be vulnerable to the kind of intrusion that Perry and his black ships represented. The Meiji reformers opened Japan to Western trade and investment but insisted that this be accompanied by Western experts who could teach the Japanese the tricks of Western industry and manufacturing. This transfer of technology led to wholesale copying of Western innovations, which the Japanese, then as now, were able to manufacture as well as the West could. Again, this pattern prefigured the modern age, not only in Japan, which still relies heavily on its superior production of Western-invented goods, but in China, which now demands the transfer of Western technology as the price of Western trade and investment there.

Japan also adopted Western methods of bureaucracy, Western forms of government, even Western dress—all in the nineteenth century. As Eamonn Fingleton writes, "Japan squared the circle: under the guise of establishing Western-style institutions, it in reality established the prototypical strong state that has since become the model for other east Asian growth economies."[15]

At the same time, the *zaibatsu*, the forerunners of today's *keiretsu*, were formed. Working with the government and bureaucracy, they quickly built mighty industrial conglomerates that seized control of Japan's trade. By the 1930s, Japan was a powerful exporting nation. Trade pressures, aggravated by reports of Japanese atrocities in China, led to Western embargoes on shipments of oil to Japan. To the Japanese, it seemed to be the black ships all over again—the use of Western, and especially American, power to control Japan's economy. Japan reacted with the attack on Pearl Harbor. Four years later, it lay defeated and ruined.

Economics as a Strategy

For Germany, the great postwar question was, Where did we go wrong? For Japan, it has been, Why did we lose? To this day, Japan, unlike Germany, has never accepted war guilt, an attitude that infuriates neighbors, like China or Korea, that suffered greatly from Japanese aggression. Instead, having renounced militarism, Japan has developed its economy with a single-minded fervor to accomplish what it could not do with arms—to ensure Japan's power in the world and its invulnerability to outside pressure.

It has done it the same way it has met every foreign challenge for 400 years:

> In the effort to avoid control by outsiders, Japan's leaders perfected systems for acquiring foreign knowledge. They built on existing patterns to develop a political, educational and ideological network that combined the strengths of big business and big government and that consistently put the interests of the greater society ahead of the comfort [of] the individual Japanese. The United States has done this in wartime: Japan has sustained it for 150 years through war and peace.[16]

Japan treated the postwar American occupation the same way it treated the nineteenth-century traders who followed the trail blazed by the black ships. They told General Douglas MacArthur and his aides what they wanted to hear, adopted Western trappings, and proceeded to build a new, powerful Japan. The *keiretsu* replaced the *zaibatsu*. The bureaucracy regained control. Trade remained tightly controlled. Much foreign investment—in autos, for instance—was virtually forbidden. New twists were added. Yukio Noguchi, a former Ministry of Finance official, told me that, in many ways, Japan's economy "is still a wartime economy." By this he means that policies adopted during the war, such as lifetime employment to minimize job changing and forced savings to create a vast pool of domestic funds for investment, remain to this day.[17]

At the same time, the United States opened its own markets and deliberately overvalued its dollar, to help both its friends and former foes to rebuild their war-shattered economies through exporting. It was a generous and statesmanlike policy that led to mature, normal trade relations with European allies, whose view of economics and trade largely meshed with America's own. In Japan, however, the mercantilist state built up its domestic industries behind a wall of tariffs and other trade barriers that kept out any foreign competition.

By the 1960s, these industries had recovered and were ready to attack. The key was "a sophisticated strategy of selected protectionism," in which Japan conquered world markets for an increasingly sophisticated range of products while its home market stayed closed to any foreign competitors for those products. "Japan protected, at all costs, a narrow moving band of products at the margin between certain lower-technology industries—the ones in which, at a given stage, it already had global superiority and no longer needed to protect—and those higher-technology industries in which it is not yet ready to launch its challenge."[18] At the start, it protected its black-and-white television manufacturers or its steelmakers while they conquered foreign markets. Once this was done, there was no more need to protect those industries, and the protectionism shifted up to the next level, such as autos and color TV. Today, those industries can take care of themselves, so Japan now blocks imports of high-tech machine tools, glass, pharmaceutical products, and other advanced goods.

Behind this wall, Japan's industries invaded the open American market and quickly overwhelmed American makers of steel, ships, autos, cameras, stereos, television sets, and, later, semiconductors, semiconductor components, fax machines, machine tools, supercomputers, laptops—all the icons of our age. Some of these industries, such as television manufacturing, have all but disappeared in the United States. Others, such as VCR manufacturing, never began. Still others, such as steel and cars, survive but much altered by Japanese cooperation. Industries such as semiconductors survive only because the American government, belatedly grasping the challenge, forced Japan to share markets. Some goods, such as flat-screen panels, were invented in the United States but are made in Japan because only Japan, having captured control of television manufacturing, has the skills and infrastructure now to make the high-tech screens that are TV's descendants.

For the past half century, the United States and Japan both had great goals. The United States wanted to defeat Communism. Japan wanted to build the world's most modern economy. They both won.

The Framework of Japan Inc.

Japan's economy is dominated by the mighty *keiretsu* or *gurupu*—corporate groups of industrial companies, centered around a major bank and linked with a network of subsidiaries, suppliers, and distributors. The best-known and biggest are Mitsui, Mitsubishi, Sumitomo, Fuyo, Sanwa, and Dai-Ichi Kangyo. Each has its own source of funding, international trading house, and distribution network through which it can control its commercial environment from the original financing through exports abroad and sales in Japan. They are simply stupendous in size; the two biggest corporations in the whole world are not the Mitsubishi or Mitsui *keiretsu* but the Mitsubishi and Mitsui trading houses, which are only part of their *keiretsu*.[19]

These *keiretsu* are the instruments of Japanese success, not the cause. Toyoo Gyohten, an adviser to the board of the Bank of Tokyo, writes that the keys are "the channeling of the great fund of domestic savings into productive sectors of the economy, the speed with which new technologies have been internalized by industry, the combination of public-sector leadership and private-sector dynamism, and the fostering of cooperative rather than confrontational relationships."[20]

Japanese savers, corporate and personal, play their part. The national savings rate amounts to one-third of the Gross Domestic Product, more than twice the U.S. rate. Japanese families save some 15 percent of their salaries, compared with 4 percent in the United States (see Exhibit 5.2). The reasons are many: a shortage of credit cards, skimpy pensions for retirees, tax laws that encourage savings and discourage big spending, an underdeveloped mortgage market that forces potential home buyers to save most of the purchase price. The result is a mammoth pool of money—about $2 trillion in savings at post offices alone, some $6 trillion altogether. This is 52 percent of all savings in the industrialized world. It gives Japanese industry a terrific war chest and has enabled Japan to be the leading creditor to the world. Altogether the world owes Japan a net $700 billion, with all the power and leverage that implies. Japan financed no less than 60 percent of all loans in 1995 to cover the deficits of the United States, Canada, and Mexico. This is one potent reason why President Clinton, a respectful student of global bond markets, has avoided trade confrontations with Japan.

Exhibit 5.2

Savings Rate
(in percent of Gross Domestic Product)

	1960–1969	1970–1979	1980–1989	1990–1994
United States	20.0	19.8	17.8	15.4
Japan	34.4	35.3	31.8	33.5
Germany	27.3	24.4	22.4	22.2
France	26.3	25.9	20.4	19.9

Source: Organization for Economic Cooperation and Development.

As Gyohten said, this national nest egg gives Japan a freedom of action that debtor nations like the United States don't have. The Japanese are less answerable to foreign creditors or foreign markets. The Ministry of Finance sees to it that much of these savings goes to Japanese industry at preferential interest rates. In addition, most stock—about 60 percent—in Japanese companies is owned by other Japanese companies; the cross-holdings between *keiretsu* is well documented. These friendly stockholders are content with average profit margins of 1.8 percent (in Germany it's 7.4 percent, in the United States 15 percent) and do not cut and run when a share price drops. All this gives Japanese industry extraordinary flexibility and a long-term horizon free from day-by-day profit pressures. It also gives it the deep pockets that make it possible to slash prices endlessly on exports, driving out the competition. The goal is not profits but market share, which means power and control. The Japanese have proved themselves ready to sacrifice profits to dominate markets. (Once those markets are dominated, of course, prices have a way of going back up.) Taggart Murphy explains the approach clearly:

> Japanese companies are best understood as alliances for mutual protection in a world where nothing is certain. The usual criteria of profitability provide no meaningful yardstick. . . . The drive for market share is not an option that can be replaced next year with a different goal, such as higher profits, as many foreign observers urge. It is the essence of the Japanese corporation.[21]

The Japanese themselves admit that their strength lies in producing, not innovating. Through history, Japanese firms have taken ideas dreamed up abroad and thrived by making them better than their inventors could. Flat-screen panels, videotape recorders, and supercomputers are major examples. Americans invented transistors, but Sony, then a tiny start-up firm, paid Western Electric $25,000 in 1953 for a license to manufacture them, changing the history of consumer electronics forever.[22]

When foreigners think of Japan Inc., they think of bureaucrats, particularly from the Ministry for International Trade and Industry (MITI), "picking winners and losers" among certain corporations and virtually running them. It was nothing as straightforward as that. Instead, MITI and other ministries tried to spot industries that had strategic significance, such as semiconductors, or could lead to dominance in other industries, such as television. It then saw to it that a chosen industry benefited from subsidized research, low-interest loans, and selected protectionism. Within this nursery, the various firms in this industry battled it out for local dominance. The winner, mightily strengthened, then went on to dominate the world. This system is far from infallible—it missed the coming predominance of software, for instance—but it has worked well enough to produce the postwar Japanese economic miracle.

At the bottom of this structure lies Japan's chaotic and inefficient retail sector. Japan, with half as many people, has more stores than the United States. In 1989, small stores, employing fewer than five persons, accounted for 57 percent of retail sales, against 3 percent in the United States.[23] Today, these mom-and-pop shops remain the bedrock of Japanese commerce and employ millions of persons who would be jobless in a more efficient economy. This make-work system depends utterly on the superstructure of protectionism, government-business cooperation, and powerful *keiretsu*. Because the nation's markets are closed, cheaper imports are kept out, and both manufacturers and retailers can charge higher prices, probably 50 percent higher or more, than would be possible with an open market. Laws discourage larger, more efficient stores. And the *keiretsu* and their distributors make sure that few foreign goods get to the shelves of these tiny shops.

All this is changing constantly. Japan's financial market is gradually opening. Banks, loaded with bad loans, are reforming, and some are closing. Convenience stores are appearing. Japanese companies are seeking more financing abroad. But the structure that has existed throughout the postwar era remains intact. So do the motives behind it: the quest for control, the thirst for invulnerability, the drive for power.

Japan Bankrolls the Reagan Debt

During the Cold War, the American trade officials who wanted a tougher attitude toward this Japanese mercantilism were squelched by the State Department and the Pentagon. Official American policy held that Japan was America's most important Asian ally, a democratic outpost next door to China and the Soviet Union. Japan's strategic value and the usefulness to the United States of the U.S. bases on the Japanese-owned island of Okinawa outweighed trade issues. In a sense, the State Department and the Pentagon became lobbyists for Japan. Unable to admit publicly that Japanese policies were causing severe damage to the American economy, these departments insisted that Japan was a normal parliamentary democracy and its economy was a normal free market. As late as 1992, Vice President Daniel Quayle denied "that Japan is radically different, that its corporations are not subject to normal market forces. [They are] subject to the same market forces as American or European companies."

That argument has been lost. President Clinton clearly is persuaded of the revisionists' argument; one revisionist, Laura d'Andrea Tyson, became chair of his Council of Economic Advisers. Yet this has not translated into a new policy. The Clinton administration has been even less ready than the Reagan administration to force Japan to open its markets, or to retaliate for Japanese protectionism.

The reason is obvious. The U.S. budget deficits of the Reagan era coincided with Japan's enormous trade surpluses. Indeed, the one made the other necessary. The massive deficits could only be financed by massive borrowing, and only Japan had the money, mostly earned by its trade surpluses with the United States. Reagan's irresponsible budget policy virtually mandated his equally irresponsible trade policy. To get tough with Japan, to insist that it buy as much as it sold, would have turned off the Japanese money spigot and choked off the deficit financing that made the phony Reagan boom possible.[24]

That boom is over now, and the American budget deficit is coming down. But the debt, quadrupled during the Reagan years, remains and is still financed largely by Japan. Japanese banks and other financial institutions hold more than $250 billion in U.S. government bonds. If they stopped buying these bonds, the U.S. government would go broke. To keep that from happening, the Federal Reserve Board would have to raise interest rates, which would discourage investment, slow down the economy, raise unemployment, and guarantee a Republican victory in the 2000 election.

In short, it is not too much to say that the Reagan legacy will keep the Clinton administration, and many administrations to come, totally in thrall to the Japanese banks.

The More It Changes . . .

Japanese government officials admit that Japan may have been protectionist in the past but insist it is no longer. They also stress to Americans the importance of the U.S.-Japanese security alliance and the strategic significance of the Okinawa bases. At the same time, they are at pains to play down the strength of Japan's economy and play up its troubles—especially its recent "recession," the woes of its banks, and the departure of its industry to Southeast Asia. Any attempt to press Japan to reform its economy might damage this U.S.-Japanese relationship, they say. Besides, they argue with a straight face, government negotiations to open the Japanese market amount to "managed trade." And anyway, Japan has already changed (or is changing). They have a ready claque abroad: the free-market economists, conservative columnists like George Will, and editorial writers from the *New York Times* to the *Wall Street Journal*.

Meanwhile, Japan is changing but less than advertised. The "recession" was no recession in the Western sense. The economy didn't actually shrink, but its growth slowed to almost nothing. By 1996 it had revived to 3.6 percent per year, the fastest among the major nations, before slumping again. The collapse of the Tokyo stock market hurt many investors. But Japanese companies, which rely more on capital markets and less on the stock market for their funding, are not seriously inconvenienced. The collapse of the real estate market has created a Japanese version of the American savings-and-loan scandal. The government bailout of the *jusen*, the Japanese equivalent

Exhibit 5.3

Foreign Direct Investment

(in percent of Gross Domestic Product)

	1983	1985	1988	1990	1991	1992
United States	16.8	19.2	26.1	27.1	26.1	23.7
Japan	0.6	0.7	1.1	1.3	1.4	1.5
Germany	16.4	15.2	13.3	16.9	18.3	17.2
France	—	—	—	34.1	34.4	—

Source: Organization for Economic Cooperation and Development.

of America's S&Ls, will be expensive—some $80 billion—but is more of a problem to be solved than a crisis. The same is true of the other bad debts held by banks, possibly worth $160 billion or more. This mess must be cleaned up, and Japan's banks will emerge with both their reputations and their balance sheets smudged. But in a system with $6 trillion in savings, an $80 billion payout is painful but not crippling.

In short, Japan's plight looks worse from abroad than it does up close. As an American executive in Tokyo told me, "Westerners always underestimate Japanese single-mindedness and its focus on countering the laws of economics as we know them. Is Japan riding for a fall? I don't think so."

Japan still keeps a tight lid on foreign investment. Such investment in the United States amounts to 24 percent of gross domestic product (see Exhibit 5.3). In France it's 34 percent, and in Germany 17 percent. In Japan, it's 1.5 percent.[25] Japan's markets are open to many goods, such as textiles, clothing, and household goods, but virtually none of these imports come from the United States. Most come from other Asian countries, often from Japanese-owned companies there. The Gap, Tower Records, and Blockbuster all have stores in Tokyo. But trade barriers keep out less visible but more lucrative industrial goods. They also bar foreign competitors for Japan's high-tech goods, which can be sold in Japan at huge markups. As many tourists and travelers to Japan have discovered, Japanese computers, CD players, and radios are all more expensive in Tokyo than they are in New York or London.

Japan's trade surplus is still huge—about $80 billion per year. About two-thirds of this, or some $50 billion, is with the United States. Free-market economists blame this on Japan's sluggish economy and the relative weakness of the yen, which make the Japanese reluctant to buy goods abroad. Soon, they predict, the economy will recover, the yen will strengthen, and all will be right again. "Trade rows, like economies, usually go in cycles," the *Economist* assured its readers.[26] Unfortunately, this deficit, like the assurances that it will soon end, hasn't changed for twenty years.

Deregulation is the buzzword of the day in Tokyo now, but it means something different than it does in the West. Every Japanese businessman and government official says that deregulation is coming, to adapt Japan to the global economy and to make foreign entry easier. Foreigners there are skeptical. The written characters for the word *deregulation* actually mean "loosening" the rules, not scrapping them. "We think deregulation is meant to help consumers," Robert M. Orr, Jr., the government relations director in Japan for Motorola, told me. "The Japanese see it as a means to help producers, to help Japan."[27]

Beyond the Bubble

Most of Japan's problems now are the result of the "bubble economy" of the late 1980s, when a policy of cheap credit sent land, property, and stock prices to ridiculous heights. The "bubble economy" began in 1986, after the Plaza Accord of 1985, in which the Americans, Europeans, and Japanese agreed to lower the value of the dollar. The dollar then was so overvalued that it was pricing American goods out of world markets. At the Plaza, Japan and Europe agreed to let their currencies rise against the dollar. But this meant that Japanese exports would become more expensive. In an economy that depended on exports to grow, such a policy could lead to recession.

So the Ministry of Finance deliberately opened the financial tap. Under MOF orders, banks lowered interest rates to the point that loans were nearly free. This cheap capital led to massive borrowing and a surge of money into the economy. The purpose was to encourage investment by Japanese companies, to enable them to compete and win without the advantage of a cheap yen. Stock prices soared and so did real estate. Using these inflated assets as collateral, businesses borrowed even more. At one point during the bubble economy, the value of land in Tokyo was greater than the value of the entire United States. Japan accounted for 60 percent of the land value of the entire earth. The Imperial Palace grounds were worth more than Canada. Some Third World nations paid off their national debts by selling their embassies in Tokyo.[28]

When the bubble burst in 1990, some *jusen* S&Ls collapsed, and banks suffered losses. Some Japanese investors had used the cheap money to buy American resorts and French art at inflated prices, and took a bath. A gallery's worth of Picassos, Renoirs, and van Goghs, bought for $50 million or even $80 million each, have since been repossessed by the banks that loaned the money and sit in bank vaults, hidden from anyone who would like to look at them.[29]

But the corporations, by and large, had used the loans to invest in modern, labor-saving equipment that will keep Japanese industry on the spearpoint of modernity for the next decade. About 30 percent went into modernization, mostly robots, that will raise Japanese productivity. Another 30 percent went into innovation. Some went into American country clubs and impressionist art, but most of the other 40 percent was used to expand industrial capacity, including heavy investment in Southeast Asia, establishing a Japanese bridgehead there both for low-cost manufacturing and for exports.

This economic invasion of Asia is a key to Japan's strategy for the future. Like Japan's banking problems, the financial woes of these East Asian nations and their effect on Japan's investment there is more of a short-term pang than a long-range setback. In Asia, Japan sees a market of 3.1 billion people, three times the size of NAFTA and the European Union put together. Japan once aimed its investments at the West; now the target is Asia. Of the 21,000 Japanese overseas subsidiaries, 9,000 are in Asia and 5,000 in North America. By the end of 1995, this investment amounted to no less than $88 billion. The East Asian financial crisis and looming depression will put a severe crimp in this Japanese strategy. But the depression is temporary: the reasons for the Asian Miracle still exist, and the area will revive, sooner rather than later, made even stronger by the purging of its excesses.

Asia will boom again. As it does, so will Japan.[30]

In a region where most persons make less than $4,000 per year, this means that the Japanese have to sell their cars and other goods under cost to compete. But with their vast savings at home and huge trade surpluses, they can do precisely that, just as they did thirty years earlier to capture the American market.

This investment abroad enables Japanese spokesmen to claim that their nation's industry is being "hollowed out." This is a fear that I've heard in Japan for more than a decade now. The reality is less stark. For the past two decades, Japanese companies have been setting up manufacturing plants abroad. The first investment was in the United States to prepare for American protectionism that never materialized. More recently, Japanese manufacturers invested in Europe, especially in Britain, in case the drive toward a single market there deteriorated into a protectionist Fortress Europe. Now they also are investing in the low-wage countries of Southeast Asia, mostly because a stronger yen has raised the cost of doing business at home.

But like many changes in Japan, there is less to this trend than meets the eye. Overseas manufacturing by Japanese companies accounts for 9.6 percent of Japan's gross national product, up from only 3.2 percent in 1985, but still minuscule compared to other countries. American companies, for instance, do 22 percent of their manufacturing overseas.

More important is what's made abroad and what's still made at home. Generally, Japanese companies have exported the manufacturing of low-tech, low-value-added goods, enabling them to use their domestic capacity for state-of-the-art production. Fujitsu, for instance, mass-produces earlier generations of printers and other goods, what it calls "past products," at its plants in Thailand and elsewhere in Southeast Asia. But its fourteen plants in Japan remain busy by concentrating on high-speed printers, flat-panel displays, impact scanners, and futuristic medical equipment.[31] If cheaper cars are being made in Southeast Asia, the high-value, high-profit cars like the Lexus are still made in Japan. Japan may be ceding supremacy in lower-end consumer goods to the Southeast Asians, but it makes sure that the cutting edge—things like mini-CD video players—is still wielded in Japanese factories by Japanese workers. These are the products of the future, the keys to the Japanese industrial kingdom, and they are not going abroad.

Cornering the Global Economy

Japanese companies are betting their future on what has worked in the past: maintaining their manufacturing base behind trade barriers, monopolizing world production of techniques such as flat panels, and when necessary, buying American ideas and using superior Japanese production techniques to dominate world markets.

Yoshihiro Suzuki, the executive vice president of NEC Corporation, the electronics giant, is an outspoken admirer of American technological creativity. When I talked with him, he had just come back from Silicon Valley and professed himself dazzled by the dynamism of the American system, where the free market spun off new ideas and businesses by the day. But like many Japanese executives, he was openly contemptuous of Americans' ability to turn these ideas into products that sell and confident that this skill will remain cornered by the Japanese.

"You Americans are good at conceiving new ideas," Suzuki told me, "but when it comes to organizing those new ideas, you're not very good. Once the technology is developed in the United States, state-of-the-art production can take place in Japan. Japanese consumers will notice the smallest surface defect. Americans are satisfied with television sets, say, that from our point of view are not of high quality. Our production is very finely tuned. It's very difficult to imagine Americans doing such things."

But surely Americans can catch up? "Not yet," he said, "and I think it's impossible. All this is based on the culture of a country. It comes from our history."[32]

Suzuki smiled politely as he said all this, as though this Japanese superiority is a gift from heaven that cannot be helped, only admitted. When the interview ended, one of his aides took me to the top of the NEC building to show me its sweeping view across the capital. In a corner was the thing that, I suspect, I was really meant to see. It was an aquarium, with brilliant fish swimming amid the bubbles. Except it wasn't a real aquarium. It was a flat-panel screen, more than forty inches across but no more than a couple of inches deep, and so realistic that I gasped when I realized what it was.

The technology for flat-panel screens was invented by two American companies, RCA and Westinghouse Electric Corporation, back in 1963. But making this technology commercially viable was a long, arduous task. RCA, beset by financial problems, licensed its technology for a fee to the Japanese. Westinghouse persisted, according to a history by Richard Florida and David Browdy. But then, in the 1970s, Westinghouse, battered by Japanese imports, decided to stop making television sets.

One technology leads to another: expertise in the manufacture of television sets polishes the skills that are needed to produce flat-panel screens. Having dropped one, the United States lost its capacity for the other, which could have given it the lead in a multibillion-dollar field.

The RCA and Westinghouse technology first developed by the Japanese involved liquid-crystal display (LCD) panels now common in laptop computers and calculators; sales of the LCDs reached $6 billion in 1995, mostly from Japanese companies. As South Korean firms begin to move into the LCD market, the Japanese companies, including NEC and Fujitsu, have developed forty-two-inch plasma displays panels (PDPs) that provide a wider viewing angle and a splendid picture. These PDPs are the screens of the future, not only in television but in computers, in office copiers, at terminals in stock markets, anywhere that pictures or information will be displayed. They are the windows into the Information Age, and their production is controlled by the Japanese.

This is far from the only example of Japanese industrial dominance, even monopoly. A fire in 1993 in a small factory in the Japanese town of Niihama wiped out 65 percent of the world's supply of epoxy cresol novolac resin, an obscure substance that is vital in the making of computer chips. American companies may produce the chips themselves, but many components or processes crucial to making these chips—not only the resin but resolving silica, steppers, ceramic substrates, sputter targets, mask blanks, and many other products that few Americans have even heard of—are controlled, either largely or totally, by Japan. The fact is that Japan could throttle America's semiconductor industry overnight if it chose, just as its bankers could strangle America's government if they chose to stop buying its bonds.

Nor are semiconductors the end of the story. Japan also dominates the laser diodes that go into laser printers (99 percent of global market share), compact disc players (100 percent), robots (80 percent), endoscopes for internal medical examinations (70 percent), high-technology machine tools (70 to 80 percent), plus copiers, fax machines, and notebook computers.[33]

One result of this dominance is that Japan, unlike the United States or Europe, does not have to move jobs to low-wage countries to meet its global competition. There *is* no competition.

Another important result is this dominance makes it much easier for Japan to keep its workers' wages high. As we saw in earlier chapters, free trade raises the wages of Third-World workers but lowers the pay of First-World workers making the same goods. Theoretically, they will meet in the middle sooner or later, which is good for the Third Worlders but hard on the First Worlders. If a country like Japan can monopolize important industries, so that nobody else anywhere makes the same goods, its workers never face this competition.

Japan Faces the Future

Japan does face challenges. One is the kind of slow growth that is endemic to mature economies. Another is slowly shrinking trade surpluses, as imports from Southeast Asia grow. Imports are imports, even if most of them are made by Japanese-owned companies. Another is the pressure this will put on unemployment. Yet another is the weakness of some banks, weighed down by bad loans, and the ability of a wounded Ministry of Finance to continue to lead the economy and, by extension, the nation. Bank reform is a clear priority and must be guided by MOF, despite the black eye it suffered when it allowed, and even engineered, the bubble economy and the subsequent collapse.

But a black eye is not a coronary. MOF is an astonishing agency that controls the national budget, determines fiscal and monetary policies, writes tax laws and then collects the taxes, supervises banks, oversees the stock market, and supervises the savings system. In other words, from its hulking headquarters in the heart of Tokyo, it controls all the powers that in the United States are spread across the Treasury, Congress, the Internal Revenue Service, the Federal Reserve, and the Securities and Exchange Commission. As former MOF official Yukio Noguchi said, "Anything related to money is controlled by MOF. So it controls the economy."

The ministry retains almost all its old powers. It recently beat off political attempts to curb these powers. It has agreed to the establishment of an "independent" bank regulatory agency, but even this agency will be primarily staffed by former MOF officials. This scattering of retired MOF officials across the boardrooms of "private" banks is a Japanese tradition—no fewer than 114 of them were senior managers at banks in 1992—and gives MOF a fistful of strings to pull.[34]

Japanese companies like NEC seem determined to keep high-end manufacturing at home. So long as Japan controls cutting-edge technology, such as flat-panel screens and many phases of semiconductor manufacturing, its trade balance should stay in surplus. The pressure on jobs is expected to ease soon, simply because the number of people seeking work will shrink. Japan already has a low birthrate, only 1.43 children per family. The number of persons between fifteen and sixty-four began to decline in 1966, and soon the labor force will follow suit. If anything, this could produce a labor shortage. Like Japan's other problems, this is not a big one; millions of women barred from work now can be recruited, as in other countries, to fill this gap.

Changes are happening now, and more will take place in the future. Japan is beginning to allow imports of beef and rice, but not enough to drive its inefficient farmers out of business. Discount retailers, like America's 7-Eleven stores, are beginning to appear. Some banks are failing, but, with one exception, they are small and medium-sized banks, not the so-called "city banks," the large nationwide banks, headquartered in Tokyo, Yokohama, Osaka, Kobe, and Nagoya, which are the financial core of the giant *keiretsu*.

Kenneth S. Courtis, the highly respected economist in Tokyo for Deutsche Bank, argues that Japan does need to restore the basic strength of its banking system, reform some regulations to increase consumer demand, and shift more manufacturing to the rest of Asia. If Japan can do this, Courtis told me, "it could come out a hell of a lot stronger, with a vibrant domestic economy, an efficient home base, and real control of strategic technologies. They've already got most of the chips in the global poker game."[35]

The Threat of a Strong Yen

There is one cloud on the horizon that alarms the Japanese. This is the growing strength of the yen and the fear that an overly strong yen could undermine Japan's exports and, by extension, its ability to support its consensual, often inefficient economy. This fear became acute in 1995, when the yen, which had been dropping since 1973 from its low of 360 to the dollar, finally peaked at 79 to the dollar.*

This strength meant that Japan was pricing itself out of world markets. The Economic Strategy Institute in Washington had estimated in 1992 that Ford and Chrysler, if not General Motors, could produce as efficiently as the major Japanese auto companies, assuming an exchange rate of 120 to the dollar. Suddenly, here was an exchange rate a full 33 percent above that level, meaning that American auto manufacturers—and the manufacturers of many other goods, in many other countries—were at least 33 percent more efficient than the Japanese.

At this rate, important changes began to happen. The export of Japanese manufacturing to Southeast Asia speeded up. As Murphy pointed out, companies had three choices: to pull out of foreign markets where profits had disappeared, to raise prices and so give up hard-won market shares, or to protect these market shares at all costs and absorb the losses. Japanese foreign trade is based on an obsession with market share, and most companies took the third choice. But profit margins fell, and corporations began to look for ways to save money. The impact cut to the heart of the Japanese way of doing business.[36]

Richard Koo explained to me that this way of doing business is based on close personal relations between manufacturers and their suppliers. There is a sense of trust built up through years of relationships between these companies, and between business and government. This is the personal basis beneath the closed Japanese market. It is not just government regulations that have kept foreign suppliers from striking deals with Japanese companies. These foreigners have found it almost impossible to overcome their personal ties.

But what foreign sales forces have been unable to do, the strong yen began to accomplish. "Everyone understood that, with the strong yen, they couldn't go on as before," Koo said. "At 80 yen, people were saying, 'I really want to buy from you but I can't. I have to buy from the Malaysians or the Americans.' Once they started doing this, they discovered that foreign goods are not only cheaper but of high quality. This is important."

---

* Readers who don't deal daily with foreign exchange markets should note the seemingly reverse logic in the thought that an exchange rate of 360 to the dollar is "low" while 79 is "high." This means that it once took 360 yen to buy a dollar, and each yen was worth less than a third of a penny. At 79 to the dollar, each yen had more than quadrupled in price and was worth about 1.2 cents.

But the yen didn't stay at 79 very long. The Japanese government, worried about its industries, and the American government, worried that the Japanese would stop buying U.S. government bonds, cooperated to reverse the trend. Within a year, the yen had weakened by 50 percent, back to 120 to the dollar.

For the moment, the crisis had ended. Japanese companies that had sought suppliers in Malaysia or America began to look homeward again. "At this level," Koo said, "people say, 'Are you going to fire us and hire the Chinese or the Americans? What kind of Japanese are you?' After all, Japanese companies do still exist to provide jobs to Japanese workers."[37]

Danger in Strength

This is a dilemma for Japan. Sooner or later, the yen will soar again, if only because its reserves and savings make Japan so strong. But a strong yen will raise costs and encourage businesses to invest more abroad. This in turn will call into question the ability of Japanese industry to keep employing Japanese workers. As Koo says, Japanese companies truly feel a duty to employ these workers and keep unemployment down. But there comes a point when a strong yen will force them to invest elsewhere.

The only way to avoid a strong yen is to reduce Japan's pool of savings, by stimulating the local economy and by opening the country to cheaper, more attractive imports. But this in turn would undercut the power of the bureaucrats, especially the men from MOF, whose authority rises from their control of Japan's ocean of money. No one—no politician, bureaucrat, or businessperson—gives up power willingly. The bureaucrats will cede power only if the government forces them to do so. But the politicians are too weak and the bureaucrats too strong for this to happen. Wishful thinkers assume this must happen, sooner or later, but this imbalance between politics and bureaucracy, like so much else in Japan, is a legacy of the Meiji era and is too deeply rooted to be easily changed.[38]

Such a reform also would force Japan to become leaner and meaner, in the American mold. In a country that depends on a vast number of make-work jobs in corporations and on a hugely inefficient retail and distribution sector, such a change would be revolutionary.

"It's a private-sector welfare state," according to Orr of Motorola, an American expert on Japan. "It's sort of remarkable. I'm amazed at how many people in Japanese companies are not doing anything. This is a welfare state that has been largely financed by foreigners, through those trade deficits. This is still going on." Orr, like many foreigners in Tokyo, is of two or even three minds, seeing the need for change, doubting it will come, and not sure it should come:

> I raise hell about a lot of barriers here. But I look out my window and I say, 'They haven't done too badly.' Real change depends on whether the rest of the world will keep allowing them to play the same old Japanese game, and I'm not convinced that the rest of the world is ready to stop this. Without this, I don't think they're capable of changing.[39]

Any regime based on control needs a strong economic underpinning. The Soviet Union collapsed when its economy could no longer support its pretensions to superpower status. The exodus of heavy industries from Chicago in the 1960s undermined the Machine's ability to deliver services, especially jobs and good schools; the Machine survives, but much diminished from its glory days, and more modest. Basic change will come to Japan when its economic system—the tightly knit machine called Japan Inc.—stops delivering the goods.

Changing Without Changing

Some of the things that almost certainly won't happen in Japan are the things that are reported daily by Western wishful thinkers: a rebellion among women seeking more independence, an uprising among young people seeking less conformity, an insurrection among consumers demanding lower prices and a more expansive standard of living. James Fallows, in his book about Asia, *Looking at the Sun*, dived into a stack of yellowing clippings and came up with stories in the American press from the 1950s and 1960s making exactly the same predictions. In 1964, Fallows found, the old *Life* magazine devoted a special issue to Japan, reporting, among other things, that "in growing numbers, the country's youth runs away from tradition, family and authority," that "the transition to a consumer economy is in full swing," and that the government was "stripping away import restrictions." The issue contained an essay by the American ambassador of the day, Edwin Reischauer, reporting on Japan's "efficiently operating democratic government" and "free economic system . . . supported by a populace devoted to the concepts of individual human rights, democracy and world peace."[40]

As Fallows points out, none of this was true then, and it's no more true now. Japan remains a nation with strong national values, which happen not to be the same values that the United States and Western Europe cherish. These values, and the economy based on them, have served it well in the past. Japan will change in the future, as it has always changed, but in obedience to these values. Root-and-branch reform, of the sort that the West is always advocating, would make Japan something other than what it has always been; if the trauma of defeat in World War II could not achieve this, pious pleas from Washington and Brussels are hardly likely to do the job. As Eisuke Sakakibara wrote, Japan certainly could reform many of the "closed aspects" of its society, "but this closedness cannot be opened unless the Japanese wish to change their regime from a noncapitalistic to a capitalistic society."[41]

To meet the global economy, Japan will change, because it has always changed. The fact of change is inevitable. But the nature of this change is not. There is no reason to think that Japan will become like the West. If history is any guide, Japan will change to become more like itself.

Japan's basic problem is that its society has had one goal ever since Commodore Perry sailed in in 1853: to catch up to the West. Well, it has caught up. Now what?

6. EUROPE:
THE APPREHENSIVE CONTINENT

IN THEIR CEASELESS search for efficiencies and best practice, the global markets are marching through country after country, Eastern and Western, developed and underdeveloped, rich and poor. In their passage, the markets are uprooting civilizations and established ways of life. Like Sherman's army, which marched through Georgia and destroyed a civilization that did not recover for a century, the forces of globalization have the power to disrupt societies that have built the lives they wanted, replacing them with something that is new but not necessarily better. These societies and civilizations have their faults, although few are so flawed or so unfairly rooted as the antebellum South. Their citizens know that the markets, like General Sherman, are too potent to ignore and must be met. But most are not ready to throw out the old order without knowing whether it will be replaced with a new order that offers something of equal value.

Nowhere are the winds of globalization sensed with more apprehension than on the continent of Europe. The postwar history of Europe describes a conscious effort to use politics and economics to create a new and better civilization from the ruins of two continental civil wars.

The old civilization that existed when Europe began this century had failed. Its brilliant exterior hid a core of ancient hatreds, inequities, and instabilities that rotted into forty years of chaos. From this failure, the Europeans built a new order carefully based on social fairness, partnership among all classes of society, political balance, and cooperation between old enemies. This project has been driven by memories that, fifty years on, still live. It has been an

157

attempt to use economics to forge not only prosperity but equity. For most Europeans, it has worked marvelously.

Globalization threatens the entire framework of this new European order. The Europeans themselves are only recently aware of this. So far, they have no idea how to respond.

A Decade of Doubts

In the past decade, the Europeans were too preoccupied with their internal affairs to pay proper attention to the growing global market outside. First came the European Union's campaign to create a single market—in effect, erasing the commercial borders between its nations—by the end of 1992. As this was going on, the Berlin Wall fell, Germany was reunited, and a galaxy of 80 million Eastern and Central Europeans, forcibly isolated for forty-five years from the rest of Europe, began to demand readmission to their historic and cultural homes. The EU expanded from twelve to fifteen nations; another dozen were knocking at the door. Yugoslavia collapsed and the EU failed conspicuously to cope with this crisis, damaging its own self-confidence in the process. Most important, the EU committed itself to creating a common currency, the Euro, by 1999. If this project succeeds, Europe will have built a truly common market, taken a crucial step toward political unity, and created a currency strong enough to challenge the dollar, a potent weapon in the global economic competition of the future.

The birth of the single market and the reunification of Germany produced an economic boom in the late 1980s and early 1990s. This enabled the Europeans to ignore the problems—the wage declines, the downsizings, the manic rise and fall of corporations, the growth of global capital markets—that were afflicting the United States. Until 1993, the Europeans generally had lower unemployment than the Americans did. Then the boom ended, and the Europeans woke from their self-obsession to discover that, while they had been remaking their continent, the outside world had changed forever.

When Americans look at Europe now, they see high unemployment and low job creation and assume that, no matter how many troubles the United States has, Europe has more. This is not necessarily true. It just has different troubles. Globalization's impact on the United States has been felt in low wages. In Europe, it's been felt in high unemployment. Europe has 18 million unemployed but supports them above the poverty line through social security. America has 6 million unemployed and another 12 million working poor, earning wages below the poverty line. Neither is happy with this situation. But neither knows how to solve its troubles without inviting the troubles of the other.

Europe, more protected than the United States and less protected than Japan, could not keep globalization outside forever. But the global market has come to Europe about ten years after it hit the United States. The Europeans know this and shudder, much as many Americans wince at the latest fad out of California.

"There's a saying in Germany that what happened yesterday in the United States comes tomorrow in Europe, necessarily and unavoidably," Albert Schunk of the giant German union IG Metall, told me. Schunk, like other Europeans, is acutely aware that the United States has already suffered the global squeeze and has reacted in its own way. This American response is summed up by Europeans as "the American hire-and-fire system," a phrase that has become almost a cliché there.

Almost unanimously, this is not the model they want. But they know change is coming. They know that Europe is less vibrant than the United States and less aggressive than Japan. They know the market must be accommodated. They know that governments can't afford their current welfare systems, nor companies their expensive workforces. They just hope they can make enough changes to survive without ripping their societies apart.

Europe's Race Against Time

After World War II, Germany had to rebuild its society, and it did so on the basis of a system of consensus, with a strong common goal shared by business, labor, and government. Its success was evident when I asked Germans in all three areas how Europe and Germany can change to cope with globalization. All three responded with a mixture of acceptance and apprehension.

"The key question is how to build a competitive economy without abolishing our environment of social protection," said Schunk of IG Metall. "Germans do accept that change is necessary. The argument is on the basis of justice. If the burden has to be put on workers, it must be put on the rich, too. This is the philosophy of justice."[1]

"Our system has worked so well in the past fifty years," Klaus Friedrich Hofman, a German Labor Ministry official, said. "But the answers of this old system are not adequate to the new challenges of globalization. If we change completely, though, we will fail. We just don't want to abolish everything. Instead, we have to reconstruct. But that's a very hard task, and for the moment, the outcome is open. It's a very risky thing. We are experimenting with our whole society."[2]

In Munich, Horst Teltschik, a member of the BMW board, agreed. "We have to be more flexible and mobile," he said, "but we don't take the American hire-and-fire system as our model. We have a different tradition and culture in Germany. Germans just wouldn't accept this. Because of global competition, we can't afford any longer the kind of social security that people are used to. But we have this idea of a Social Market Economy, a consensus that those who are skilled, able, successful have to be ready for solidarity with those who are handicapped, for whatever reason. This culture is a precondition for our social peace."[3]

In many ways, Europe is in a race against time. The Europeans are working to unite their continent in two ways. First, they want to deepen their own unity through economic union and growing political cohesion. Second, they want to expand it to include the most advanced of the formerly Communist nations of Central Europe. Their hope is to have this continent stable and secure in time to withstand the global winds blowing in from the Third World to the south, from Central Europe to the east, and from across the Atlantic to the west.

Europe is more skeptical of the free market than the United States. Most of its major institutions, such as government and unions, and its intellectuals instinctively favor a more collective and consensual society than most Americans do. Its corporations share this cultural belief but are less protected from globalization than the Japanese corporations. And so they are beginning to move abroad, downsize workers, undercut unions, and attack welfare, as American corporations have been doing for the past two decades.

In the postwar years, the United States amassed more might across the board than any other country and the Japanese created an economy of unparalleled focused power. But the Europeans, more than either of these rivals, built an economic and political structure that combined prosperity, equality, and security. It realizes this structure is at risk now, and it has not decided what to do about it.

The European Union and Its Parts

This chapter will talk about Europe as a whole, or rather the European Union, which is an association (not really a union yet, despite its name) of fifteen Western European nations. These nations, with varying degrees of fervor, aspire to become a United States of Europe but are far from that goal.

The EU, now more than forty years old, is probably the single most visionary and successful political and economic experiment since the creation of the United States itself, but it is still a work in progress, and its success is not guaranteed. It is a lodestar for a dozen or so other nations that want to join it, especially those—like the Poles, Czechs, and Hungarians—for whom the end of the Cold War meant nothing less than a "return to Europe." Globalization will affect this project deeply and could defeat it.

In looking at Europe, I will focus on its two leading nations, Germany and France. Old enemies and allies, the Germans and the French are often seen by the rest of the world as the core of Europe, two nations that have merged their economies to provide the foundation on which Europe is being built. In fact, they are two very different nations, with different histories and cultures and, hence, different economies. Since the war, these economies have been able to work together without really converging.

The rest of Europe orbits around these two giants. Some other nations, like the Netherlands, have been able to institute reforms—the modernization of industry, the reform of welfare states—but may be too small to be models for their larger neighbors. Others, like Spain and Italy, are wrestling with economic problems more severe than those of France and Germany but will be powerfully influenced by the direction set by the French and the Germans.

Britain is a special case. The British, holding to a chimerical "special relationship" with the United States, came late to EU membership, have never made up their mind whether they truly belong to Europe, and hence have much less influence in EU affairs than their size and history would dictate.

In her eleven years as prime minister, Margaret Thatcher changed Britain utterly. She destroyed the power of the unions, privatized much of industry, opened the country to market forces, and revolutionized Britain's class-based politics. In so doing, she mirrored the similar revolution across the Atlantic carried out by her great friend Ronald Reagan. The result is that the British economy today resembles the American economy more than the continental model and so is a poor guide to the present and future of Europe. The political debate in Britain today sounds much more like that in the United States than that on the continent, with which the British seem to have little in common.

I lived in London at the start of the 1990s and traveled regularly to Brussels, Paris, Bonn, and other European capitals. I was always astonished at the degree to which the British and the other Europeans were, literally and figuratively, speaking two different languages. The British seemed fixated on issues—including whether European unity was a good idea or not—that the other Europeans had long since settled. The fears of the British Euroskeptics are no more than an irritation or an amusement for the Germans and French, who are increasingly prepared to leave Britain behind on such all-important issues as a single currency.

Despite all the changes and progress of the Thatcher years, Britain still seems more an appendage of the United States than it does of Europe, and neither a power nor a paradigm in its own right. This is the reason that the economic reaction of Britain to globalization, while interesting in itself, gets fairly short shrift in this book. My intention is to look at the way in which four very different economies—the American, Japanese, German, and French—are dealing with this problem. But in dealing with it, they would be smart to look at the impact of globalization on Britain—not only on its economy but its society.

The Legacy of Thatcher

Because of Thatcher, Britain is definitely more open to the global market and, at the moment, enjoys an economy that is expanding faster than any other in Europe. But many British feel this has been a Faustian deal that has cost their nation its soul. John Major, Thatcher's successor, and his Conservative Party lost the 1997 election in a landslide, which wasn't supposed to happen to an incumbent party in a time of prosperity. Whence this sense of dissatisfaction?

One reason, certainly, is that the average Briton, like the average American, has not shared in the nation's overall prosperity. As in the United States, the markets and their manipulators become ever richer, while median wages stagnate or shrink, ancient industrial cities crumble, public services deteriorate, and a new class system—based more on wealth this time than on birth—disfigures the society.

But I think a truer reason is that Thatcher destroyed the old structure of British life, which, for all its faults, provided a framework within which people knew who they were and could organize their lives with confidence and stability. The old class system may have pinched and limited lives, but it also defined them. It is largely gone now and has been replaced by the market—and the market isn't enough. There's a feeling in Britain now of corrosive instability. The pubs are full of drunken yuppies, loudly celebrating their new wealth. Outside, the doorways are filled with the unemployed sons of coal miners who have fled to London from their jobless Midland villages in search of low-skilled jobs that don't exist.

John Plender, a British author, puts it this way:

> The transmission mechanism that leads from economic growth to a sense of well-being has broken down. Bracing Tory radicalism gave confidence and [stock] options to the business community, while failing to give ordinary people any sense of a stake in national prosperity. In the workplace, aggressive human resource management has replaced paternalism. Resulting insecurity has not been mitigated by any sense of increasing wealth stemming from a soaring stock market. [This] version of capitalism, for all its strengths, has delivered a feel-good factor to companies but not to individuals.[4]

To an American, the British class system was an abomination, with the lower classes knuckling their brows to well-born toffs. But it also embraced a sense of noblesse oblige upstairs and service belowstairs, and both are lost now, replaced by scorn above and hopelessness beneath. This is not a nostalgic bleat against progress but simply a recognition that, when we remove a structure of shared values, we must replace it with new values that go beyond material wealth.

Thatcher and her successors had no such vision. Thatcher herself once said, "There is no such thing as society. There are individual men and women, and there are families."[5] She was wrong. Civilization is not a shattered prism of individual men and women, connected only by blood, but depends on the links that unite these people and these families in a common history and understanding. Thatcher transformed Britain, and not for the better. The shared values of Britain's continental neighbors are under attack now, and the Europeans should look to the British experience and hark to Plender for an example of how the market can both enrich and wreck.

The Romance and Logic of Europe

Germany and France, if not Britain, see their future tied to the European Union.

The Anglo-Saxon mind, in Washington or in London, is a rigorously logical instrument that insists on facts, figures, and proof, and therefore often misses the truth. This sort of mind likes its dreams programmed on computers or mapped in equations. It is very good at creating markets, not so good at squishier subjects like philosophy. It computes, therefore it is.

One of the problems with this Anglo-Saxon rationality is that it is forever underestimating the romanticism that is the key to European unity. France and Germany are romantic nations, with the poetry and bloodshed to prove it. If the Marshall Plan was an act of generosity based on self-interest, European unity is an act of imagination based on history. Its purpose, from the moment of its founding with the European Coal and Steel Community, was to entwine the German and French economies so thoroughly that another war between them would become impossible. Jean Monnet, the French brandy salesman and visionary who is the father of European unity, believed that the edifice could be built by simply adding agreement upon agreement, minor treaty upon minor treaty, like bricks upon a wall. This is basically what has happened. Thousands of directives and decisions, issued by drab bureaucrats in Brussels or agreed upon by weary politicians in hundreds of all-night meetings, have gradually built the House of Europe.

Occasionally, this process has required a grand and romantic gesture. In 1985, the EU (then more prosaically called the European Community) roused itself from the doldrums of Eurosclerosis by drafting a plan for a "single market," to be in place by 1992. This program, with its goal of erasing the frontiers between the European countries, was so improbable that few persons in Europe and almost no one in America even noticed it at the time. Typically, this grand scheme became reality brick by brick. It was achieved by drawing up a list of 282 things that had to be done—standardizing industrial norms, harmonizing public procurement policies, ironing out differences in taxes—and then doing them, one by one, with bureaucrats and politicians ticking them off the list like so many shoppers in a grocery store. By the end of 1992, it was done.

The latest grand scheme is currency union, or the establishment of a single European currency, the Euro, which is to replace the fifteen national currencies. A single currency is a logical outgrowth of a single market. The single market marked the evolution of Europe from fifteen national markets, divided by restrictions and barriers, into a single continent-wide economy as open to the free flow of goods as the fifty American states. But a single market with fifteen national currencies is no single market at all, any more than the United States could be a single market with fifty currencies, rising and falling against each other. The establishment of the Euro will cure this.

Not all fifteen EU nations will qualify to convert their currencies into Euros in the first phase. According to the EU's timetable, those that do will be chosen in 1998. In 1999 the exchange rates of these countries' currencies will be fixed against each other, removing them from speculative pressure. At the same time, the Euro will be introduced but only as a unit of account, for use between central banks. Over the next three years, the Euro will be phased into business and banking. On January 1, 2002, Euro banknotes and coins will be introduced. By July 1 of that year, the national currencies will be withdrawn, and the Euro will become the only legal tender. Bratwursts in Berlin or *poulets* in Bresse will be on sale for Euros only, not for deutsche marks or francs.

The creation of the Euro is a complex and risky venture, and much can go wrong. The infant currency will be under constant attack from global money markets, which could destroy the project. This will require some steady political nerves, especially in Germany and France. But the austerity needed to lay a solid fiscal base for the Euro has helped increase European unemployment, while forcing cuts in welfare budgets. Already one French government has fallen over this issue. Voters in France did not reject the Euro itself, but they felt it could be brought in with less pain. Orthodox economists, particularly those in Germany, doubt this is possible. The road to a single currency is still more of a tightrope than a garden path.

This battle over the Euro demonstrates vividly the power of the global economy to complicate the established order. The Europeans know that their nation-states are too small and too weak to carry out any sort of an independent economic policy in the face of the global markets: the French tried in 1983 and failed. If the Germans, French, and other Europeans are to exercise any power in this world, it will be through a large, powerful, and cohesive European Union. For this sturdy EU to work, the single market must be completed through the creation of the Euro.

But what the global market demands, it can also destroy. Until the year 2002 at least, the Euro project will be under assault both from the global currency traders, who doubt the Europeans can carry it off, and from European workers unwilling to pay the price in joblessness and stagnant wages. These same workers are already seeing the global economy take their jobs, as their employers move manufacturing to lower-cost countries in North America, Eastern Europe, or the Third World. The French elections may have been the first sign of a voter backlash that could sink the Euro.

Like most EU projects, the single currency has baffled the Anglo-Saxons. The British, who still think the EU should be little more than a customs union, oppose it as a Teutonic plot for continental domination, and, until recently, vowed never to enter it; but they will someday, after it is a proven success. The Americans, who never thought it would work, mostly ignored it. But the EU today is the result of a string of improbable projects that succeeded, mostly because the Europeans wanted them to succeed. Both the United States and Britain have failed to understand the emotional ramifications of the Euro and, hence, have missed the romantic impetus behind it. If the Euro succeeds, it is because the Germans and the French believe it will succeed and are willing to overlook all the reasons why this should be impossible.

Basically, the Euro is a bureaucratic procedure with immense historic implications. The logic of Europe goes like this. France and Germany don't like each other. When they fight, the continent convulses. To prevent wars, their economies must be interwoven. This is a continuing process, a brick-by-brick approach, that cannot be stopped and may never end. If it stops, Europe will unravel. Monetary union is the next step. Therefore, it must be taken.

Behind this logic is a fear of Germany as the loose cannon on the European deck. A powerful, untethered Germany has wreaked havoc on its neighbors twice in this century. Therefore, Germany must be embedded in a strong, encompassing Europe. If that Europe can be expanded to include Poland, so that Germany no longer lies exposed on Europe's eastern frontier, so much the better. Nowhere is this fear of Germany felt more strongly than in Germany itself. The Germans know their own history and are appalled by it. Europe is seen as the guarantor that this history will not repeat itself. Therefore it must grow.

This is the dream of Europe. It remains a potent dream, even as the last generation that vividly remembers the war passes from the leadership. So far it has worked. France still doesn't trust Germany, nor Germany France. But because of the European Union, they are not going to fight about it. Nothing in Europe's history in the twentieth century is so important.

Europe and Globalization

The global economy is one reason for this millennial dream. It also could destroy it.

The EU has more people, 371 million, than the United States' 261 million. Its gross domestic product of $8.42 trillion is larger than

America's $7 trillion. It is the biggest single economic unit in the world. But it doesn't act as a single unit, especially in monetary affairs. The smaller United States and its single currency, the dollar, are the giants of the global economy. The lira, the peseta, the franc, even the deutsche mark, remain relatively minor currencies. More to the point, the economies they represent can be held hostage to the dollar's power and the policy of the U.S. government.

This was shown in the mid-1990s in the travails of Dasa, the aerospace arm of Daimler-Benz. Dasa restructured itself, moved production, and laid off thousands of workers to meet losses that it blamed on the dollar. The dollar was relatively weak against the deutsche mark at the time, which was Dasa's problem. As a company with most of its production in Germany, it paid its workers and suppliers in strong, expensive deutsche marks. But as an aerospace company, Dasa and its other European partners in Airbus sold their planes on a world market where prices were quoted in weak, cheap dollars. These weak, cheap dollars were the same dollars that Boeing, Airbus's leading rival, used to pay *its* workers and suppliers. Dasa had other problems at the time, including the fallout from earlier mistakes by its management. But the currency complications were real, to the point that its program of layoffs was introduced under the name of Dolores, which stood (in English) for DOllar LOw REScue.[6]

The Euro would be a currency big enough to compete with the dollar on all levels, meaning that the Europeans would have one more tool to compete with the Americans on all levels. In a world of integrating markets, size counts. The United States is recruiting Canada and the Latin Americans into its trading bloc. Japan is expanding its reach into China and Southeast Asia. A united Europe would be a mighty bloc through which the voices of the European nations, inaudible on their own, could be amplified into a roar.

It has become a cliché to note that, as the world economy becomes more global, the interests of nations become more regional. This may be true, but only if the nations themselves are secure within a regional grouping that can enable them to cope with the global economy outside it. "Divided and disunited, the nation states and their puny borders can offer no real resistance to the globalized capitalist economy."[7]

The Europeans know this. Both France and Germany do more than half their trade within the EU. Both have been preoccupied in recent years with strengthening Europe as a whole, and themselves only indirectly. They know that a vibrant home base built on trade with their prosperous neighbors is a precondition for survival in a world filled with low-cost producers. Germany, having accumulated surpluses on the world trading market, has used these surpluses to finance its reunification with its eastern lands. This reunification, paradoxically, has made Germany much more powerful but less global.

In Paris, I talked with government officials, businesspeople, and union leaders about France's role in Europe and the world. All vividly remembered the lesson France learned in 1983, when the Mitterrand government, then new, tried to expand its economy at a time when the rest of the world was fighting inflation with restrictive policies. This go-it-alone policy achieved nothing for the French but higher inflation, high interest rates, and an economic black eye. It proved the limits of independence in an interdependent world. What I heard from these leaders could be paraphrased and summed up this way:

> We want to survive. We want to keep France, our language, our nation-state. We feel that being a nation is still important. Globalization poses a new version of this old problem, of national identity. Our solution is to be strongly French in an environment that is strictly European. We have no choice but to exist within a strong Europe. We can have a voice, we can defend our interests, but only through Europe. We have to transfer to this larger field, in Brussels, the impact of our own interests.
>
> This is necessary for the reforms ahead. Our public opinion is not really ready to sacrifice what we have gained to a mythic and unknown globalization. If we say they have to reform their social security because of globalization, they refuse. If we give the public the feeling that the government is not in control and that the life of a Frenchman will be affected by the fact that some Chinese tycoon did something, then we're in serious trouble. But this Frenchman will accept a change dictated by Europe, because he has already taken advantage of Europe.

There is in Europe a feeling of a rich society, in every sense of the word, that must be protected. To the French and Germans, the global economy is not something to be embraced, as the Americans have embraced it. Nor is it possible to keep it totally at bay, as the Japanese hope to do. Rather, it is a beast to be accommodated and, if possible, tamed.

Japan, as we have seen, can be defined as a noncapitalist market economy. Germany and France, along with the other European nations, are indisputably capitalist nations with free markets. Like the Americans but unlike the Japanese, the Europeans are open to both imports and immigrants. Perhaps nowhere else, even in New York, is there the sense that one gets in Europe of being at a global cross-roads, with the winds of the world passing through, bringing news, goods, and ideas from far lands.

But the economies of Germany and France—especially Germany—are not like the American model in their assumptions, goals, or practices. Nor are they like each other. Perhaps, after another century of European unity, they will be, but not yet.

Germany in Globalization's Path

Germany, like America, is based on the market, private property, and free enterprise. Both nations, unlike France, share a devotion to economic liberalism and free trade. Both shun central economic planning. Both are dominated by large corporations but reserve an important role for the *Mittelstand*, as small and medium-sized companies are called in Germany.

It is the differences between Germany and America that are under attack by globalization, with most of the pressure on the German way of doing business.[8]

In Germany, banks, not stock markets, have traditionally played the major role in the financing of companies. Business is part of a social structure that includes government and labor and sees social harmony as the greatest good. Workers in particular have a direct role in management, and the priority of ownership extends beyond profit.

If global capital markets are changing the financing of economies everywhere, the effect will be greatest in places like Germany, where these markets have never had much to say about who got the money. Wall Street has nine times the capitalization of the Frankfurt stock exchange. Instead, German companies have received their financing through their nation's huge banks, which have a power that American law forbids to U.S. banks. These German banks, like Deutsche Bank or Dresdner Bank, not only lend money to companies but own shares, sometimes 25 percent or more, in their clients and sit on their boards. These banks manage company treasuries, provide invest- ment advice, and run networks of business and industrial informa- tion for their clients. As such, they have a long-term stake in their clients' growth and prosperity that no American stockholder, focused on short-term profits and stock prices, can offer. There is an old-boy aura about this, with bankers protecting their pals in the executive suites of German firms. But this structure also provides patient cap- ital that permits long-range thinking, encourages product develop- ment, and prevents hostile takeovers.

This system of stable financing lies directly in the path of global capital markets. These markets couldn't care less about the social con- cerns—for national cohesion, worker protection, or political stabil- ity—that underlie the German economic structure. Everything that the German system of financing represents is challenged by the global capital markets. Already, many German firms are looking to these markets for financing, and German workers are feeling the results.

Tens of thousands of workers in steel, mining, shipbuilding, autos, and electronics have lost their jobs. Others are working short hours for short pay, in an attempt to keep some semblance of their jobs. Wages are still rising but not much faster than inflation. Com- panies that once proclaimed their loyalty to their workers talk now about "shareholder value" instead.

The company that exemplifies this trend is Daimler-Benz, Ger- many's biggest corporation. DB was the first German firm to regis- ter itself on the New York Stock Exchange; so far, it is the only big firm to do so, although others are expected to join it. Already, share- holder value has become a buzzword in DB's Stuttgart headquarters. When DB's chairman, Jürgen Schrempp, was asked if profitability was "the only criterion of any significance," he answered, "At the moment, it has priority. We owe this to our shareholders."[9] In a speech at the 1996 shareholders meeting, he added, "We are meeting the expecta- tions of the international capital markets. For if one does not want to fall behind in the worldwide competition for a short supply of funds, one must satisfy the demands of international investors."

In the same speech Schrempp announced that Daimler-Benz has started to give stock options to its executives. Not coincidentally, the company has downsized by 70,000 jobs over the last seven years.

The Social Market Economy

Schrempp's sentiments are second nature to any American corporate chairman. But they are a new sound out of Germany, where these market pressures threaten the nation's social structure. For Germany, this development is every bit as dangerous to national stability as the shredding of the American middle class is for the United States.

This German social structure is based on the Social Market Economy, or *Soziale Marktwirtschaft*. This idea, enshrined in the nation's Basic Law, or constitution, proclaims a market economy but embeds it in a "social dimension" that guarantees rights to workers and sets off areas of society where the market cannot intrude. It is based on the belief that capitalism untamed is a raw power that can both create and destroy, a force so strong that it must be controlled for the stability of the country and the well-being of its people. This is not a unique notion; every capitalist nation has its economic rules and regulations. But nowhere is this principle, that an economy must be both "market" and "social," so developed and rooted in society.

In practice, this means a strong welfare state, with a national health system, strict rules on the firing of workers, high unemployment benefits, generous sick pay, and a comprehensive pension system. Behind this lies a genuine national sense of common responsibility. This belief in society's obligation to protect the weak is so strong that, so far, Germans have been willing to put up with some pretty blatant abuses—the average German worker calls in sick twenty days a year and stays home on full pay—rather than question this duty.

Other countries have lavish welfare states, but only Germany has the cohesion and cooperation between business and labor that distinguishes the Social Market Economy. Nationwide and regional unions, for instance, negotiate labor contracts, including pay, with nationwide and regional employer associations, a process that gives unions great power and keeps individual employers from driving down wages.

Perhaps the most dramatic example of this cohesion, and the one that is best known abroad, is *Mitbestimmung*. The word means "co-determination," and it describes a system that literally gives workers an active voice in company management. Not only are workers represented by workers' councils within companies, but in companies with more than 2,000 employees, workers' representatives have half the seats on the board. A chairman, usually loyal to management, can break tie votes, but in practice, the system promotes cooperation, stresses compromise, and has given Germany one of the world's most strike-free labor records.

Another aspect of the Social Market Economy is the apprentice system. Youngsters leaving high schools and even universities go into a training program of two to three years, working with "masters," who teach them their craft. The tradition is an outgrowth of the medieval guilds but continues in Germany not only among factory workers and carpenters but for young bankers and other professionals, even preachers. This apprenticeship is the root of Germany's world reputation for craftsmanship and high-quality products. Government, unions, and companies set nationwide standards. The government and unions share the costs, but most of the expenses are borne by companies, who pay knowing that, if an apprentice jumps ship for another company when the training ends, the nation is full of other young workers who have gone through identical apprenticeships.

This description states the ideal but also depicts the reality of the Social Market Economy. It established a highly egalitarian society, with close and sincere cooperation among big government, big business, and big labor. In essense, it represented the "stakeholder principle" in practice. This is the idea that the fruits of the economy belong not only, or even foremost, to the shareholders in a business but to all the stakeholders—share owners, to be sure, but also workers, families, suppliers, communities—who contribute to the economy.

This sort of cooperation within a structure of rules and regulations is an American manager's nightmare. But it succeeded. Germany, as everyone knows, is one of the economic success stories of the postwar years. It has high production, strong exports, enviable quality, good workers, few strikes, a stable currency, mighty banks, and, by all signs, contented owners. It also provided its workers with the highest wages, shortest workweeks, longest vacations, and richest benefits in the capitalist world. American companies, including major automakers like General Motors, invested massively in Germany, learned the German way of doing business, and prospered.

For German workers, writes British historian Harold Perkin, the system "delivered the goods, not only in the material form of a high standard of living with all the luxuries, gadgetry, cars, foreign holidays, of modern consumerism, but in the psychologically satisfying form of a meaningful vote in the political process and a say in the running of the companies that employed them." He continues:

> Above all, West Germany offered an alternative model of professional society, a third way between the extremes of individualism and collectivism, between soulless communism and the mindless and materialist free market. The social market [is] a carefully regulated free market with all the choices that an affluent person could reasonably want plus the protections and benefits that the same person might need in the exigencies of life. [It] squares the circle of combining individual ambition to rise as high as one's abilities will reach with collective insurance against falling to the depths of poverty. . . . It achieves the best of both worlds, competitive efficiency and a concern for every citizen. Society, in fact, is a great insurance company against the ill winds of life which only the most reckless and overconfident of free-marketeers would be foolish enough to reject. The social market is the best compromise between the adventure of risk taking and the safety net of community.[10]

The Social Market Economy grew out of German history, ancient and recent. Martin Luther was, in a sense, protesting against the misuse of the market when he nailed his Ninety-Five Theses to the Castle Church door in Wittenberg in 1517, attacking the Vatican's custom of selling indulgences, or pardons of sin. Luther maintained that some things, like forgiveness of sins, are beyond the market's reach. The Christian traditions of both the Roman Catholic and Protestant churches in Germany have engendered a communitarian feeling and a belief in social solidarity and responsibility; socialism and social thought, not only in Germany but in much of Europe, owe more to the church and less to Karl Marx than is generally supposed. German miners in the Middle Ages invented social security by setting up joint funds to support needy colleagues, and the Iron Chancellor, Otto von Bismarck, gave Germany the world's first comprehesive social security system in the 1880s with laws establishing insurance for health, accidents, and old age.

None of this prevented the economic collapse of Germany in the 1920s, followed by the rise of Hitler, the Holocaust, and World War II. After 1945, Germany, unlike Japan, knew it could not simply recreate its prewar society because that society had failed. In its place they carefully crafted a cooperative society with political power diffused through federal and provincial governments, and economic power shared with the stakeholders. The *Wirtschaftwunder*, or economic miracle, quickly followed, and Germany and the system have remained intact, until now.

"We Germans don't have much to be proud of in this century," a government official once told me, "but we're proud of our Social Market Economy, and we'd like to keep it." The question now is whether the global economy will permit countries like Germany to keep the good things they have developed, or whether the Social Market Economy is about to be strangled.

Challenging the Consensus

"The priorities that underpin this consensus—the primacy of collective over individual interests, the power of trade unions and the voluntary sector, co-responsibility in company management—are proving vulnerable to new and destructive forces." This is the judgment of Michel Albert, a French banker who has written about the difference between capitalisms. "Finance . . . is one of the two or three most powerful vectors involved in the spread of the neo-American model. Just as a lever multiplies the force applied to it, finance is the perfect tool for adding strength to the capitalist ideology: what it does spectacularly well is to reinforce the status of the market as the most powerful economic mechanism and the ultimate arbiter of the fortunes of business and industry."[11]

The German Social Market Economy depended on a relatively closed system. German industry got most of its financing from German banks, which also owned blocks of shares in their clients. These companies did most of their manufacturing at home, providing steady jobs within a German framework for German workers. Foreign trade played a major role, but mostly with other industrial countries. The European Common Market was founded on the basis of a French-German deal, embodying protection for French farmers and markets for German industry. Other nations, as they joined, bought into this deal. As Europe grew, it grew in a German pattern. The deutsche mark became the strongest currency. Social protection for workers became the rule of the workplace. Stock markets remained second to banks. (Britain—with its own proud currency, adversarial labor relations, and mighty stock exchanges—never fit this pattern.)

This closed system is no longer closed. The Social Market Economy may have only been possible in a closed, bank-dominated system in which companies were allowed to serve not just shareholders but workers and communities, too. As we saw above, international finance has bulled into the boardrooms of Daimler-Benz and other German companies. As global capital markets penetrate Germany, the German banks lose control over the economy. As trade with the Third World and, especially, with the former communist nations of Central Europe increases, German workers find themselves priced out of the market. Companies listed on international stock exchanges find the demands of global capital for best practice clashing with the Social Market Economy, which guarantees the protection of workers against these very demands.

Hoechst, the chemicals and drugs giant, has cut about 12,000 of its 65,000 jobs in Germany to increase profits and raise its share price. Volkswagen workers accepted a twenty-eight-hour week rather than lose their jobs. Sixteen percent of all employed persons are working part-time. The 100 percent sick pay allowance has been reduced to 80 percent. In early 1997, Krupp Hoesch Steel announced 2,000 job cuts, Thyssen Steel announced 6,000 cuts, and machine builders warned that they planned to cut 10,000 jobs. The same year, Siemens, the electronics group, announced 6,000 job cuts, on top of 30,000 cuts over the previous three years; most Siemens workers will be outside Germany before the century ends. Continental, which makes tires, cut 10,000 jobs and moved some production to Portugal, Thailand, and the Czech Republic. Robert Bosch, which makes car parts and electronics, says half its employees now work outside Germany.

"We have been forced to globalize all branches of our company—R&D, production, sales, financing," BMW's Teltschik said. "We're still a German company, even a Bavarian company. But only 40 percent of our employees are in Germany. And we no longer say we are 'made in Germany.' Instead, we say, 'made by BMW.'"[12]

Already, German unemployment is 10 percent, or nearly 4 million persons. Forty percent of all workers still belong to unions, but the number is shrinking. IG Metall, the metalworkers' union, had 2.6 million members in 1989 when the Berlin Wall fell. It immediately gained 1.3 million more members in East Germany, but as Germany's metal industries contract, it is almost back to its 1989 membership.

German Workers Get Squeezed

The time-honored custom of national or regional labor negotiations between the big unions and employers' associations is breaking down. The overall agreements are still being negotiated, but increasingly they are being violated by companies pleading that they need to cut costs, with the acquiescence of workers who fear for their jobs.

Daimler-Benz insisted that workers at its Stuttgart engine factory and its Gaggenau small tractor factory work Saturdays at no extra pay, or their factories would close. At the same time, Daimler, which traditionally has done the bulk of its manufacturing in Germany, opened plants in places like Hambach, over the border in France, and in Tuscaloosa, Alabama. The Stuttgart and Gaggenau workers got the point and are working Saturdays now. This may seem like no big deal in the United States, where weekend work is common, but it is a major departure in Germany, where factories have kept to seven-and-a-half-hour shifts from Monday through Thursday and a five-hour shift on Friday, ending early enough to give workers a running start on the weekend. The Daimler plant in Untertürkheim is working three shifts a day. Daimler's rival, BMW, has 290 different forms of work schedules, a radical shakeup of a once rigid system.

In one celebrated case, Viessmann, a medium-sized maker of heating systems, planned to build a new factory near Prague, in the Czech Republic, figuring it could save some $12 million per year because Czech wage scales were about one-tenth the German level. At the Viessmann plant near Kassel, frightened workers agreed to work an extra three hours per week for free, which would also save the company about $12 million. Viessmann accepted the deal and was sued by IG Metall, the union, on grounds that workers at individual factories do not have this freedom to negotiate their own wages and hours. A court agreed with IG Metall, but with so many conditions that the union's victory was meaningless.[13]

Other manufacturers and their unions have since worked out similar deals. The *Mittelstand* companies are beginning to drop out of employers' associations so they can negotiate contracts directly with their workers. *Mitbestimmung*, the power sharing within companies of management and labor, still exists but is being questioned. The average manufacturing wage in Germany, including benefits, is $30 per hour, compared to $20 in the United States, $15 in Britain—and only $3 in the Czech Republic, which for much of Germany is about an hour's drive away. Already companies in places like Bavaria, which borders the Czech Republic, are outsourcing component purchases, if not all manufacturing, to the east. "Our Asia is right next door," a worried trade union official in Munich told me.

German companies complain that they pay the world's highest wages, highest social costs, and highest corporate taxes. Much of the debate from the employers' side is based on the concept of *Standort*, or whether Germany remains competitive and a good place to invest. The global verdict seems to be negative. While Germany has been investing some $80 billion overseas, virtually no foreign investment has entered the country in recent years. The place is just too expensive.

Mitbestimmung and the other facets of the Social Market Economy promote social harmony and allow change to take place with a minimum of friction. But the system, based on consensus, requires a great deal of time and negotiation. It moves slowly. Lacking consensus, it doesn't move at all. In a fast-moving global economy, it is an anchor that German businesses doubt they can afford. In good times, it was a marvelous mechanism to spread the wealth. In harder times, it is proving less adept at spreading the pain.

Fewer Days at the Spa

German president Roman Herzog has said, "Firms that close down factories and jobs in Germany and pay almost no taxes are no longer German firms in my book." Not that a lot of firms would care. German manufacturers have invested $80 billion overseas in the 1990s. About $6 billion of this investment is in Eastern Europe. But some of it is in the United States, such as the Daimler plant in Tuscaloosa and the BMW plant in Spartanburg, South Carolina. Daimler makes 95 percent of its top models in Germany now; it says it will be making 30 percent overseas within ten years.

The German companies claim that increased business overseas will mean more jobs at home, but it's not working that way. German industry has shed 1.1 million jobs in the 1990s. Daimler has told its employees that globalization "not only opens up markets but also safeguards domestic employment." Meanwhile, the company has eliminated 70,000 jobs in this decade.

Exhibit 6.1

Unemployment Benefit Replacement Rate

(percent of previous salary covered by unemployment benefits,
for worker with dependent spouse)

	First Year	Second and Third Years	Fourth and Fifth Years
United States	26	10	10
Japan	25	0	0
Germany	41	36	36
France	58	37	28

Source: Organization for Economic Cooperation and Development.

But if workers' security is part of the Social Market Economy, an equally important part is the welfare state, and that also is under attack, from three directions. First, there is general political agreement in Germany that taxes are as high as they can go. Second, businesses say that global competition makes them unable to afford paying benefits that add an extra 80 percent to their wage bills. Third, the issue has become complicated in the drive toward a single European currency, which is Europe's passport to global economic power. (Exhibit 6.1 gives an example of this European welfare load.)

To ensure that the new currency would be stable, the framers of the EU's Maastricht Treaty insisted that any nation joining the Euro have its own economic house in order by meeting five criteria. The first three—low inflation, low interest rates, and a stable national currency—have not been much of a problem. But the last two—a national budget deficit of 3 percent or less, and a total public debt of less than 60 percent of gross domestic production—became huge barriers. When the 1999 deadline for the inauguration of the Euro was confirmed, only two tiny EU members, Ireland and Luxembourg, had deficits under 3 percent.

Any common European currency without France and Germany is doomed. So both nations began to reduce their budget deficits. One way to do this was to reduce welfare spending, which in Germany is one cornerstone of the Social Market Economy.

The first reductions, by non-European standards, were not exactly draconian. The Germans suggested a reduction in sick pay, which lets workers take six weeks of sick leave at 100 percent of pay.

Another reform reduced the amount of paid time employees could spend at health spas from four weeks every three years to three weeks every four years. In France, the government tried to raise the retirement age of fifty for train drivers, which was set in the sweaty age of steam locomotives.

In both countries, workers protested, which was to be expected. What wasn't expected was the degree of public support they got. Polls indicated that both French and Germans recognized that some cuts were necessary, if only to keep taxes from rising too high. But there also is widespread support for the ideologies—of solidarity and social responsibility—that underlie the welfare state. The Germans in particular see that their social welfare state is a tapestry of many strands, and no one knows how many strands can be pulled out, or which ones, before the tapestry itself begins to unravel.

German companies discovered this when some of them, including Daimler, showed undue haste in taking advantage of the reduction in sick pay benefits from 100 percent to 80 percent. The new lower level was to apply only to new employees, or when new labor contracts were negotiated. But Daimler and Siemens said they would impose the cuts at once and unilaterally. Even Germans who felt the sick pay benefits were ludicrous opposed this breach in Germany's consensual system of labor relations. Massive protests appeared. Unions claimed they had been deceived. The conservative government was furious. Siemens backed off at once, and Daimler caved in several days later.

Since 1989, Germany has coped with the biggest economic shock that any country has faced since the oil crises: reunification and the incorporation of East Germany's primitive economy into the West German system. The effort was made, the taxes were paid, the sacrifices were suffered, and the job, so far, has been done. But it helped create the deficit that is causing so much pain now. And it left the country exhausted, its goodwill spent and its workers, faced for the first time with cheap competition from the east, resentful and looking for scapegoats.

The German government drew up a fifty-point "Action Program for Jobs and Investment" that contained proposals for deregulation, corporate tax reforms, and incentives for company start-ups. By the standards of Germany's competitors, it was a mild menu of reforms that would loosen some of the regulations on the economy without ripping out its structure by the roots. Some of it, no doubt, will be adopted. But it is seen, correctly, as a collective of half measures—scorned as too little by business, which must cope with the global economy, and feared by those who see globalization shredding the Social Market Economy that has done so much good for Germany in the past half century.

"It is so much more difficult for this culture to get down to reform," a foreign ministry official, Klaus-Peter Klaiber, told me. "The Social Market Economy has developed into a real culture. For forty-five years, it was the culture of success. It worked. But the social dimension has got the upper hand—it's less economic now and more social. And now we have globalization, and we must reform. Just a little squeeze won't do it."[14]

Germany's success is crucial, not only to Germany but to the United States and other countries facing the global economy. If Germany can preserve its Social Market Economy, it will prove that it is possible to have a socially conscious capitalism within the global economy. If the Germans fail, then the hire-and-fire system has won.

There is a growing fear in Germany, that most egalitarian of countries, that the price of reform may be the creation of a permanent underclass. As jobs disappear, apprentices vanish, too. Young workers become less skilled and less able to find jobs, and sink into permanent unemployment. A Social Market Economy built on a mass of unemployed workers may be economic, but it's no longer social. Yet this may lie ahead.

"We could keep our Social Market Economy, our consensus, but only for two-thirds of society, and accept that the other one-third don't take part," said Dietmar Herz, a professor in Munich, who was clearly appalled by the prospect. "Of course, the welfare costs would be high. But that's the price that a lot of people are willing to pay to preserve the rest of the system. I agree that it's unfair and dangerous. But it's part of the debate here now, this two-thirds–one-third idea."

Why one-third?

"Because we can control that many," Herz said.[15]

France: The Pull of Tradition

France, Germany's great partner and rival, runs its economy in a different way. For more than two hundred years, it has followed a tradition called social Colbertism, after Jean Baptiste Colbert, Louis XIV's chief minister, whose statue still stands outside the parliament building in Paris and whose ideas still hold a powerful influence over the French economy. Under Colbertism, France until recently relied on a strong central government to direct the economy. It was a mercantilist policy involving trade protection and a strong core of state-owned industries, plus other companies, privately owned, that enjoyed public monopolies. The state, rather than banks or the bourse, dominated financing. Unions, often Marxist-influenced, were adversarial and fractious. Unlike Germany or the United States, France's regions and provinces have little power to balance or restrain the central government. A strong and expensive welfare state enjoys public support. So does the protection of key industries, such as agriculture.

France, in short, is not a country run by the textbook of Adam Smith. But, like Germany, it is an undeniably successful country. Living standards are high. Heavy state investment has given France the world's most modern railroad system, good airports, fine roads, an excellent telephone network, and one of the most admired educational systems on the globe.

All this was done by a country devoted to the glory of the nation-state. This nationalism, epitomized by the policies of Charles de Gaulle, exasperated France's partners within the European Community, which France too often saw as a body that existed solely to serve France, and the United States, which frequently saw France as a not-too-friendly antagonist rather than an ally.

This caricature was overdrawn by both sides. France and French ideas have been the guiding force in the development of the European Community and, later, the European Union. Even after it dropped out of the military arm of NATO, France remained a loyal ally with a great deal of quiet military cooperation behind the scenes. No matter how great its devotion to French independence and glory, the priority of every postwar French government was the relationship with Germany. If Germany was the economic leader of Europe, France saw itself as the political leader. Their partnership was the guarantee of stability in Europe and the bulwark against another war.

The primacy of French-German partnership remains. But much of the rest has changed in recent years, part of it because of the Cold War's end, more of it because of globalization.

The end of the Cold War drastically altered the balance between Germany and France. A reunified Germany has emerged as the powerhouse of Europe, both economically and politically. Strong and newly confident, Bonn is no longer content to hide its political light and let France assume the leadership of Europe. France, therefore, has lost this leadership and feels this loss keenly. It is as anxious as ever to keep Germany within the European structure, so that it does not once again float free through central Europe. But where it often acted before as first among equals, it no longer is equal.

At the same time, the global economy has affected France as it has affected every industrial nation. The growing single market gradually opened France to foreign competition, both within Europe and outside it. French companies have joined foreign stock exchanges. Lacking strong sources of finance at home, they have sought it on global capital markets. State-owned companies are being privatized. Mergers and takeovers on the American model are increasing. For years, French laws have limited Japan's share of the French auto market to 7 percent; now Toyota is building a factory in northern France that will turn out 200,000 cars per year.

French companies have been restructuring longer than those in Germany, but job cuts have usually been by attrition. Renault, France Telecom, Giat—all have wiped out thousands of jobs. Now the focus is on the nation's respected but overstaffed civil service.

To many French, this is heresy. A poll showed that 66 percent would prefer the high benefits and high unemployment of France over the low unemployment and low welfare system of the United States. The national attitude toward globalization seems to be thumbs down. Marc Blondel, the embattled president of Force Ouvrière, a powerful union, thus speaks for many:

> Globalization is the extension of an economy around the world and, for me, this idea just doesn't exist. This expression of globalization is used by capitalists to get the best results all over the world, particularly with the fewest rules. This is a predatory culture. To me, it means the freedom for money to go where the workers have the fewest rights.[16]

A Refuge in Brussels

Most crucially, France has realized that the day of the independent medium-sized nation-state, secure behind its own borders and running its own economy, is over. France has cast its lot totally with the European Union, even if the new power of Germany means that the EU no longer dances to a tune called in Paris. To the degree that France can force events, it will be through influence exercised in Brussels. France, with Germany, is driving the campaign toward a united Europe, and especially toward a single currency. But its budget deficit, well over 3 percent, has meant that France itself risked not qualifying for membership in the Euro. As in Germany, this has meant proposals for cuts in welfare, raising the pension age, and other adjustments to public spending.

The French system is less delicately balanced and less philosophically cohesive than the German Social Market Economy. Reductions in welfare and changes in the balance between unions and businesses, therefore, do not affect the core of society, as they do in Germany. But in a country that already has accepted much change, there is opposition to more, and a longing—expressed in demonstrations and at the polls—to protect the gains of the past.

Even city dwellers support the French farmers in their protests against a more efficient, less protected agricultural system. When French truck drivers tied up the country for two weeks with a strike, members of the public showed up at the truckers' blockades with food, drink, and offers of a clean bed and a hot shower. And in the 1997 elections, the voters replaced the conservative government with a socialist one that had promised to create jobs *and* protect pay and benefits—in other words, to bring globalization without pain. The new French government may or may not be able to deliver on this promise. But clearly the voters were demanding that their leaders meet the challenge of globalization by reaffirming the nation's social contract, not by an American-style acceptance of the market. (Exhibit 6.2 demonstrates this greater government role in Europe.)

"The American idea that consumers may benefit from lower prices is hard to sustain in France," said Francis Kramarz, a professor at INSEE, a research institute in Paris. "The effects of what market competition can do for consumers is hard to understand by workers who already have a job, with a salary, and is also hard for the elite here to understand. The French really don't believe in a free

Exhibit 6.2

Public Social Protection Expenditure
(Health, Unemployment Pay, etc.)
(in percentage of Gross Domestic Product)

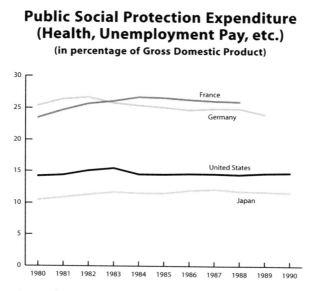

Source: Organization for Economic Cooperation and Development.

market. The idea that you should leave all firms to do their jobs is hard to accept here."[17]

The same impulse can be seen in the French reaction to globalization. President Chirac, as quoted in the first chapter of this book, wonders if France is "condemned" to choose globalization. The intellectual climate is equally hostile to a global system that elevates the values of the market over the more graceful and gentle values that the French prize. A government adviser, quoted by the *New York Times*, warned, "The French are confronted by a lot of changes. Are they prepared to accept them all? France disappearing into the Euro, disappearing into NATO, at the same time as we demand more mobility, harder work and sacrifice? An upheaval cannot be ruled out."[18]

A Warning from the Clubhouse

European economists and businesspeople are readier than Americans to recognize that the global economy can cause pain as well as gain, producing a worker backlash that would be only too justified. Klaus

Schwab and Claude Smadja run the World Economic Forum at Davos, Switzerland, which is where the world's economic and political elite meet each year to wine, dine, ski, and talk. If the global economy has a clubhouse, this is it. So Schwab and Smadja, the keepers of this clubhouse, drew wide attention with an article warning, "Public opinion in the industrial democracies will no longer be satisfied with articles of faith about the virtues and future benefits of the global economy.

"The mood in these democracies is one of helplessness and anxiety," they write. "In the famous process of 'creative destruction,' only the 'destruction' part seems to be operating for the time being." The two men caution that globalization is moving too fast for societies to adjust, that it is creating more losers than winners, and that corporations are profiting at the expense of their workers. "The globalized economy must not become synonymous with 'free market on the rampage,' a brakeless train wreaking havoc. The social responsibilities of corporations (and governments) remain as important as ever."[19]

Compare Schwab and Smadja's perspective with the heedless greed of American downsizers like "Chainsaw Al" Dunlap, the Sunbeam Corporation CEO, or the dictum of Milton Friedman that business's only social obligation is to make profits. Europeans such as the two men from Davos are caught between the demands of global markets and the knowledge that they are in charge of a delicate society that has already collapsed twice in this century.

The European Union is the place where these stresses and tensions will be played out. Germany, one of the EU's two leading members, is struggling for its soul against the lures of the global market. Its business community wants to seize the riches of globalization, its workers fear for the structure of their lives, and the government is caught in the middle. France, the other leading member, is sheltering against the global winds within the EU. Its powerful government, committed to the European experiment, is openly skeptical about the virtues of globalization.

As go these two powers, so will Europe. And Europe, remember, is already the biggest, richest single economic unit in the world. The debate going on there now will have much to do with the future shape of the global economy.

PART III

Common Pressures, Different Responses

7. A QUESTION OF FAIRNESS

INEQUALITY IS BUILT into the capitalist philosophy. Few persons in any of the great market nations of America, Japan, or Europe would quarrel with the notion that the person who invests more, works harder, has the better ideas, or takes the bigger risks deserves to end up with more of life's marbles. Even these societies' ideal of a broad middle class implies that there will always be some people—an upper class—who are richer than the rest. In most capitalist countries, the rich are envied and admired in equal measure but are, by and large, accepted. The rich, like the poor, are always with us.

But this acceptance has its limits. Capitalism and democracy are uneasy partners, and a balance between them must be struck in any nation that tries to live by both creeds. The driving force behind capitalism is inequality—the dream of making more money than other people. The driving force behind democracy is equality—one person, one vote. If a democrat is born equal, a capitalist intends to die as unequal as possible. In the balance between these two great strivings lies the health of nations.

Globalization and the growth of unfettered global markets is hazardous to this health. George Soros, perhaps the world's most skillful player of these markets, writes in the *Atlantic Monthly*, "The main enemy of the open society, I believe, is no longer the communist but the capitalist threat."[1] Global markets, freed from the kind of regulations that restrict national markets, pursue a pure laissez-faire capitalism. This theory holds that markets are perfect and that the common good is best served if they are left free to work their magic. But Soros argues that markets are no more perfect than communism, which also claimed infallibility, and, like communism, can lead society to a breakdown.

If capitalism is not to breed its own destruction, it has to be fair, which is to say that the steeds of inequality must be guided by the reins of democracy. People will support a capitalistic system only so long as they feel they're being treated fairly. If they play by the rules, they feel entitled to be rewarded. Promises made should be promises kept. The rich can get many of the marbles but not all of them. Inequality is fine but blatant inequality is not. A rising tide should lift all boats.

These are maxims, if not clichés. But they have real meaning to people who, as long as they can vote, have the power to judge the system. Fair treatment or blatant inequality cannot be precisely measured, but most persons feel that, as with love or pornography, they know it when they see it.

There is a growing feeling in the United States that the markets are in the saddle and unfairness rides. Part—but only part—of this feeling is the unease over the soaring compensation for the top executives of America's giant corporations. The other part is that, while wealth at the top is growing rapidly, the rest of America is barely holding its own or is falling behind. In the new globalized market, the top 20 percent, and especially the top 5 percent, are prospering. The bottom 80 percent is not sharing this prosperity. The tide definitely is rising, but it is lifting only the yachts, not the tugboats.[2]

Only America, among all the leading capitalist nations, is experiencing this new inequality. Even other nations' leading executives, who could be expected to be envious, say they are appalled. Is this, they wonder, where globalization will lead? Germans and Japanese, who like the Hungarian-born Soros have a keener respect than Americans for the fragility of society, fear the results of this inequality.

There are two aspects to this imbalance: the income and wealth of those at the top, and the well-being of the rest of society. Let's begin at the top.

The Suite Life

In Europe and Japan, executives are well paid by the standards of their own countries, if not by American standards. But in all these countries, pay is rising at both the top and the bottom; if the rich are getting richer, so are the poor and the middle class. There is a slight trend toward greater inequality in most nations, but this is because the rich are getting richer faster than the poor and middle class are, not because incomes for the nonrich are falling. In its divergence, America stands alone.

Is this American trend the wave of the global future? Non-Americans fear it may be. In his Tokyo office, Yoshihiko Miyauchi, the president and CEO of Orix Corporation, a worldwide leasing and financial firm, told me, "If the world becomes one big free market, the standards will be set by the United States."[3]

Like most Japanese businessmen, Miyauchi was coy about how much money he himself makes, but he said his paycheck was a fraction of what it would be if he were in America. Most experts who have compared pay across countries agree he is telling the truth. To a great degree, this reflects a different cultural slant on the role of a business leader in society.

"In Japan, executives are like army generals," Miyauchi said. "There's a lot of responsibility and status but little pay. We do have respect, and this respect gives us social influence."

Everything, of course, is relative. Even Japanese executives do better than the average general. Eamonn Fingleton, a Tokyo-based author, estimates that the CEO of a big Japanese firm might make $1.2 to $1.5 million per year.[4]

The story is the same around the world. In France, the news that Pierre Suard made $2.5 million in 1994 as chairman of Alcatel Alsthom, a telecommunications and engineering firm, stirred a scandal, especially since his company reported record losses the next year. In Germany, Jürgen Schrempp, chairman of Daimler-Benz, the country's largest industrial firm, makes an estimated $1.5 million per year.

Even in Tokyo, Paris, and Stuttgart, this kind of income keeps the wolf from the door. But it's a far cry from the salaries and other income brought in by executives in the United States, where million-dollar-plus salaries are common, the twenty highest-paid CEOs each bring in more than $11 million a year, and a relatively obscure boss like Lawrence Coss of Green Tree Financial Corporation made $65 million in 1995, then upped that to $102 million the next year. J. P. Bolduc, forced out as chief executive of W. R. Grace & Company after allegations of sexual harassment, left with a golden parachute of about $43 million.[5] Robert Allen, CEO of AT&T, made $16 million after announcing plans to chop 40,000 jobs. CEOs Sanford Weill of the Travelers Group brought in $97 million in 1996, Theodore Waitt of Gateway 2000 made $81 million, and Anthony O'Reilly of H. J. Heinz made $64 million, even though investors in his company would have done better picking stocks on a dartboard. Amid these excesses, the news that Jack Welch, CEO of General Electric, made $27 million in salary, bonus, and share options barely lifted eyebrows.

How much the *average* executive makes depends on the measurement, and estimates vary. But by any standard, it's a lot. One measure, by Pearl Meyer & Partners, said the average CEO of a major U.S. corporation made $4.3 million in 1995, counting salary, bonuses, stock options, and other forms of payment. In 1996, according to *Business Week*, the *average* CEO of *all* U.S. companies made $2.3 million in salary and bonus alone; add in stock options, and this went up to $5.8 million. This amounted to a 54 percent raise over 1995 income, which itself was up 30 percent over 1994—at a time when the average employees of these CEOs' companies were barely staying even with inflation.[6]

Towers Perrin, the international executive search firm, using different figures, tried to compare this bonanza with CEO salaries in other countries. In 1995, it said, the average CEO of all U.S. corporations, big and small, made $927,896. By contrast, Towers Perrin said, the average total pay was $600,052 for a French CEO, $512,651 for a German, $483,815 for a British, and $558,457 for a Japanese.[7]

"What are they going to do with that much money?" wondered Yoshihiro Suzuki, executive vice president of NEC, the Japanese electronics giant, about the American salaries. "How are they going to spend it? These people should ask themselves, 'Why am I making this much money?' "[8]

In France, Denis Kessler, vice president of the Patronat, the French employers' association, called these pay levels "very awkward."[9] Hans-Olaf Henkel, president of the Federation of German Industry and an outspoken proponent of the free market, said, "All German busi-nessmen would say that these American salaries are absurd."[10]

This sanctimony toward American excess might be more impres-sive if non-American executives were more willing to publicize their own paychecks. The law in most countries, unlike U.S. law, does not require publicly held companies to tell how much they pay their top executives. In France, companies report the total compensation for their top ten executives, but not how much each one made. The exec-utives themselves seldom volunteer the information. French execu-tives have sued muckraking reporters who found out their salaries and published them. One CEO, Jean-Marie Messier of Compagnie Générale des Eaux, told a magazine impertinent enough to ask that it was guilty of "voyeurism."[11]

Despite this secrecy, all evidence indicates that the U.S. salaries are in a class by themselves. For instance, Patrick Ponsolle, co-pres-ident of Eurotunnel, the giant British-French Channel tunnel project, made $348,000 in 1995, small change by American standards.

Why American Executives Make More

There are reasons, cultural and financial, for these differences. One lies in tax laws. It makes less sense to demand a high salary if the tax man is going to take most of it, and American executives simply pay less tax than those in other countries, even not counting the cre-ative ways they find to avoid tax. The top tax rate in the United States is 39 percent; it's 50 percent in Japan and 57 percent in Germany and France.[12]

Instead, many foreign executives worry more about perks like housing or, in Japan, golf club memberships than they do about salaries. Daniel Jouve, president of his own head-hunting firm in Paris, told me, "When I'm recruiting an executive here, I spend more time negotiating the type of car he's going to get than his pay."[13]

Another factor is the makeup of the boards that set executive salaries. In Germany, the *Mitbestimmung* (codetermination) system gives workers a voice in management, with workers' representatives fill-ing half the seats on the boards of most big firms. This puts a power-ful brake on any temptation to raise CEO salaries at the expense of workers' pay. In Japan, board members are mostly other executives who are less inclined to give mega-raises to CEOs than are U.S. boards, which are often dominated by outside directors, most of them highly paid CEOs themselves and pals of the executives whose salaries they set.

Too often, these high payoffs go to the executives who have laid off the most employees. When he was CEO of Scott Paper, Albert Dunlap laid off 35 percent of the company's workforce, merged the company with Kimberly-Clark, and left with a $100 million payoff. The Institute for Policy Studies looked at the twenty-two American firms that announced layoffs of at least 3,000 workers in 1995 and found that their CEOs, on the average, got a 13.6 percent raise the following year, compared to 10.4 percent for chief executives overall. These CEOs—heads of such firms as AT&T, Boeing, Chase Manhattan, and Eastman Kodak—earned an average of $4.5 million. One CEO, Lucio Noto of Mobil, saw the value of his stock options go up by $23.9 million the day after he announced he was cutting 4,700 jobs.[14]

In most differences between capitalist nations, culture and tradition play a big role, and this is true in executive salaries. Japan and Europe have a tradition of equality that doesn't exist in the United States. At $5.7 million, the CEO of a top American firm makes 209 times the pay of an average manufacturing employee.[15] This is an insulting figure on its own, and it becomes absolutely foul in comparison with other nations. Japanese CEOs, for instance, make only 9 times as much as the average manufacturing employee in their plants.[16]

One reason for this American gap is the fact that American CEO pay is going up faster than anywhere on earth. Another reason, according to Cornell University researchers John M. Abowd and Michael L. Bognanno, is that the United States is the only major industrialized nation where pay for the average worker is actually going down. The two researchers looked at twelve nations and found that, in 1984, American CEOs and manufacturing workers both ranked first in total compensation. By 1992 the American CEOs were further ahead than ever, but the workers ranked tenth. (Not only shop floor workers are suffering, Abowd and Bognanno found. Middle-level executives, members of the middle class, aren't doing so well, either. In 1984, American human relations directors, like the CEOs and workers, ranked first. By 1992, the human relations directors, like the workers but unlike the CEOs, ranked tenth.[17])

Riding the Options Rocket

Apart from culture, the key difference between executive compensation in the United States and that of other countries is the degree to which U.S. executive pay is linked to stock prices. Under heat for paying their CEOs too much in base salary, American boards began tying compensation to the price of the company's stock, so that the companies and their executives thrive, or suffer, in tandem. One way was to simply give executives shares in the company. Another was to award share options, which give the manager the right to buy shares at a set price; if the price of the stock rises above this set price before the option expires, the executive can buy and then sell the stock and keep the profit.

This sounds good, but the long American bull market on Wall Street turned these stock options into an historic honey pot. In 1996 one Chicago executive, U.S. Robotics CEO Casey G. Cowell, earned $3.4 million in salary—and $30.5 million in stock options. In 1995 another Chicago CEO, John N. Brincat of Mercury Finance Company, collected nearly $11 million in stock options, more than five times his basic pay. Within a year, Brincat was out of a job, and his company's stock had collapsed after allegations that it had falsified its profit statements.[18]

Stock options clearly have gotten out of hand. Many CEOs have seen their total pay go up by 50 percent or more because of the bull market. The average increase in total pay for CEOs was about 15 or 20 percent in 1996, a year in which the pay of their employees barely kept up with inflation. For these CEOs, stock options now account for 45 percent of this total; their salary, by contrast, is only 22 percent.[19] These executives maintain that, if their genius raises shareholder value, then they should benefit, too. But in a boom, when virtually every stock is going up, it takes no genius—just an ability to avoid disaster—to ride the wave. The options trend is, in fact, hurting the companies it is meant to help. In 1996 options cost MCI $97 million, Pepsico $68 million, and Travelers $51 million—all money that could have gone to stockholders or, better, been used to create jobs, prevent downsizing, and raise the pay of the ordinary mortals who, day in and day out, kept their companies going.[20]

Stock markets go up and down. Executive compensation, theoretically tied to stock values, only seems to go up. Executives have been demanding—and getting—revaluation of their options to ensure that, if their company's stock falls, their income won't fall with it.[21] This only underlines the unfairness of the use of options. Ostensibly, they are based on performance. At too many companies, they are based on nothing but greed.

The Options Game Spreads

Stock prices in most other countries aren't as important as they are in the United States. Japanese and European countries get more of their financing from banks than from stock markets. Stockholders in these companies often are banks or other companies more interested in a long-term investment than in the ups and downs of a stock market.

But this is changing. As more foreign companies go to the New York Stock Exchange and other markets for financing, share prices will loom larger for their management. Daimler-Benz, for instance, recently became the first German firm to be listed on the NYSE. Not coincidentally, 170 of Daimler-Benz's executives have been given stock options. By American standards, these options are small. Schrempp, the chairman, received options worth about $65,000. By contrast, of the twenty best-paid U.S. executives in 1994, all but two made more by exercising options than they did from their basic pay.

There is a suspicion that European executives may have more stock options than they let on, but hide them behind the secrecy permitted by their corporate laws. As more European companies are listed on the NYSE, they come under American reporting laws, which requires disclosure of these options. When Axa, the French insurance giant, bought the U.S.-based Equitable Companies, American regulators forced it to disclose executive pay, including $27 million in stock options held by its chairman, Claude Bébéar.[22]

Daimler-Benz and other European and Japanese firms live in a globalizing world. They are getting more of their money from global markets and face the same demands from these markets that American CEOs do. If most big companies are still national in their culture and character, some are becoming global and will recruit their executives from an international pool of executive talent. It is only a matter of time before non-American executives, competing more directly with Americans, will demand American-style compensation.

Exhibit 7.1

Gaps Between Low- and High-Income Individuals
(ratio of top 10% to bottom 10%)

United States	5.67
Germany	2.98
France	3.51

Source: Timothy M. Smeeding and Peter Gottschalk, "The International Evidence on Income Distribution in Modern Economics: Where Do We Stand?" Presentation at the annual meeting of the Population Association of America, New Orleans, 1996.

The towering U.S. levels of pay disturb many Americans but at least conform to the individualistic American creed. Similar pay for European and Japanese executives will clash with the more egalitarian tradition of their nations. How they deal with this clash will determine whether these nations are more successful than America has been in creating a society based on fairness.

An Unequal Nation

The salaries earned by America's chief executives are the most visible sign of a trend toward concentration of wealth that has its counterpart possibly only among the oligarchies of Latin America. (See Exhibit 7.1 for a comparison to Germany and France.) These figures are well known by now and have received plenty of outraged comment, but this outrage has produced no countertrend, so they are worth repeating.

The problem is not with the economy itself. Between 1983 and 1989, total personal income of Americans rose by $2.8 trillion. Despite the mild recession in the early 1990s, it has certainly gone up since then by as much again. Yet virtually all of this increase—$2.75 trillion, or 98 percent—went to the top 20 percent.[23] The top 5 percent of wage earners, those making more than $120,000 per year, command a bigger chunk of the national income than the bottom 50 percent put together.[24]

If 98 percent of the increase in personal incomes went to only 20 percent of all Americans, that means the other 80 percent barely held their own. In fact, most of them didn't do that well.

Beginning in the mid-1970s, median wages in the United States began to fall. The process began with manual workers and high school dropouts, and caused no particular anxiety among the rest of the population. These people offered strong backs but few skills; their situation was sad but nothing that the better-skilled had to worry about.

But then the process moved up the ladder. Median wages began to fall for high school graduates, then for those with some college education, and then, in the late 1980s, for male college graduates, when inflation is counted in.* By the mid-1990s, the only broad category for whom wages were still rising was female college graduates, mostly because they had started from a lower base, and even their pay was beginning to stagnate.[25] By the late 1990s, pay for the lowest-paid Americans finally began to rise again, by about 1 percent, after falling by more than 20 percent since the 1970s.

For many Americans, debt became the answer. Total consumer debt in the United States is $1.3 trillion. Between 1989 and 1995, debt for the bottom 80 percent rose by one-fifth. Personal bankruptcies rose even faster, by 30 percent. For the global citizens at the top, the cost of transatlantic telephone calls and computer capacity is falling by the day. But for the 12 percent of Americans at the bottom, those who don't have checking accounts, the system stacks the cards against them. According to the Consumer Federation of America, the currency exchanges where these people cash their paychecks and Social Security checks have raised their prices by some 40 percent in the past decade.

Rising productivity, we are told, means rising wages, because it creates more wealth to be invested or shared. Lagging productivity is occasionally blamed for this decline in wages. But the truth is that the average worker's productivity went up by 25 percent from the mid-1970s to the mid-1990s—not a good record by historical standards, but better than nothing. Meanwhile, this worker's wage fell

---

*This inflation factor is highly contentious. The distance these "real wages" have fallen depends on the rate of inflation used. I am using the rate reported in the government's official Consumer Price Index (CPI). Many economists feel the CPI overstates inflation; an official panel said this overstatement could be as much as 1.1 percent per year. If the official CPI is lowered by that amount, much or most of the decline in wages disappears. So do many of the nation's other problems, such as the expected shortfalls in Social Security funds, even the federal budget deficit. A reduction in the CPI, in fact, would solve so many problems so painlessly that skepticism in this new math is warranted, and, indeed, many other economists dispute it.

18 percent. In purchasing power, 75 million Americans by late century were back where they had been in 1956.

The pundits have an answer to that. Household income, not individual income, is what really counts, they say, because it really determines how much food gets eaten, how big a house gets bought, how long a vacation gets taken. Family income, unlike individual income, has at least held steady over the years because of the rapid increase in the number of wives in the workforce, giving the average home two incomes instead of one.

But too often, even that doesn't do it. Gary Burtless, an economist at the Brookings Institution in Washington, says that for the bottom 60 percent of two-income families, total income is less now than it was twenty years ago. Put another way, the addition of the wife's income in these families has not offset the decline in the husband's income.

How can this be? A bit of thought supplies one answer. Most people marry spouses with similar background, education, and skills. A modestly skilled husband and a modestly skilled wife, perhaps a construction worker married to a store clerk, have both probably suffered layoffs and falling wages over the years. Two married lawyers who met in law school have both seen their incomes soar. For these two couples, the addition of the wives to the workforce increases rather than shrinks the gap between them.[26]

I found another answer while talking with John Grand, a Chicago banker who spent twenty-four years with First Federal Savings and Loan Association of Chicago and then with Citicorp after it bought First Federal. He rose first to branch manager, then to vice president of sales, and was flying high—two cars, two kids, a three-bedroom home in the suburbs. Then he got caught in a downsizing and was out of work for seven months, until he found a new job as a sales representative with another bank.

Grand wouldn't tell me exactly how much money he made in his old job or his new one. But he said he took a 28 percent cut in pay. His wife, Julie, who had chosen to stay home to look after their two school-age children, returned to her old job as a schoolteacher. Her salary, he said, just barely made up for what her husband had lost.[27]

Here was the story of the American economy, played out within one family. Before, one member of the Grand family worked; now two of them have jobs. Twice as many people are working, and that's good;

it's one reason why President Clinton can brag about the number of jobs created on his watch. But the two of them together haven't added a cent to what only one of them used to make, and that's bad. It explains why more Americans are working, and working harder, without bringing in any more money.

Where the Wealth Is

If income figures are wildly skewed, the accumulation of wealth—the household assets such as homes, bank accounts, insurance policies, stocks, bonds, real estate, and other investments—is positively Brazilian in its unfairness. Edward N. Wolff, a professor of economics at New York University, has calculated that, between 1983 and 1989, "the top 20 percent of wealth holders received fully 99 percent of the total gain in national wealth: the wealthiest 1 percent enjoyed 62 percent of that increase."[28]

America has no fewer than 129 billionaires, led by such modern descendents of Croesus as Microsoft's Bill Gates with a fortune of $39.8 billion, the duPont family with $10 billion, and Micromedia's John Kluge with $5.9 billion. The average American family has a total worth of $52,000, leading Wolff to comment that it would take 248,000 average Americans, a city bigger than Rochester, New York, to equal Gates's wealth.

As important as the distribution of this wealth is its composition. As you would expect, about two-thirds of middle-class wealth is invested in the family home. About 7 percent is in stocks and other financial investments. But the superrich, the 1 percent at the top, have 80 percent of their wealth in investment real estate, corporate stock, financial securities, and unincorporated businesses; their homes account for only 7 percent of their holdings.

The makeup of this wealth is important. The bottom 80 percent has most of its wealth tied up in houses, which can't be cashed in quickly when money is needed for a medical emergency or to pay tuition bills. Virtually all of the nation's liquid assets, or ready cash, is held by the 20 percent at the top.

Wall Street likes to boast that more than 40 percent of all Americans own stock and have shared in the bull market, which, as this is being written, is still roaring. This figure is true, but misleading. Most of these holdings are in company ESOP or 401(k) programs or

Exhibit 7.2

Share of Total Financial Wealth Owned
by Different Income Groups

Year	Top 1%	Next 19%	Bottom 80%
1983	42.9%	48.4%	8.7%
1989	48.2%	45.7%	6.2%

Source: John T. Cook and J. Larry Brown, "Asset Development Among Low-Income Households," report issued by the Center on Hunger, Poverty, and Nutrition Policy, Tufts University, Medford, Mass., December 1995.

represent a tentative dip into the mutual fund market; overall, the holdings represent a small fraction of the wealth of most families.

The real wealth is still at the top, Wolff says, among the super-rich 1 percent of Americans with $2.3 million assets or more. This elite crust owns 46 percent of all outstanding stock, more than 50 percent of financial securities, and 40 percent of investment real estate. The top 10 percent of families had 90 percent of the stocks and bonds and 80 percent of the nonhome real estate. Overall, he says, the top 1 percent has 39 percent of the wealth, and the top 20 percent has 84.6 percent. Both these figures are rising; the bottom 80 percent, which had 19 percent of the wealth in 1983, held only 15.4 percent by 1989 and only 6.2 percent of the stocks, bonds, and other financial wealth.[29] (See Exhibit 7.2)

All these figures were for 1989, the most recent year for which complete figures are available. Incomplete statistics indicate that the gaps narrowed a little between 1989 and 1992. Since then, however, the bull market has tripled or quadrupled the value of most stocks, bonds, and other financial securities. The price of houses has lagged behind. This means that the skewing of wealth reported in 1989 probably looks positively egalitarian next to the imbalances of the late 1990s.

Wolff has calculated one graphic implication of this skewed wealth. If the top 20 percent lost all their income today, he says, they have enough wealth and savings to go on spending as they do now for the next year and a half before they go broke. For the bottom 40 percent, that cushion is two weeks or less. Another study, by RAND researcher James P. Smith, found that among families headed by adults in their fifties or older—those facing retirement—the bottom ten percent had accumulated savings of $800 or less. Among older black and Hispanic households, four out of ten had no assets at all.[30]

As usual, wealth breeds wealth. Investments in stocks and other financial instruments create more wealth, much more than houses or savings accounts do. At the same time, federal laws cosset the wealthy by allowing, for instance, deductions for charitable contributions and trusts to escape inheritance taxes. At the bottom, laws discourage those with minimal assets from getting more. For the elderly, Medicaid only begins when assets give out; if you're old and sick, it's financially better to be broke, too. For younger families, welfare—even the new, reformed welfare—is a disincentive to save and build wealth. The rules differ from state to state: in Illinois, help for poor families, called Temporary Assistance for Needy Families (TANF), is cut off for families with $3,000 in assets. This is better than the program it replaced, Aid to Families with Dependent Children (AFDC), which had a $1,000 cutoff, but it still penalizes thrift and investment. Most likely, any savings will go into the mattress, safely hidden from government bureacrats but earning nothing.[31]

Why Is America More Unequal?

There are reasons for all this inequality. Surprisingly, inequalities in wealth owe little to inheritance. Smith and other researchers say that when inheritance is discounted, 90 percent of the inequalities remain. Instead, unequal wealth flows largely from unequal incomes, and it is in these skewed incomes that we must seek the answer.

As we saw in Chapter 3, the decline in median wages began in 1973 and had several reasons—the birth of the global capital market, the OPEC oil crisis, the double-digit inflation that led to high interest rates, an overpriced dollar, and the sudden surge of imports, mostly from Japan. American companies fought back by moving overseas or laying off workers at home. As trade competition grew and technology took over the workplace, this process moved up the pay and skills ladder, engulfing more and more workers.

All this history begs the question. The United States, with its high wages and relatively open market, was the first of the wealthy nations to feel this blast of globalization. But since then, globalization has struck the entire First World. Why has its impact on America—particularly on the incomes of its workers—been so different from its effect elsewhere? As we saw before, American manufacturing employees, whose wages ranked first in the world in 1984, had fallen to tenth out of twelve industrial countries surveyed eight years later. If the trade and technological forces of globalization are penalizing American workers with falling wages and shrinking standards of living, then this should be happening in all other countries, too. If the same forces are rewarding executives and other high-paid, high-skilled employees at the top of the information society, then inequality should be growing across the First World.

Neither is happening. All available statistics show that the United States has become by far the most unequal nation in the First World. If inequality is growing in other countries, the growth is minimal compared to the glaring inequities of wealth and income distribution in the United States.

Wolff says that all nations, including the United States, became more equal from the 1920s through the late 1970s. Inequality existed in the United States, but by international standards, this was a country that took the ideal of equality seriously. In class-ridden Britain, for example, the top 1 percent owned 44 percent of total wealth; in America, it was 28 percent. By 1981, the situation had reversed.

In 1983, the top 1 percent in America controlled 33 percent of the wealth. The share was 26 percent in France, 17 percent in Canada, and 11 percent in Sweden. In Japan, the top 5 percent owned 25 percent of the wealth, compared to 87 percent at that time for the United States.

Latest statistics show that the richest 20 percent of Americans are eleven times richer than the the poorest 20 percent. The ratio in France is about six, and the ratio in Japan, the most egalitarian rich nation, is only four. The U.S. standard of living is the highest in the world—some 20 percent higher on the average than that in Finland, the Netherlands, or Italy. But the poorest Americans live at levels about 20 percent below those of the poorest Finn, Dutch, or Italian.[32]

If globalization tends to increase inequality, why should these other nations be coping with the problem so much more fairly than the United States? The answer lies in the institutions, described in Chapter 3, that promote equality.

Strong labor unions are important. More than 40 percent of German workers belong to unions, and these unions carry out regional or nationwide bargaining with equally powerful employers' associations. Although this system is beginning to fray under the pressures of globalization, German workers still have a strong voice when wages are set. The same centralized wage bargaining system exists in France, where union membership is relatively low—only 10 percent of workers—but the unions negotiate wages that apply to 80 percent of the workforce.

In the United States, only 11 percent of private-sector workers belong to unions, and these unions themselves have lost power since the 1980s under a battering from globalization, the hostility of the Reagan administration, and union-busting tactics by employers who have become skilled at using the law, technology, and replacement workers to defeat strikes, organized labor's strongest weapon.

In Britain, the destruction of the power of the unions by former Prime Minister Margaret Thatcher has led to an increase in inequality. Even there, wages for the lowest-paid workers are still rising, but wages at the top are rising faster, increasing the gap.

A strong minimum-wage policy promotes equality. The American minimum wage stood at $4.25 per hour for five years until it was raised to $5.15 in 1996. Even with this raise, minimum-wage workers in the United States had less purchasing power than they did in 1967. Thirty years ago, a worker making the minimum wage could support—barely—a family of three at the poverty line. By 1996, a minimum-wage worker with a three-person family brought in $2,442 below the poverty line.[33] By contrast, the minimum wage in France, set on a monthly basis, works out to about $6.60 per hour; counting health coverage and other benefits, it's actually closer to $11. There is no legal minimum wage in Germany, but that country's welfare policy, by setting a high level of unemployment pay, enforces a de facto minimum wage of $12.37 per hour.

Inequality Is Not Inevitable

The fact is that inequality is not foreordained by globalization. In countries where governments remain committed to social solidarity and where strong unions are accepted by management as legitimate voices in the economy, the gap between rich and poor, between boardroom and factory floor is not growing.

Robert Reich, the former secretary of labor, has written eloquently that the idea of inevitable global inequality is wrong:

Evidence from other countries and U.S. history shows inequality rises and falls with the choices that a nation makes. Nations are not merely economic units but also societies. Should a nation choose to push against the economic forces that would otherwise divide it, it has the ability to do so. The consequence of choosing otherwise—of pretending the choice is not ours to make—is eventually to cease being a society.[34]

Throughout this book, we have seen that governments and their people are reacting to globalization in different ways, according to their own culture and beliefs. Americans like to think that the American way is the only way, but as Reich said, this isn't true.

Businesses everywhere try to make money, and to ask them to stop is both futile and unnatural, like asking a duck to stop quacking. But no business is damaged by demands that it share its prosperity with its workers. To allow businesses to do otherwise is to undermine society and to invite retribution.

The overpaid executives of American companies are guilty not only of greed but of an ignorance of history. Over the centuries, societies afflicted by blatant inequality have restored the balance, often destructively. The boyars and nobles of Russia paid the price in 1917. Seventy-four years later, the cynical, grasping *nomenklatura* that ruled the Soviet Union "destroyed the moral mainspring of their society and brought it down around their ears," David Marquand writes. "On present trends, the over-rewarded and socially irresponsible corporate elites of the U.S. and Britain are threatened by the same fate."[35]

Maintaining the social contract has become harder in a time of globalization, because businesses have the means to escape both the jurisdiction and the moral restraints of their home nations. American business executives have clearly succumbed to the temptations offered by these global freedoms. So far, most of their First World allies, for reasons both cultural and legal, have resisted these temptations and, in the face of globalization, have kept their contract with the workers beneath them.

8. THE EFFICIENCY OF BEER

THE IOWA OF MY boyhood was a galaxy of neat, prosperous towns, most of them small, all of them little civilizations unto themselves. Some of them were strung along railroad lines, with a town every ten or fifteen miles, wherever the engineers who laid out the Union Pacific or the Milwaukee Road or the Chicago & North Western had decided to put a station. Other small towns had been broadcast like seed across the soft, rich countryside, radiating out from the county seats of Iowa's ninety-nine counties. These little communities had a few hundred or a few thousand people and existed to serve the surrounding farms or coal mines that powered the state's economy. Each had a school, feed stores, a cafe, a doctor, a bank, a movie theater.

Fiercely self-sufficient, these towns and villages gave the Midwest its sturdy nature of independence, hard work, and rugged responsibility. "A great place to raise kids," the residents said, even when those kids grew up and moved to the city to find work. The towns they left behind seemed rooted in the soil, dependable as the changing seasons, a symbol of the American character. With their white clapboard houses, elms, and water towers, they looked like everybody's hometown.

I recently drove around Iowa, stopping off in towns with names like Grand Junction, Promise City, Cincinnati, and Gravity. Each was a rural slum, all but abandoned except by its elderly, old folks waiting to die, or by welfare mothers and their children who washed up there, living in mobile homes on the edge of town because it was a cheap place to live. In each town, at least one-quarter of the people lived below the poverty line. None had a school, a bank, a doctor.

207

Each had more residents over seventy-five than under five; Iowa, as a state, ranks third in the nation (behind Florida and Pennsylvania) in the percentage of its people over sixty-five, and first—even ahead of Florida and Arizona—in the percentage over eighty-five. In some little towns, a retirement home has replaced the school. Between 1980 and 1990, ninety-two of Iowa's ninety-nine counties lost one-quarter of their population or more; most of them had been bleeding people for years before that.

The town of Gravity sits on high ground in southwestern Iowa. It once had 1,000 people and a Main Street, two blocks long, lined with two groceries, a drugstore, a jewelry store, a dance hall, two taverns, a movie theater, a bank, insurance offices, barber shops, and farm implement dealers. A high school stood down the street, and there was a gas station in the valley below town, next to the highway.

Today, Gravity has 218 people, mostly elderly. Main Street is derelict. Three empty stores lean on each other at one end of the street, waiting to be torn down. A bank, closed a decade ago, stands vacant at the other end. The stores in between are long gone. Weeds grow through the foundations of shops that once served a close-knit little community. The gas station is closed. So is the school, shuttered since 1959. The only "business" is a nonprofit cafe that a few women run on a volunteer basis, just to give people somewhere to meet.

Some neat white houses remain, with generous porches and gliders for summer sitting. But they're surrounded by tattered mobile homes or the kind of shanties that always seem to have three rusted cars and a pickup truck parked in the littered yard. Some houses burn. Others just cave in.

I called on Helen Janson, now in her seventies, who came to Gravity in 1944 as the bride of the town veterinarian. As her retired husband snoozed in the living room, Mrs. Janson, the town historian, served me iced tea on her porch and talked about Gravity and its destruction.

"It was a busy town, but when we lost the school, things started disappearing," she said. "You talk to every little town like Gravity, you find the same thing. The school was the center of activity."

In 1992 a reporter for the *Des Moines Register* organized a charity fix-up day for the town. Hundreds of people came to paint houses and plant flowers. In the evening, they reopened the school, and four bands played. It was the first dance in Gravity in the thirty-three years since the school closed.

"It made you think of the times, many, many years ago, when everybody attended all the functions in town," Helen Janson said. "For years there was always a weekly dance here. Now there's nothing. It's depressing if you let it be. To those of us who care, yes, it is depressing. It's a part of life that's gone that you wish hadn't gone."

Across the Midwest, hundreds of little towns like Gravity are shrinking and dying. Corn grows where neighborhoods stood, and the countryside reclaims towns, as surely as the jungle overwhelms the Mayan ruins of Mexico. As with the Mayan remains, Gravity and the other little towns like it are a lost civilization.

Not long after I talked with Mrs. Janson, I was driving through the eastern Dordogne Valley in France, through the little towns near Aurillac. Set in rolling countryside away from the highway, these little places are pretty and nondescript, looking in their French way like Gravity used to. Each has a school, a bank, a post office, a gas station, a butcher shop, a grocery. In one town, the main street widened out into a square anchored at one end by Cathy's Cafe, where the eponymous Cathy and her terrier Lucky presided over the town's social life.

Across France and the rest of Europe, you'll find thousands of healthy little towns like these. Some, in the more scenic areas, thrive because the young people who grew up there return in later years to retire. But mostly they survive to serve the farms that surround them. In these villages, there is no clear dividing line between town and country. Farmers with loads of hay drive their tractors through the center of town or stop off at Cathy's on the way back to the farm.

Why should the small towns of Iowa decay into the soil while the villages of Europe flourish? There are many contributing causes. Better highways and better cars draw small-town residents of Iowa into county seats to shop. Then a Wal-Mart opens nearby, and the shops on Main Street, already weakened, give up. Young people leave and don't come back. The school is consolidated into a larger school in another town, and young families stop moving in. A mine closes. A railroad abandons its passenger service. The bank, burdened with too many bad loans on overextended farms, goes broke, and no other bank moves in to buy and reopen it.

But the real reason can be summed up in one word: efficiency. It's a word that is becoming more important every year, as global lenders and global markets demand ever higher profits, ever lower costs, ever greater efficiency. Machines often are more efficient than people. Big stores are more efficient than small stores. Mass production is more efficient than craftsmanship. It often is more efficient not to do a job at all than to do it inefficiently.

Saving Small Civilizations

The American farm system is a model of efficiency. Its aim is to keep grocery prices low, squeezing the farmer to the benefit of the shopper. Both the United States and Europe have support prices for many crops, setting floors that guarantee a minimum income. But the European prices are set high, usually above market levels, assuring farmers in France and other European countries not only a minimum income but a living wage. The American prices, by contrast, are set low, usually below market levels (and there are no support prices at all for livestock or chickens). The result is that, when the market price falls, the farmer's income falls with it. Farmers do have the guarantee of a minimum price, but it's not enough to support a family, pay off the debt to the bank, or buy new machinery.

And so the small farmers go broke, or lose their farm to the bank, or flee into town in search of a decent life for their families. This has been going on for decades, as small farms have been consolidated into larger farms. A farming family that once had all it could do to farm 160 acres, and made a decent living from this land, has been succeeded by a well-capitalized farmer who farms 2,000 acres with the aid of a million dollars' worth of equipment in a shed and a computer in the house to monitor the corn futures market in Chicago. When a farmer retires or goes broke, there's always another farmer nearby, or a rich dentist in the county seat, ready to buy him or her out and create one bigger farm where two farms used to be.

This is what really happened to towns like Gravity. As farms grew bigger, the number of farmers and their families shrank. Towns that existed to serve the people who lived on a hundred small farms have no purpose and no customers when the same land is farmed by two or three families, especially when these families buy their machinery and fertilizer from giant corporate suppliers hundreds of miles away. Gravity's problem is that its reason for existence has simply vanished. "If you have half as many farmers, you have half as many people buying shoes or groceries or going to the show," said Clete Swackhamer, a state agriculturalist in the Iowa town of Corydon.[1] He's right, except that it's not half as many farmers. It's even fewer.

"My son and two nephews are farming three farms that twenty-one families lived on thirty years ago," Willis Rowell, an economist with the National Farmers Organization in Ames, told me. "That's pretty typical. That's why we are boarding up the windows in these little towns."[2]

American farming today is a cruelly competitive but very efficient business. One result is that American shoppers probably pay the lowest grocery prices in the world. According to the Department of Agriculture, the average American family used to spent 30 percent of its income on food. Now it's barely 10 percent, which is great for shoppers but not so good for farmers, or the towns that once nourished them.

The French farm system is not a model of efficiency. In fact, French farmers are notorious around the world for the loutish ferocity with which they defend their high prices, crop supports, government help, and guaranteed markets. The European Union's Common Agricultural Policy (CAP), which has been the bane of generations of American trade negotiators, was literally invented by the French, who insisted that it be adopted by the EU's forerunner, the Common Market, as the price of French membership. It is an expensive, wasteful system based on high price supports, export subsidies, and trade barriers. It exists to prop up relatively inefficient farmers. One result is that French shoppers, like those in most European countries, pay grocery prices half again as high as those in the United States.

There may be only one good thing to say for the CAP, and that is that it has helped to preserve the little farm towns around Aurillac, while the American system is extinguishing little farm towns like Gravity. The French, given a choice between efficiency and their rural civilization, have opted for the civilization. Even Parisians who've never been on a farm in their lives say that the French heart beats to rural rhythms. When French farmers snarl city traffic with their tractors or block highways with tons of dumped produce, the world may snicker or groan, but the rest of France applauds. There is virtually no sentiment in France for a leaner, meaner agricultural system. French shoppers may pay more for their food than Americans do, but they aren't complaining. Besides, no one can argue that the French eat badly.

It is hard to make an argument for inefficiency, and true unrelenting inefficiency is doomed even in the most forgiving countries. The Soviet economy institutionalized inefficiency and collapsed. Despite the protests of French farmers, the CAP is being slowly reformed, to conform to world trade laws and to escape the ruinous costs of all those price supports. French farms are growing in size and shrinking in number.

But throughout the industrialized world, ordinary citizens are rebelling against a newly efficient world. Others are giving in grudgingly to the demands of a global market that values efficiency above all. Some of the struggles center on nothing less than the preservation of a civilization. Gravity is gone and is not coming back, but other communities, dependent on an industry that the market deems inefficient, continue the fight.

Some battles, like those in rural France, are fought over issues that would strike outsiders as trifling but that symbolize a way of life to those involved, who are being asked to give up something of value without seeing what they will get in return. Grave or frivolous, these feelings must be honored if the global economy is to get the political support it needs.

This is another way of saying that compromise—between global efficiency and human emotion—is a precondition for the new civilization being built.

Never on Sunday

In Germany, where laws regulate the days and hours when stores may open, parliament approved an extension of these hours late in 1996 only after a bitter national debate. Before then, a law called the *Ladenschlussgesetz* dictated that most stores could be open only from 7 A.M. to 6 P.M. on weekdays and until 2 P.M. on Saturdays. As a concession to madcap consumerism, there were exceptions—until 4 P.M. on one Saturday each month and until 8:30 P.M. on Thursdays, except for Maundy Thursday. The law forbade any shopping at all on Sunday, except at newsstands, which could open for two hours around noon. Drugstores and gas stations could stay open whenever they wanted, but only to sell drugs and gas and a few basic items—milk and bread for two hours on Sunday, flowers for six hours. In an emergency, these basic items also could be bought at railway stations.

The *Ladenschlussgesetz* was passed in 1956 to keep mom-and-pop stores in business and protect them from large stores or chains without making them work long hours or weekends. Recently, large retailers began lobbying for longer hours, until 10 P.M. on weekdays and 6 P.M. on Saturdays, by claiming this would force stores to hire 50,000 more workers—not a bad argument in a country with 10 percent unemployment.

Few Germans were persuaded. Even the big stores admitted that two-thirds of their customers opposed longer hours. Other polls raised this to 80 percent. On an idle afternoon in Bonn, I conducted my own informal poll and found no one—neither shopper nor store-owner—who favored the new hours.

A woman named Christine Sick said she worked all day at a men's clothing store called Pohland Exklusiv. By the time she got off work at 6:30 P.M., all the other stores were closed, so she had to do her grocery and other shopping before 2 P.M. on Saturdays. To an American, it seemed obvious that longer store hours would give her a more relaxed and better life.

Not at all. "Personally," she said, "I'm not very amused." Rather than shop at all hours, American-style, "I prefer to be home with my family." But what if she were cooking the Sunday dinner and discovered that she lacked a crucial breast of goose or red cabbage, and the nearest open grocery was in, say, Belgium? "Well," she said, "that's my mistake. You have to think ahead."

I wrote a lighthearted article about this tempest and then began to think about what Christine Sick and other Germans had told me. They were perfectly aware of the shopping habits in other European countries, which are more liberal than in Germany, or in the United States, where Americans can shop 'til they drop, at all hours of the day and night. They know that big chains and Wal-Mart–style super-stores are making headway throughout Europe, but less so in Germany than elsewhere. They have traveled enough to have seen wee-hour shopping in America, with its underpaid assistants working night shifts, and the swamping of small shops by huge chains. They are stodgy enough, or human enough, to think they have found a better way. Given the chance to spend more time in stores, the majority of Germans, like Christine Sick, said they'd rather spend the time with their families.

In the end, parliament extended the hours, but not by much—until 8 P.M. on weekdays and until 4 P.M. every Saturday. Sundays stayed holy. Clearly, the Germans intend to take their efficiency in small doses.

The Efficiency of Globalization

As we saw in Chapter 6, the entire German social and economic system is based on a balance of interwoven interests, called the Social Market Economy, that is inefficient by its very nature. Germany now is being challenged by a global market that insists that it become more efficient, and threatens it with growing unemployment if it fails. But the Germans know that sweeping efficiency, at the cost of social cohesion, could unravel this balance and, with it, their entire society. This is the real meaning of the debate going on there now.

Germany relies on a balance among big business, big labor, and big government, with no one of these three partners getting too much power over the others. The exemplar of this balance is *Mitbestimmung*, or codetermination, in which workers in large companies are guaranteed a voice in management, including half the seats on the board. Workers' representatives must be told well in advance of any changes that could cut employment, and they have the legal right to challenge those changes. Endless negotiations ensure that everyone's voice is heard and everyone's rights are upheld. It is a tedious, time-consuming procedure that certainly makes many German industries less competitive than their American rivals.

Yet even German executives say they support *Mitbestimmung* and would oppose attempts to scrap it. It ensures stability within the corporations. It has given Germany the West's best record for labor peace. If it enables the workers' voice to be heard by management, it also enables management's voice to be heard by the workers. It establishes openness, trust, and a professionalism that are fading from American companies.

The Germans fear centralized power. Not only is power diffused within their companies, but their federal system makes the American version of states' rights look like a dictatorship. Bonn must negotiate most policies with the *Länder,* or states, which have more power than any American state.

The global market likes centralized power. It likes the ability to pass judgment on a company or a nation, and to force that company or that nation to change its policies. In this way, the market gets maximum return on its investment, and it gets it fast. If lives are damaged in the process, or social contracts broken, or civilizations upset, the market replies that this is the price of progress and perfection, and that everyone will end up better off, sooner or later.

The Germans and the other Europeans aren't so sure. They know their own history, and they think they have found a way to avoid repeating it. This way is the European Union, which is an economic entente originally based on an agreement between Germany and France, its two leading members. This agreement rested on the interests of German industry and French agriculture. And both of these, as we have seen, not only have built-in inefficiencies but rely on those inefficiencies to function. If French farming were as efficient as American farming, or if German industry scrapped *Mitbestimmung* at the market's behest, then not only farmers and factory workers and their towns would be hurt. The entire foundation of the European Union could be at risk.

"No segment of the body politic, in France or in Europe, wants this system dismantled on the basis of economic efficiency," a French economist told me. "This is the consensus throughout Europe."

A Nation Based on Inefficiency

If commercial inefficiency is a cultural preference in Germany, it is crucial to the national economy in Japan. Anyone who visits Japan is immediately struck by several things: the high prices, the huge number of tiny shops, and the overstaffing of larger stores, mostly with

Exhibit 8.1

Distribution of Employment by Size of Enterprise, as Percentage of Total

	1–19 People	20–99 People	100–499 People	500–Plus People
United States	24.6%	18.8%	13.5%	43.1%
Japan	36.4%	17.7%	18.3%	27.6%
Germany	25.9%	18.7%	18.2%	37.2%
France	29.1%	21.0%	16.2%	33.7%

Source: Organization for Economic Cooperation and Development.

young women who seem to have little to do but bow as customers come and go. All this seems inefficient, even wasteful, to a visiting Westerner who would prefer a little less personal service in exchange for lower prices.

There's a reason for this inefficiency, and it's built into Japan's dealings with the world, as described in Chapter 5. Japan, as we saw, runs huge trade surpluses with most other countries. One major reason is that the Japanese market remains closed to many of the goods the world would like to sell there, especially goods that would compete with Japanese products. Some of these imports are blocked by outright trade barriers, as foreigners have found out when they tried to ship rice or baseball bats to Japan. But more subtle barriers are built into the inefficient structure of retailing. The tiny mom-and-pop stores that dominate Japan's shopping streets don't have the time or personnel to seek out exotic and low-priced foreign goods. Instead, they buy from wholesalers linked to major Japanese manufacturers. It is a distribution system designed to keep foreign goods off Japanese shelves. (Exhibit 8.1 shows the concentration of Japanese workers in small business.)

This means that low-priced imports are all but kept out of stores. Lacking this competition, Japanese suppliers and stores are free to charge the high prices that startle so many foreign visitors. These high prices serve several purposes. First, they enable Japanese manufacturers to make huge profits from domestic sales, which are then used to subsidize exports to other countries: Japanese goods abroad, unlike those at home, are priced so low that they sometimes drive the local competition out of business, as American television manufacturers learned. Second, high prices in Japan discourage consumption, which encourages savings. These savings are an important weapon in global competition for Japanese companies, which are assured of a vast pool of homegrown capital to finance investment.

Perhaps most important, these high prices are the key to Japan's social contract with its workers. Full employment is national policy. Government and business are dedicated to keeping all Japanese—or at least all Japanese men—on the job. High prices make this possible. No company has trouble meeting a payroll when it can charge what it wants, secure in the knowledge that it will not be undercut by low-price competition.

This is how Japanese companies keep workers on the job or find new jobs for them with subsidiaries, even when times are hard. This is how those tiny shops stay in business. This is how big stores afford platoons of nearly idle employees, like the thirty-two sales-women that I counted one afternoon in the costume jewelry department in the Matsuya Ginza store in central Tokyo. Back home in Chicago, twelve employees ran a jewelry department of about the same size at a Marshall Field's store.

This sort of inefficiency makes no sense to a Western economist. But it underpins the whole Japanese system, which consists of a superefficient industrial superstructure on an immensely wasteful base. Foreigners stand in awe of the Toyotas and Fujitsus of Japan, but these efficient superstars employ only 30 percent of Japanese workers; if Japan depended on them for jobs, it would have European-level unemployment rates. The other 70 percent work at jobs where inefficiency is not only tolerated but planned, especially in the inefficient retail and service sectors, where productivity is less than two-thirds of the American level.

When American negotiators demand that more U.S. consumer goods be allowed into Japan, or when they try to open up Japanese services like insurance to American competition, they are arguing in the name of free markets. When Japanese negotiators resist these demands, they are defending the social structure of Japan, even if they don't say so in those words.

The United States is probably the most efficient nation of all. This was true even during the 1970s and 1980s, when Japanese exports were driving many American businesses to the wall. Productivity is the output that countries and companies produce compared to the input, in capital and labor, that they spend. Statistics for the 1970s and 1980s show the overall U.S. economy performing consistently better than the Japanese economy and well ahead of the Europeans. Specific Japanese industries—the auto industry, for instance, or branches of the electronics industry—outperformed their American competitors. But these Japanese industries also had the advantage of a huge war chest, built up from high profits at home, that enabled them to cut prices far below what the Americans could afford.

That Japanese edge, even in the industries where Japan is strongest, has largely disappeared. This is partly because the edge was based on a weak yen, meaning that Japanese costs were relatively low compared to American costs paid in more expensive dollars. As the yen has strengthened, Japanese costs have gone up. The Japanese edge also has vanished because the American companies, or at least those that survived the initial Japanese assault, got leaner, tougher, and more efficient. It was America's first experience with mass layoffs due to the global economy, and if it caused hardship for thousands of workers, it restored American competiveness. According to the Economic Strategy Institute in Washington D.C., Ford and Chrysler were more efficient than their Japanese competitors by 1992.[3]

According to a study by the McKinsey Global Institute, Japan is more productive than the United States in some important industries, such as auto parts, steel, and consumer electronics (see Exhibit 8.2). But Japan is less productive in such areas as soap and detergent, beer, and food processing, which is only 33 percent as efficient as American food processing.[4] Many more Japanese, however, work in food processing than in steel—deliberately so, as we saw, because food processing is a protected industry where inefficiency is endemic.

Japan, like Germany, has built inefficiency into its social contract. If the Japanese factory floor is a model of efficiency, the Japanese office is a paradigm of waste. The reason is job creation. It has been estimated that Japan's rate of unemployment, now a little more than 3 percent, would be closer to 9 percent if the nation's companies fired the window-sitters and other unproductive employees. But this would upset the Japanese system in which companies assume responsibility for their employees and get the employees' lifelong loyalty in return.

Exhibit 8.2

Labor Productivity in Selected Industries
(in percent of U.S. productivity)

Industry	Germany	Japan
Autos	66	116
Auto parts	76	124
Metalworking	100	119
Steel	100	147
Computers	89	95
Consumer electronics	62	115
Food	76	33
Beer	44	69
Soups and detergents	76	94
Total*	79	83

*Based on total employment
Source: McKinsey & Company Global Institute.

"All of the techniques to promote efficiency developed in Japan, including lean production, just-in-time inventory management, small group activities and employees' proposals, are concerned with manufacturing processes in the narrow sense," writes Yutaka Kosai, president of the Japan Center for Economic Research. "On the contrary, decision-making in Japanese management based on consensus formation from below (in which white-collar employees are mainly engaged) is regarded as inefficient, slow, and time-consuming, since complicated processes of organization coordination are necessary. Productivity improvements in office operations have been left aside."[5] Japanese economists like Kosai are perfectly well aware of the problems from the market's point of view. But the rest of Japan sees the cure as worse than the disease.

Beer and the Global Market

One eye-opening statistic in the McKinsey study showed that German beer producers are only 44 percent as productive as American breweries. This attempt to judge beer by its quantity reminded me of the *Chicago Tribune*'s claim, during the reign of its fabled late publisher, Colonel Robert R. McCormick, that it was a better newspaper than the New York newspapers because it weighed more.[6]

Seeking greater insights, I dispatched a colleague in Frankfurt to test the other attributes of German beer efficiency. He reported back that the chosen draft beer, a Warsteiner, was so rich and produced such a thick head that it took no less than ten minutes to pour: in other words, the delivery of German beer to the thirsty customer is some 2,000 percent less efficient than the pouring of a Budweiser in an American bar. On the other hand, my colleague said, the German beer tasted precisely 248 percent better than the Bud.

This is the point to be learned in Gravity, in Aurillac, in the shopping streets of Germany. Efficiency enables businesses and societies to produce more with less, and rising productivity frees resources for new and often useful production. No one, in Iowa or Japan, wants to return to a hunter-fisher economy. What we are hearing is not the cry of the Luddites. Instead, we are hearing people who have created a decent society. If change comes, as it must, it should come in ways that enable them to enhance that society, not diminish it. Efficiency for its own sake, as the global market demands, too often destroys without enhancing. To those who must live with the consequences, this is a bad trade-off.

Lowell Bryan and Diana Farrell, the McKinsey consultants who wrote *Market Unbound*, are unabashed enthusiasts for the ability of unfettered markets to shift the world's resources toward the highest profit and productivity. In their view, the global market is burgeoning not because it benefits the people who live within it but "because it is so profitable for the participants in the market."

Bryan and Farrell are talking mostly about the capital market, but they predict that global markets in stock ownership, production, and services will grow rapidly for the same reason—that's where the money is. They say this relentless mating of technology and low wages adds up to the "best practice" that drives the market.

They concede that, for workers who depend on a "social contract" with their employers, or who expected lifetimes of work to lead to decent pay, health care, and pensions, this process "can be truly devastating. On the other hand, the economic rent to those who are highly skilled, or to those who own the innovations and best practices across industries, has probably never been greater."

In other words, the disruption of stable societies and decent lives is the price that inevitably, and rightly, must be paid to achieve the profits of efficiency and the high incomes for those who own or exploit it.

Backlash

There is a growing backlash against this kind of thinking. It was dramatized in the public repentance of Stephen Roach, the Morgan Stanley chief economist, for his earlier praise of American business's ability to raise productivity through technology and downsizings. Roach said bluntly that efficiency is not enough. Business undeniably was more efficient, he said, but it was a phony efficiency based on a one-shot downsizing that would not last and was profoundly unfair to the American workers who bore its brunt:

> Surging profits, sustained low inflation, improved competitiveness and a record run in the stock market are all unmistakable byproducts of spectacular improvements in business efficiency. But it is increasingly apparent to me that these are the result of plant closures, job cuts and other forms of downsizing that are not recipes for lasting productivity enhancement.
>
> The distinction between efficiency and productivity goes to the heart of America's competitive dilemma . . . In the face of intense competition, managers may simply have pared the largest chunk of their bloated costs—worker compensation . . . If that is so, the so-called productivity resurgence has been built on slash-and-burn restructuring strategies that have put extraordinary pressures on the work force. This approach is not a permanent solution. Tactics of open-ended downsizing and real wage compression are ultimately recipes for industrial extinction . . . Some form of worker backlash is an inevitable byproduct of an era that has squeezed labor and yet rewarded shareholders beyond their wildest dreams.[7]

This view is taken for granted in Europe. Dominique Moïsi, the deputy director of the French Institute for International Relations (IFRI) in Paris, went to a roundtable for American and European businesspeople and found them reacting according to their national genes. Americans, he said, "could see no alternative to the ethic of individualism." To the Europeans, though, "the need for a new ethical revival in an era of globalization appeared fundamental. . . . Multinationals cannot take on the ethical responsibilities of the state or churches, nor can they neglect the ethical and social consequences of their actions."[8]

Many commentators predict that Japanese industry will abandon its policy of protecting jobs at all costs, as companies begin to move manufacturing abroad, especially to Southeast Asia. "But this argument underestimates the importance Japanese people attach to maintaining employment for their fellow Japanese," says Richard Koo, the chief economist for Nomura in Tokyo. "It will be very difficult for Japanese managers to sacrifice jobs of Japanese workers at home to hire Vietnamese or Chinese abroad when the yen is weakening. When push comes to shove, many Japanese executives may choose to maintain employment at home at the expense of idling more efficient foreign operations."[9] Procurement officers at Japanese companies say they will pay 20 percent more for telecommunications components and other supplies made in Japan, rather than buy a cheaper foreign product that is just as good.

How Efficient Do We Want to Be?

This sounds blasphemous to the ears of many American businesspeople, including Albert "Chainsaw Al" Dunlap, the downsizing CEO of Sunbeam Corporation. Dunlap joined a panel convened by *Harper's* magazine and ran into the heresy of Edward Luttwak, a fellow at the Center for Strategic and International Studies, who put the case against efficiency:

> When a country is as rich in GNP and as poor in social tranquillity as the United States, it makes no sense to purchase more GNP, through deregulation and increased efficiency, at the expense of tranquillity. It's like a man with 24 ties and no shoes buying himself another tie. And efficiency is always purchased at the expense of stability. A society that is rich in GNP and poor in tranquillity ought to be thinking of ways to impede change, to secure and stabilize, not ways to increase change for the sake of efficiency.

This was too much for Dunlap, who is so efficient that he laid off 11,000 workers at his previous company, Scott Paper, while raising the stock price by 225 percent. "With all due respect," he said without any noticeable respect at all, "that has got to be the biggest bunch of rubbish I've ever heard in my life. To say that we shouldn't be efficient? That's nonsense!"[10]

I bounced this thinking off a European businessman I know. He shook his head. "Dunlap's right," he said. "Businesses aren't there to create jobs, they're there to make money. But how far can you take this philosophy and still have a society?"

Some writers, such as Robert Kuttner, have argued that we can have it both ways, that limits on markets actually improve efficiency. He presents some compelling examples. National health systems in Europe, for instance, deliver more care to more people at lower cost. I'd like to think that Kuttner is right, and perhaps he is. Luttwak argues that the sheer pursuit of efficiency causes more instability than it's worth, and instability can only damage a nation's economy in the long run. Roach adds that efficiency as a means to productivity is a false goal, unless the gains of that productivity are shared with workers.

But we may not be able to have it both ways. The global market will demand efficiency, no matter the price. The only true response is a political one by citizens who say that efficiency is not the only goal, or even the ultimate one. Protection for society may require a trade-off in efficiency. This is a political decision, and societies must choose, as the French have chosen in their decision to keep the villages of the Aurillac region viable and vital.

The remnants of the societies that have paid the price of efficiency can be found not only in the small towns of southern Iowa but in the old steelmaking neighborhoods of the American Midwest, the British Midlands, and the French Lorraine. French farmers and German shoppers seem determined to resist; so do Japanese workers. To the prophets of the market, this is both futile and wrong. But to the people involved, it is a fight for the right to lead predictable lives, to raise stable families, and occasionally, to enjoy a slow, inefficient beer.

9. THE FIRST WORLD GOES GRAY

THE GLOBAL ECONOMY is often seen as an arena for a clash of economies between the wealthy nations of the First World and the still-poor nations of the Third World. It is more than that. It is also a clash of generations—great armies of young, hungry workers in the Third World who want the jobs, opportunities, and incomes that now belong to a smaller, well-fed corps of First-World workers who are, literally, old enough to be their parents.

Consider these statistics: In Japan, the average manufacturing worker is forty-six years old. In Indonesia, he—or, more likely, she—is twenty-one.[1] This fact carries immense political, social, and economic significance. Japan, and the other First-World nations, are running out of younger workers. These nations have aging workforces that soon will be retiring, straining government pension and health programs. This in turn means increasing government welfare expenses at a time when global bond markets are insisting that the same governments cut spending to the bone.

It also means that hundreds of millions of young workers in Indonesia and other developing countries are going to want work. To meet this demand, the world must create no fewer than 1.5 billion jobs over the next twenty-five years—as many jobs as it has created in the past fifty years. More than 90 percent of this horde of hungry young workers will be in the Third World, and most will be willing to work hard for wages far below First-World pay levels. At the most basic level, this portends a clash of the haves and the have-nots, of the comfortable and the unfulfilled, of the old and the young.

This aging of the wealthy industrial nations, and the growing age gap between them and the developing countries, will be the most important demographic fact of the twenty-first century. Americans, faced with rising Medicaid bills and warnings of a crisis in their Social Security system, are aware that something important is going on. But few of them realize that the aging is faster and the financial squeeze worse in most other industrialized nations. In the United States, the aging population is a problem; in Japan and much of Western Europe, it's a crisis.

The Aging Boomers

Social security programs date back to 1889, when Otto von Bismarck, the Iron Chancellor of Germany, created the first government-sponsored pension program. Under Bismarck's program, workers could collect pensions when they reached sixty-five—a safe bet for the German government in that era, when the average life expectancy was forty-five. The American program was instituted in 1935. Many others grew out of the postwar era and adopted the Bismarckian benchmark of sixty-five as the proper age to retire. This benchmark remains fixed to this day, more or less, in the psychology of most workers and in many national laws, even though life expectancy has soared into the seventies and eighties in most industrial nations. The only change has been downward; as people live longer, they are retiring earlier.

In 1950, when many government pension programs were being designed, the over-sixty-five population still was fairly small. In the United States, it amounted to 8.1 percent of all Americans (see Exhibit 9.1). In Germany, it was 9.3 percent; in Japan, only 5.2 percent.

That has gone up a little since then. Now, as the baby boomers age, it is about to take off. In the 1990s, the percentage of those over sixty-five has risen to about 12 percent in the United States and Japan, 14 percent in France, and 16 percent in Germany. For the next forty or fifty years, these statistics will surge, peaking around the year 2040. At that time, fully 20 percent of all Americans will be sixty-five or older. This is about where Florida, the grayest U.S. state, is now.

But this is blithe youth compared to other major countries. By 2040, Japan's over-sixty-five population will be nearly 23 percent, or

Exhibit 9.1

Projected Age Structure, as Percentage of the Population

Nation	Age	1950	1980	1990	2000	2010	2020	2030	2040
United States	0–14	26.9	22.5	21.8	21.2	19.3	19.2	18.9	18.9
	15–64	64.9	66.2	66.0	66.8	67.9	64.7	61.6	61.3
	65+	8.1	11.3	12.2	12.1	12.8	16.2	19.5	19.8
Germany	0–14	23.5	18.2	15.1	15.5	13.2	13.4	14.9	15.2
	15–64	67.1	66.3	69.4	67.4	66.5	64.8	59.3	57.2
	65+	9.3	15.5	15.5	17.1	20.3	21.7	25.8	27.6
France	0–14	22.7	22.3	20.3	19.2	17.4	17.0	17.4	17.9
	15–64	65.9	63.8	65.9	65.5	66.3	63.6	60.8	59.4
	65+	11.3	14.0	13.8	15.3	16.3	19.5	21.8	22.7
Japan	0–14	35.3	23.5	18.3	17.5	18.3	16.8	17.3	17.4
	15–64	59.5	67.4	70.3	67.3	63.0	62.3	62.7	60.0
	65+	5.2	9.1	11.4	15.2	18.6	20.9	20.0	22.7

Source: Organization for Economic Cooperation and Development.

more than double the present rate. The rate in France and Canada will be about the same. In Italy, it will be 24 percent, in the Netherlands 25 percent, and in Germany no less than 27.6 percent. In other words, one out of four people in most of the First World will be over sixty-five. In Germany and Japan, one out of every three persons will be sixty or older. (We know all this, of course, because all these people have already been born and are nearing adulthood now. One thing we don't know is how long they will live. If genetic engineering fulfills its promise, many of today's young adults could see the twenty-second century.)

The World Bank figures that there are now about 500 million persons in the world over sixty, which is about 9 percent of the world's population. By the year 2030, this army of the old will have nearly tripled to 1.4 billion, or 16 percent of the world's people. In the wealthy countries, about 18 percent of the total population is sixty years old or older right now; by 2030, it will be 31 percent.

This, of course, is progress of the highest degree. People live longer. Many of them live healthier. It is a triumph of economics, prosperity, technology, and health care. No one would wish it otherwise.

But the problems besetting the world's economies and pension systems, and the coming generational conflict between the rich and poor nations, are only more examples of how the solutions to yesterday's problems create new problems for tomorrow.

The Aging of Germany

Americans will be wise to keep an eye on how these older societies handle the aging problem; wherever the United States is going, other countries will get there first. The debate over the American Social Security system is focused on the time when the bulk of the baby-boomer generation hits retirement age and erodes the system's trust fund—its cushion against insolvency. This crisis is timed to hit around the year 2020, when 16.2 percent of all Americans will be sixty-five or older. Germany has already hit that level, and if the German social security system is not in crisis, it is feeling the pinch.

The growing German imbalance is not so much due to a surplus of aging workers—Germany didn't experience a postwar baby bulge comparable to that in the United States—as it is a shortage of younger workers. The country's birthrate is only 1.51 children per household, meaning that the average couple aren't replacing themselves. It is one of the lowest birthrates in Europe—only Italy, at 1.29, is lower—and it means the German population will fall, unless it can be supplemented by immigration. For years, Germany imported "guest workers," mostly from Turkey or the former Yugoslavia, to take the jobs that Germans themselves didn't want. After the Berlin Wall fell in 1989, a flood of refugees, many of them ethnic Germans, flowed in from the former Soviet Union and Eastern Europe. Two years later, unification added a population that was, on the average, younger than the West German population.

This influx postponed the crisis of aging but hasn't solved it. These new Germans arrived at a time when the global economy was already beginning to draw German jobs overseas and create unemployment at home. Jobs in shipping, defense, electronics, and autos—all mainstays of the postwar German economy—were declining. Many of these new arrivals, including the former East Germans, lacked the skills and work habits necessary to compete in this new, tougher market, and went straight from the refugee hostels to the dole.

This has produced a backlash among German workers against these Easterners, similar to the resentment felt in California and Texas against Hispanic immigrants. I talked in Munich with a BMW union official named Manfred Schoch, who echoed the bitterness heard around Germany from workers who, coming under new pressure from global markets, have picked out the most visible target—the Eastern immigrants—as scapegoats. Schoch talked about the longer hours and added shifts that BMW has demanded to meet competition from lower-wage nations. Then he complained that the workers' wages had stagnated for the past four or five years: "We are getting more and more the American system," he said. But what really made him mad was the opening of the eastern borders "that brought 15 million people to us, many of them without work, many of them retired, and now they get money from our system. We had to pay for thirty years into our retirement fund, and overnight, the government decided that somebody else gets money from that fund. Some Russian is collecting money from my insurance. That's what we're angry about."

This widespread anger means that Germany, a relatively crowded and still ethnically homogeneous nation, is already trying to control immigration. With the flood from the east having crested, it is not going to be anxious to bring in more workers from abroad. But because of the aging of its workforce, it must find younger workers, if only to pay the pensions of the retirees.

These workers are not being born, and that portends a shortage of future funds for the pension system. Germany, like the United States and all other major industrial nations, runs a pay-as-you-go pension system, with deductions from workers' paychecks going directly to support retirees. At the moment, there are only two German workers to support each retiree. By the year 2020, according to the demographers, there will be only one worker for each retiree. No one thinks the system can survive this pressure. Intergenerational responsibility is one thing; robbing the young to support the old is something else. But the solution is nowhere in sight.

Again, for Americans, the German situation provides a glimpse of the future. The American birth rate also is declining, especially in contrast to the growth of the baby boom generation. At the moment, there are three American workers to support each retiree. By the year 2020, there will be only two—which means the United States will be then where Germany is now.[2]

The Contradictions of Aging

Across the First World, the generational balance is complicated by many forces, many of them contradictory.

In countries with high unemployment among young people, governments want older workers to retire to make room for younger workers. But they also want the older workers to stay on the job to save welfare costs. In time, they know, lower birthrates will mean smaller workforces, so lower unemployment rates should follow. But the same shrinking workforce means there will be even fewer active workers to support tomorrow's retirees.

Within this shrinking workforce, more and more people—in Europe, Japan and the United States—are working part-time, by choice or by necessity, or have dropped out of the official labor pool into the gray market, where payments are by cash only and taxes are neither withheld nor paid. This trend means the social security burden falls even more heavily on the dwindling number of full-time official workers.

If today's workers are blocking jobs for young people, it would help if they retired as early as possible. But this would defeat the campaign of governments to reduce their spending, including spending on social security and other old-age costs. Governments under pressure to get this spending down will be urging their workers to stay on the job longer. If government pensions are cut, many workers certainly will choose to work longer and retire later.

The state of private pensions in most countries will reinforce this choice. In Europe, most income for the elderly comes from public systems; the private pension system is relatively undeveloped. In Germany, for instance, government pensions amount to an average of 60 to 70 percent of workers' income. The American equivalent is about 40 percent. Private pensions, an important supplement for many American workers, are only about 10 percent as big as government pensions in Germany.

If government pensions in Germany are cut back, corporations will be asked to fill the gap. But German employers already claim that their government welfare contributions put them at a competitive disadvantage with the rest of the world, especially with rivals in low-cost countries. "Thirty percent of our GDP goes for social benefits already," said Hans-Olaf Henkel, the president of the Federation of German Industry. "Our customers don't want to pay for this anymore."[3]

Already Germans pay an amount equal to 21 percent of their paychecks into the government pension system. Workers pay half of this, or an amount equal to 10 percent of their pay, and employers pay the other half. By the year 2030, this will rise to at least 26 percent, if benefits hold steady. This is four times as much as American workers pay now. This doesn't count other deductions and spending for health care, unemployment pay, and other welfare benefits, which more than doubles the current total deductions, to some 42 percent. Add on to this the burdens on national health systems that go with an aging population, and the costs become stratospheric.

Postponing retirement would help lower these costs by shrinking the number of retirees. But this goes against the trend of the times. The average retirement age around the world is falling, not rising. In 1970, 20 percent of all Germans over sixty-five were still working; now it's barely 5 percent. Americans work longer, but not as much as they used to. Fifteen percent of America's over-sixty-fives are still on the job, but this is about half the 1970 rate.

In most countries, workers do not wait until they reach sixty-five to retire. The official retirement age in France, Japan, and Italy is sixty. In Germany, it's sixty for women and sixty-three for men, soon to be raised to sixty-five. In fact, Germans often retire between fifty-five and fifty-eight, take a lump sum payoff from their companies and then survive either on unemployment pay or disability allowances—easily available through the country's generous welfare system, with a certificate from a friendly doctor—until partial pensions kick in at age sixty.

Everywhere, even in Japan, people are retiring earlier than they used to. The trend is clear. To make their people work longer, governments would not only have to pass new laws; they would have to engineer a social revolution amounting to no less than teaching old dogs new tricks.

France Says No

France, a traditionally paternalistic country, has the same financial problems as Germany. The average French wage is lower than that in most countries, but a panoply of benefits—medical care, vacations of five weeks or more, children's allowances, maternity leaves, free daycare systems, free university education—raise standards of living to a level as high as anywhere in Europe. Among these benefits are generous retirement provisions. Train drivers can retire at age fifty, blue-collar workers at fifty-five, and most white-collar workers at sixty. (This retirement used to be sixty-five but was reduced to sixty in 1982; once reduced, any retirement age is very hard to increase again, as the French government is finding.) Retired blue-collar workers get pensions equal to up to 70 percent of their final salaries; for white-collar workers, it's up to 80 percent.

One result is that the nation's social security fund runs an annual deficit of some $17 billion. Because of its commitment to join the European single currency, France had to cut its annual overall government deficit from 5 percent to 3 percent, and this welfare deficit was an obvious place to start. Some savings were made, but the government struck out in its attempt to raise the retirement age for train drivers. The retirement age of fifty was set in the age of steam, when driving a train was hard, dirty labor. Today, engineers in comfortable cabins send their high-speed trains whisking across the French countryside at the push of a button. Raising the retirement age would seem reasonable to most people—but not to the French. The train drivers staged a one-month strike and won, mostly because of widespread support from a public that saw them not as the coddled beneficiaries of unjustified perks but as important workers fighting to keep a right they had acquired justly. Eighteen months later, French voters threw out the conservative government that tried to institute these reforms and elected a socialist one that promised a less painful, more French path to the future.

"We have an expensive but good health system, so people don't die anymore," one exasperated French businessman told me. "So they vote—and we have a system tilted to old people. They have money and power, and they don't die. Young people don't have a chance."

But for the French, this protection by the state is not only a perk but a guarantee of the social contract. Government leaders know this relationship must be protected if France is going to take its place in the global economy without ruinous strife. "We need to think about giving our people the skills and confidence that they will be employable for life, even if they have to change jobs," the president, Jacques Chirac, said in an interview with the *Washington Post*'s William Drozdiak. "This is how we can make globalization succeed and still remain faithful to our own cultures and history. For me, that goal is based on the European social model, where the state is the guardian of unity."[4]

The Threat to Japan Inc.

Japan's population is aging more rapidly than that of any other industrialized country, presenting a problem in two stages. The first threatens the tradition of lifetime employment, which is a key to Japan Inc. Fewer than 40 percent of Japanese employees enjoy lifetime employment, but they are the employees with the best jobs, the "core" around which the rest of their corporations spin. These employees and other older workers benefit from a seniority system that overpays older workers while underpaying younger workers. These practices, which originated during World War II, are intended to promote stability for both employer and employee. Employers benefit because workers stay with a single company throughout their careers, instead of taking their skills and knowledge to new employers. Employees benefit because they know this loyalty will be rewarded in the long run with job stability, an eventual high salary, and an honorable retirement. Younger workers put up with this institutionalized exploitation because they know that their time, too, will come.

But the system depends on a steady, orderly turnover at the top, as older workers retire and younger workers take their place. In the next few years, there is going to be a glut of older workers at the top, blocking promotion to the best jobs, plus another glut of older workers in the middle, keeping the youngsters out of the line of advancement. As with everything else in Japan, this twin system of lifetime employment and seniority preference is a consensual, cooperative arrangement that relies on the approval, or at least the acceptance, of everyone involved. If the smart, young workers now entering the workforce aren't allowed to take their place in the system, this acceptance could break down.

In the longer run, these older workers will retire en masse, creating a huge budgetary problem for Japan. Within the next thirty years, the percentage of the population over sixty-five will double. One reason for this, as in Germany, is the nation's low birthrate, which is 1.53 children per household, not much better than the German rate.[5] On the one hand, this will help keep unemployment down, as more Japanese manufacturing moves offshore and as the nation's service and retail sectors, with their large numbers of underemployed workers, gradually become more efficient. But there will also be a shortage of workers—not much more than one worker for every retiree—to support the nation's social security system.

Even at present levels of support, this Japanese system is relatively spartan. If Europeans rely on public pension plans and Americans benefit from both public and private plans, the Japanese emphasize private plans over public ones. Public old-age spending is about 11.5 percent of gross domestic product in Germany, 7 percent in the United States, and only 5 percent in Japan.

Corporate pension programs help, but not enough to keep Japanese pensioners out of poverty. This is one of many reasons for Japan's high savings rate. Aging Japanese, knowing their pensions will be far from lavish, save heavily against their retirements. Many of them also rely on their families to a greater degree than in either America or Europe, where younger generations are more mobile and extended families are breaking down. In Japan, 57.6 percent of the elderly live with their children, compared to only 14.7 percent in the United States.[6]

There have been fears of a looming labor shortage in Japan. Paul A. Summerville, an economist at Jardine Fleming Securities in Tokyo, writes, "Japan is slowly running out of Japanese." The aging population and low fertility rate, he says, will mean a dearth of people to carry out future economic growth. Women, who tend to drop out of the workforce when they get married, are hard to lure back because of the lack of child-care facilities. Higher immigration is one solution but not one that Japan, one of the world's most xenophobic countries, is likely to adopt. Summerville notes that Japan allowed only 6,333 foreigners per year to become naturalized citizens in the early 1990s; the United States naturalized that many every ten days. The upshot is that less than one-half of 1 percent of the labor force are legal non-Japanese workers, a figure that could grow but probably won't. Nor is there much hope of alleviating a labor shortage by keeping older workers on the job. Summerville writes that Japan already "has by far the highest participation rate of workers over the age of 60 of any industrialized country"—37 percent, compared to 6 percent in the United States and only 2 percent in France and Germany—a tribute to Japan's underdeveloped pension programs.[7]

Summerville's fears seem to me to be overdrawn. Japan definitely faces problems in supporting its elderly in the future, but probably not much of a problem in finding enough workers. The most efficient Japanese industries, such as automaking, already are highly automated and employ relatively few workers. In many companies, the tradition of lifetime employment has forced employers to find make-work jobs for underemployed workers, the so called "window tribe." Many other Japanese industries are notoriously inefficient. Its food industry, for instance, is only 33 percent as efficient as the American food industry, and its retailing sector isn't much better, only 43 percent as efficient as the American one.[8] These industries are deliberately kept inefficient to keep Japanese unemployment low. They could easily be modernized, freeing millions of workers for jobs in an economy beset by a shortage of labor.

Social Security and Snake Oil

In all these countries, "the key social policy concern . . . is whether society, and in particular the working population, will be able to or willing to bear the additional financing burden" of an aging population, reports the Organization for Economic Cooperation and Development. Most countries accept that society must carry this burden but haven't figured out how they are going to do it. The German system, despite its high costs, is still a national icon, and no one suggests throwing it out or even reforming it radically. But this seems to have more to do with national character and tradition than economics. In the United States, by contrast, Americans are seriously debating whether to junk their entire system and go to a new, riskier system based on the market.

If anything shows how different cultures lead to different economics, it is this question of pensions. Seen from Europe, the American debate about a system that—to outsiders—looks extremely strong and relatively inexpensive makes no sense at all. The solution to this puzzle lies in Americans' traditional scorn of government programs and the growing adoration of the market as the solution to all problems. A lot of snake oil is being peddled by participants in this debate, who know that only Americans are likely to swallow it.

Purveyors of this snake oil, such as the libertarian Cato Institute in Washington, D.C., and billionaire presidential candidate Steve Forbes, say the American Social Security system "is in profound crisis" (Cato) and "is going bust both morally and financially" (Forbes). Neither statement is remotely true, but they've been repeated so often that they have led to a broad belief that the vast federal pension program is near collapse. In one poll, which Cato loves to distribute, more young Americans said they believed in flying saucers than thought they'd get any money from Social Security when they retire. (Since 46 percent of them said they believed in flying saucers, this probably says more about young Americans and the education they received than it does about Social Security.)

Social Security, like public pension programs around the globe, has problems, but nothing that will pinch for thirty years or so and that cannot be fixed by a nip or a tuck before that pinch is felt. The problem, stated briefly, is this: American Social Security, like that in other countries, is basically a pay-as-you-go system. It is financed by payroll deductions of 12.4 percent, paid half by employees and half by employers. But it has one significant difference from those in other countries. Demographers, looking ahead, knew the time would come when there would be more retirees and fewer workers than now. So rates were set so that today's workers would pay in more than is strictly needed to pay for today's retirees; in effect, they prefunded part of their own retirement. The result is a "trust fund," a surplus that now amounts to about $70 billion per year. This is invested in government bonds, which help fund the federal deficit. The surplus will keep growing until about 2013, when it will peak at $1.3 trillion. Then, as baby boomers begin to retire in large numbers, the system will go into deficit, and that surplus will begin to shrink.

By 2029, the surplus will be gone. When reformers say that Social Security is "going broke," this is what they mean. There won't be any surplus anymore. But there will still be enough money coming in from current payroll deductions to pay 98 percent of all pensions. This deficit in the system, however, will be real, and it will grow. Sooner or later, Social Security will be in real trouble if nothing is done.

How to Fix Social Security

But something will be done, probably quite soon. Where Social Security is concerned, something is always being done. Ever since it began, Congress has tinkered with Social Security, raising a deduction here, increasing a benefit there. Demographers traditionally peer 75 years into the future; at that distance, the view is not always clear, and mistakes are made that must be corrected. But they have always been corrected in plenty of time. Critics of Social Security like to call it a "giant Ponzi scheme," meaning that its ability to pay past contributors depends on a never-ending flow of new contributions. But the constant tinkering by Congress has guaranteed that, for more than six decades, Social Security has been able to meet all its obligations and even raise the benefits to the point that America's elderly have one of the lowest poverty rates of any group in the population. A record like this could give Ponzi schemes a good name.

The projected shortfall by 2029 can be headed off now in a number of ways. Raising the retirement age to 70 would help. So would taxing Social Security benefits. So would ending the separate pension programs for state and local employees and bringing them into the federal system, which will almost certainly be done. So would recalculating retirement benefits. So would changing the way that inflation is calculated; lowering the consumer price index by 1 percent, as some economists want to do, would automatically lower the cost-of-living allowances that retirees get and would solve the problem at a stroke, although this handy tool is both mathematically suspect and politically dishonest.

Robert Kuttner has calculated that a return to real annual wage growth of 1.7 percent per year would also increase deductions and solve the problem forever. This 1.7 percent is, in fact, the average annual real wage growth over the past 75 years. Current official projections foresee a real annual wage growth of only 1 percent per year, which, as Kuttner points out, is becomingly modest but not necessarily realistic. He may be right, but only if the global economy relaxes its grip on wages in industrial countries. These wages have declined for the past 20 years because of the global drive for efficiency, and there is no reason to think this force will relent any time soon.[9]

A surer way to help Social Security would be to raise the cap on contributions. At the moment, wage earners' annual contributions apply to only their first $62,000 of income. This means that a worker making $62,000 pays 6.2 percent of her income while her boss making $620,000 pays only six-tenths of 1 percent of his. It's one of the most inequitable taxes around; raising the level would ease Social Security's problems while hitting the people most able to afford the pain.

There's another way. Henry Aaron and Barry Bosworth, two Brookings Institution economists, figure the shortfall could be solved for the next seventy-five years by increasing the contributions, which are currently 12.4 percent of income (split between employee and employer) by 2.2 percent. This could be done in stages—half a percent now, another half percent ten years from now, and so on.[10] A presidential commission appointed to study the future of Social Security rejected this approach as politically impossible in an America that has become positively allergic to taxes, even to keep its elderly off the poor farm. Citizens of other countries, of course, pay more than Americans toward this generational obligation. Americans, too, may accept a higher contribution once their prolonged dalliance with Reaganism ends.

The longer any solution is delayed, the more painful the fix. But anything done soon would guarantee the future of a system that has brought millions of elderly Americans out of poverty and solidified all Americans, young and old, in a common national purpose.

The Markets See a Bonanza

It is hard to think of this marginal, long-term problem as a crisis. But a well-financed campaign has begun to treat it as such. Using public alarm as a battering ram, this campaign aims to destroy the present Social Security system and set up a new market-based program in its place. It caught the ear of that presidential commission. A majority of the commission recommended a partial privatization, by taking some of the Social Security fund away from government bonds, which are safe but pay only about 2 percent per year after inflation, and investing them in the stock market, which has an historic return of about 6 to 7 percent.

The difference in potential return is so substantial that, at first glance, the privatization proposal seemed to make a lot of sense. The presidential commission's report came out during the prolonged bull market, making it look even better. Wall Street firms, which stand to reap a bonanza from the fees on an extra $150 billion per year in investments, began lobbying for the reform. From campuses to editorial pages, free marketeers began beating the drums for privatization.

But there were second thoughts. The privatization plan had lots of little problems and one big one. The little problems included the possibility that a prolonged dip in the market, as happened in the 1970s, could erode retirees' nest eggs; it's no help to know that the market will start growing again by and by if you need the money right now. In addition, the plan seemed to stack the deck against the poor, who need Social Security the most, because they could not afford the sophisticated investment advice available to the wealthy and would be more likely to fall for a sales pitch for penny stocks or Singapore derivatives. This could be avoided by letting the government invest the money, but then where would it go? Into politically connected companies? Tobacco stocks? Foreign economies?

Finally, there is the matter of a transition tax. Under privatization, each worker would have his or her own account to invest, which would grow over the years until the worker retires. This is fine for young workers, but there are millions of middle-aged and older workers who have invested in the pay-as-you-go system over the years and expect to get something from it when they retire. This system has to be funded, too. In other words, the reformers are talking about maintaining two systems, for several decades at least, and this isn't cheap. Even the advocates of privatization concede that there would have to be a special tax—sometimes called a "liberty tax"—of 1 percent or so, necessary to cover the $7 trillion that the transition would cost. But this ends the "crisis." A tax of this size would be enough to wipe out most of the projected deficit in the Social Security fund after 2030 and solve the problem.

What Is Social Security For?

The big problem is philosophical, not economic. Social Security is a great national pension fund intended to cushion everyone, especially the poor, from the shocks of old age. Its name is Social Security, not Social Maximum Return, and its purpose is to assure a minimum level of comfort, not wealth. It is a commitment that all working Americans make to each other, the sort of commitment that children make to their parents, generation after generation. It is the closest the United States comes to making its society into a family. In a nation that is fragmenting before the forces of economic change and globalization, this benefit should not be lightly discarded.

Yet privatization would discard this and would break the generational commitment. The universality of Social Security—the feeling that all elderly are in the same boat—would be lost and, with it, the willingness of wealthier taxpayers to keep supporting it. Social programs should be supported for no other reason than good citizenship, but that's not the way it works. Taxpayers have to see that government programs benefit everyone, or else they wither whenever the economy begins to tighten. This is what happened to welfare.

The privatization of Social Security would make it more lucrative but far riskier. The privatization campaign comes at a time when another source of security for the elderly—private pensions—is also under attack. Corporations, responding to the market's pressure to reduce costs, have reversed years of progress toward solid private pensions for their employees. The percentage of workers with employer-paid pensions dropped from 80 percent in 1985 to 56 percent in 1993.[11] This doesn't count the millions of workers who have lost their jobs and, with them, their pensions. A downsized middle manager who has set up shop as a self-employed consultant needs also to be a smart investor, or may never be able to afford to retire.

Just as important, if less noticed, is the shift of a majority of companies from defined-benefit pension systems to defined-contribution systems. A defined-benefit system—the traditional form of private pensions in the United States—means that employees are guaranteed a certain pension when they retire. Companies fund all or part of the pension fund and then invest it so there will be enough money to pay the pensions when they come due. If the investments do poorly, then the company has to top up the fund—a potential expense that few companies want these days. If they do well, that's just as bad, because the windfall creates a surplus of cash that can attract a hostile bid from a corporate raider.

Defined-contribution plans involve regular contributions into the fund, which is then invested. But benefits are no longer guaranteed. If the investments—often in the stock of the company itself—do well, then the retiree is ahead of the game. If they do badly, the retiree suffers. As with so much else in the modern economy, no promises are made. But these defined-contribution systems have become the pension of choice. As of 1995, 42 million Americans participated in defined contribution plans, against about 25 million in defined-benefit programs.

These programs can be run in conjunction with Employee Stock Ownership Plans (ESOP), which also depend on the value of the employer's stock for their value. Or there are 401(k) savings programs, often supplemented by employers, which can be invested in stocks, bonds, money market funds—or the employer's stock. About 75 percent of American workers belong to 401(k) systems. Many of those without these programs work for employers that have also dropped their traditional pension plans. In addition, employees may borrow from their 401(k) plans, and many do; some never repay. This is not possible with a traditional pension.

The picture is a grab bag of options that leave American retirements more confused—and much riskier—than ever before. First, Social Security may be privatized. Second, fewer employers offer company-sponsored pensions. Third, those that do are switching to riskier defined-contribution plans, with no guarantee of a set pension at the end. Fourth, employees can top up or replace their pensions with 401(k) plans, but not all of them do.

This element of risk is crucial. Once companies carried the risk of pension investments for their employees, but no longer. With defined-contribution plans, employees now bear the risk. But this erodes even further the social role of the corporation as a stable focus for the lives of its workers. Once upon a time, these workers counted on their employer for a regular paycheck and then, when that ended in retirement, for a regular pension. Security was both promised and delivered. In its place is a corporation that has become "a more fragile community," in the words of the *Financial Times* of London. "Is the company merely a bundle of assets with an income stream, a net present value and a market price? Or is it a social organism, part of a historical continuum stretching back to its founders and forward to those future employees who will carry on its name and values?"[12]

This move toward defined-contribution systems and toward private pensions is not limited to the United States. Both trends are taking place in Britain. Several European nations—Italy, France, the Netherlands, Belgium, Denmark—are experimenting with private programs as either a partial replacement for government programs or a supplement to them. Not surprisingly, American investment advisers are playing a major role in these nascent programs.

Pressure on Aging Minorities

Experimenting with pensions and Social Security can affect the retirement of anyone who expects them. But the impact is disproportionately large for poor families, and even more so for black and Hispanic households. A RAND study showed that the average American white household with one member in his or her fifties—in other words, in the preretirement years—has two-thirds of its total wealth in such assets as its home, savings, stocks, bonds, and the like; for these people, Social Security and pensions make up only one-third of their total wealth. The situation is reversed for blacks and Hispanics. Black households at this age have more than two-thirds of their wealth in Social Security and pensions; the percentage for Hispanic households isn't much less. Any decline in the value of the programs would be disastrous for these aging minorities.[13]

Despite this, the RAND study found that most persons in their fifties and sixties were saving enough for their retirement. Not so for younger generations. A number of studies have shown that the job and wage squeeze affecting American workers is having a major impact on their ability to save up some of life's rewards and make plans for their future. Sixty-year-olds and seventy-year-olds typically have more wealth of all sorts now than did sixty-year-olds and seventy-year-olds a decade or two ago. But below this age, Americans are falling behind. As you would expect, most fifty-year-olds have more wealth than they did when they were forty. But the problem is that they have *less* wealth than fifty-year-olds did in the 1980s or the 1970s. The same is true of forty-year-olds now, and thirty-year-olds. Each generation is poorer than the generation that preceded it.

Even in home ownership, the very symbol of American middle-class life, the trend is down. Home ownership as a whole declined in the 1980s, from 65.6 percent to 63.9 percent of all households—the first decade-long decline since the 1930s. Between 1983 and 1993, the percentage of sixty-year-old Americans owning their own homes went up. But for every age group below sixty, the rate went down.[14]

Given this decline in their ability to accumulate private wealth, younger Americans should be getting greater pension protection, not less. But the opposite is true. According to the RAND study, some 62 percent of all workers between thirty and thirty-five had private pension plans back in 1979; the percentage for workers aged twenty-five to thirty was about 52 percent. By 1993, the rates had fallen, to about 50 percent of workers in their thirties, and to about 40 percent for those in their late twenties.

Aging and the Global Markets

Not all of this, of course, can be charged to globalization or the pressures of global markets. The sheer mass of the baby boom generation would be enough on its own to strain any economy and its pension systems. But no economic or social trend happens in a vacuum. As we saw in earlier chapters, the people of the First World are living in the middle of a new industrial revolution that is upsetting virtually every structure and certainty erected since the war. Global capital markets, reinforced by global trade and global technology, are pushing employers everywhere into a race to the bottom, a frantic scramble to cut costs, reduce labor, raise profits, and increase their return to shareholders. This scramble takes different forms in different countries. In Japan, workers are still employed but often underemployed. In Europe, employed workers are secure, but unemployment is rife and younger workers in particular are despairing. In the United States, a turbulent economy is spinning workers in and out of jobs, to the point that security and stability have nearly disappeared.

Now even old age is becoming globalized and marketized. This gap in the average age of workforces in the First and Third Worlds is going to force changes not only in pension programs and retirement ages but also in whether aging workers can hold on to the higher pay and perks they have come to expect. Norbert Walter, the Deutsche Bank economist, warns, "If you have pay based on seniority, as the Japanese and Europeans do, then you're going to have massive difficulties with an aging population. Globalization gets into the picture here. If your average wage costs are exploding and the rest of the world is still juvenile, you've become less competitive."[15]

So the problems of aging and of pension security are as vulnerable to globalization as any other part of society. In an era when employers need to reduce costs, pension systems—both public and private—stand out as vast money trees ripe for the pruning. They inhale great sums to be spent on people who, by definition, no longer contribute to the bottom line. Yet they are becoming more important by the day for younger workers whose ability to save for their own futures is being undermined by the turmoil in their working lives.

In the United States in particular, the trends in Social Security are part of the other swings and lurches of a stormy economy: the widening divisions in society, the lack of social cohesion, the unwillingness of the rich to help support the poor. The question is why this should be so in the United States, and not elsewhere. The American debate over Social Security—whether it should be scrapped and replaced with a new market-based system—simply is not taking place in other countries.

"The demographic structure is much worse here [in Germany] than in the United States," said Karl Hinrichs of the Center for Social Policy Research in Bremen. "So why is there no intergenerational equity debate here, as you have in the States?"

Hinrichs cited several reasons, some political, some cultural. At one time, he said, the public pension systems in both countries existed outside politics. The social security systems in both countries worked automatically and were seldom questioned. Pension policy in both was set mostly by experts, insulated from political pressure. This arrangement broke down in the United States in the 1980s, when advocates of smaller government within the Reagan Administration tried to trim Social Security. They failed, but their attempt hurled the system into the political arena and ignited the debate. "There is something here that has to do with our political culture," Hinrichs went on:

> We have what we call the "moral economy" of aging. Older people have paid for these pensions. They've done what was expected of them, and they deserve what they get. But in the States, young people who suffer from low wages and bad job prospects are expected to finance the elderly now, without expecting to get benefits themselves. Your thirty-year-olds have less income than the previous generation, so you have this large inequality between the age groups.[16]

Economic hard times cause social resentments, and Germany is not immune to this. But resentment there tends to exist more between the employed and the unemployed, and between native Germans and immigrants from the east, than between generations.

There have been suggestions for reforms of the German government pension program, but no pressure yet for privatizing it. Instead, one suggested German reform reflects a peculiarly German problem, the nation's low birthrate. Under this reform, Germans would collect pensions only if they make two contributions—in money and in children. Childless Germans, or those with only one child, will be judged to have cheated the future, because they failed to put their ante into the intergenerational pot. Therefore, they'll get no pensions.[17]

The Elderly Are Not Helpless

It is tempting to see this intergenerational battle as a one-sided affair, with the young taking their revenge on their elders for their postwar prosperity and denying pensions, health care, even a seat on the bus to these oldsters, now helpless in their dotage. But the older generation is not so defenseless as that, at least in the mass.

As we saw, the over-sixties, as they age, are becoming one of the biggest groups in the population—over one-third of their societies in some countries, such as Germany and Japan. They generally have more money than their juniors and give it to political parties and causes. They have more time and spend it in political campaigns. Of all the age groups, they vote most enthusiastically, possibly because the democracy of the postwar years has been so good to them. If roused, they are capable of turning into a ferocious single-interest bloc, and that single interest, such as pensions or health care, usually has something to do with age.

No politician anywhere is likely to ignore this bloc. When the Reagan administration tried to tamper with Social Security in 1981, it was abandoned by Republicans in Congress listening to elderly voters at home. As one congressman told David Stockman, then director of the Office of Management and the Budget and a leader of this putative reform, "My phones are ringing off the hook. I've got thousands of 60-year-old textile workers who think it's the end of the world. What the hell am I supposed to tell them?"[18]

No other nation has an organized bloc of senior citizens with anything near the power of the American Association of Retired Persons, the largest organization in the United States. But seniors everywhere are willing to make their voices heard. When the French government tried to raise retirement ages for train drivers, among others, public support for the drivers forced it to back down. When the German government tried to raise the retirement age for both men and women, 350,000 persons traveled to Bonn to protest. It was Bonn's biggest protest since World War II, and while the proposal for men went through, the proposal for women had to be delayed.

As we've seen, the solution to the problems raised by the graying of the First World is not at all clear. Every solution creates another problem. Raising the retirement age to lower pension costs only blocks the workplace door for younger workers, raising unemployment costs. The young, hungry workers of the Third World cannot be denied. But the older, comfortable workers of the First World have earned their comforts and possess the political clout to keep them. Between societies and within societies across the globe, the young and the old are fighting over the future.

PART IV

Epilogue

10. HARD CHOICES

WHEN I WAS A correspondent in Moscow in the late 1960s, my family and I lived in an apartment building on Kutuzovsky Prospekt, the broad boulevard that starts at the Kremlin and runs across the Russian plain to Poland and on to Berlin. A Stalinesque hotel, inhuman in its bulk, stood across the street, and a number of shops—a cafe, toy store, shoe shop, souvenir shop—lined the sidewalks outside our compound.

I returned to Moscow from time to time over the years. On one visit in the late 1980s, after Mikhail Gorbachev came to power but before the Soviet Union collapsed, I took a walk along Kutuzovsky Prospekt to see what had changed in the twenty years since I lived there. The answer was, nothing. There were the same shops—the cafe with its steaming windows, the dispirited toy store, the shoe shop with its plastic shoes, the souvenir shop with its nesting *matryoshka* dolls, the hulking hotel. Their signs were the same, and so were the displays in their windows. The goods looked the same, unaltered and unmodernized over two decades; for all I knew, they were the very same items, sitting unsold on the shelves for twenty years. Even the prices had not changed. In 1965 I had bought a wonderfully warm rabbit-fur hat for the equivalent of $18. In 1987 I bought exactly the same kind of hat for exactly the same price.

This was stability squared and cubed. Most Westerners thought of the Soviets as a bunch of revolutionary bomb throwers, but the truth was just the opposite. The Soviet Union was the most conservative society on earth. No, conservative is the wrong word. This was a stagnant society, utterly unchanging. Stores never changed, never went out of business, never threw out old styles, never brought in new styles. New jobs were created if people needed work, not because they were necessary. No one was fired or transferred. No factory ever closed or made something different from the product it produced the day before.

Everyone had a job, a paycheck, a roof over his or her head, food on the table. It was a dull job, a mean paycheck, a leaky roof, bad food, but they were guaranteed. Russia then was a society based on total safety, total stability, without change or risk or innovation.

Mikhail Gorbachev tried to reform this economic system by scraping the barnacles off its hull. The poor man never realized that, after seventy years of communism, the barnacles were all that was left. When he removed them, the water rushed in and the ship sank. And that was the end of the Soviet Union.

It often seems to me that the United States and, to a lesser degree, its First-World allies are mirror images of the old Soviet Union. If the Soviet Union depended on stability, the First World enshrines change. If the Soviets prized predictability and total protection for workers, the West and Japan worship innovation and risk.

The Soviets carried stability to the point of paralysis and collapsed, but in the First World, and particularly in the United States, change is in the saddle and guiding events. Global capital markets prowl the world on a relentless search for best practice, lowest costs, highest efficiency, and biggest profits. Winners are richly rewarded, and losers ruthlessly punished. Today's winner often is tomorrow's loser. Global trade pits $1-a-day Chinese workers against $20-per-hour Western workers. Global technology ensures that the West's onetime advantages—skills, training, higher productivity, sheer proximity to the customer—are advantages no longer.

This global economy demands constant change, constant innovation, constant cost cutting, constant turmoil, constant hiring, constant firing, constant risk, constant winning, constant losing. No society can live with this much instability, any more than a society can live without a steady flow of change and new ideas. If the Soviet Union failed to renew its inert society with change, the challenge for the First World is just the opposite: to temper change with stability, to tame the tyranny of the global market and permit change while ensuring its benefits to the people who must live with it.

Where Markets Belong

Believers in the market insist that the growth of globalism demonstrates the genius of capitalism at its keenest. In this view, markets are perfect. Markets reflect supply and demand at work. They exist on the abiding search for maximum utility between buyer and seller. They are the center point where the interests of buyer and seller meet and are consummated. By this reckoning, markets, being the common ground between two rational and informed persons, are always efficient, and the price they establish is always the right one—indeed, the only conceivable price at that time. If capitalism is the economic system that delivers the highest standard of living to the most people, then markets are the mechanism of this system and must be allowed to have their way. The most liberated market is the best market and, in the long run, the most beneficial market for everyone.

This is to argue that if liberty is preferable to slavery, then unbridled liberty is ideal. Or, as the social philosopher Mae West put it, "Too much of a good thing is terrific." But unbridled liberty is another word for anarchy, and unbridled markets are nothing more than the jungle.

Robert Kuttner, in his excellent book *Everything for Sale*, demolishes the idea that markets are perfect, or even efficient, compared to what he calls the "second best" outcomes of a mixed economy.[1] Such an economy lets markets do what they do best, which is allocating goods within a society through the price mechanism. Prices are the way that buyers talk to sellers. Through this "conversation," buyers tell sellers what they want, and sellers deliver it to them. If this doesn't work perfectly, it works much better than any other system yet tried. I recall another day in Moscow spent at the State Pricing Board, where I was shown shelf after shelf of short, fat books crammed with lists of tiny figures, each representing the set price for every item in the Soviet economy. Staggering in its assumption of omniscience, this attempt to outthink the market was as much a cause of the Soviet collapse as those drab, unchanging stores along Kutuzovsky Prospekt.

But, as Kuttner points out, it is one thing to give the market its due and quite another to entrust it with the running of our lives. The efficient allocation of goods is necessary to prosperity, but it has nothing to do with such issues as decency and fairness. There are areas, such as education and religion, where the market is not trusted, and others, such as public transportation and utilities, where it is permitted to intrude in some countries and not in others. In Germany, wage setting is only partially the task of the market. In America, public radio and television are an important balance to the private media. In Japan, as we have seen, financial markets, ostensibly free, are heavily monitored by the government. In no country are banks totally unregulated, nor is the right of doctors to practice unpoliced. The alternative would be a savage place indeed. A nation where the market made all decisions on health, education, protection from crime, and the safety of savings would be a Darwinian bearpit, uninhabitable except by the wealthiest, and after a while, not even by them.

Beyond that, markets by their nature cannot deal with the questions of morality, decency, and the ability of free people to choose the kind of lives they want, instead of submitting to the dictatorship of distant and impersonal economic forces with no interest in the quality of the civilizations they affect. The economist Robert Heilbroner writes, "It is part of the nature of capitalism that the circuit of capital has no intrinsic moral dimension, no vision of art or idea aside from the commodity form in which it is embodied. In this setting, ideas thrive, but morality languishes."[2]

Can Democracy Survive the Market?

Market theory is beyond the scope of this book. Instead, we have been concerned with how the globalization of money markets and trade, propelled by technology, is affecting Japan, the United States, and Western Europe. Especially, we have studied the ability of those nations, their governments, and their people to control or channel the impact of these markets so they can benefit from the global economy without losing the economic gains of the past fifty years or the stability and democratic freedoms that these gains have supported.

During this half century, the people of each of these countries and regions reached the highest standard of living in their history. These economic gains and their blessings bloomed from market economies, which differ in every nation but are alike in their trust in the market as the best mechanism available to meet human needs and wants. Each country has limited, regulated, and directed the free market to its own needs. Each country has adjusted its treatment of the market constantly, while never abandoning it as the economic basis of its civilization. Each has become a center of finance, has led in the development of technology, and has prospered mightily from trade. None wants to abandon the market, close its borders to trade, or smash its technology in a spasm of Luddite reaction.

Yet a backlash against globalization is already visible, especially in the United States and Western Europe. If the markets have their way, the blessings of postwar capitalism can be eroded so drastically, and so many people can be hurt, that this backlash could turn into a rage against the market, trade, and technology. Any economic system in a democracy exists at the sufferance of the people. If the people and governments of the First World want to preserve what they have achieved, and hope to extend these achievements to the people of the Third World, then they must insist that the global market serve humanity, not the other way around.

Even the drumbeaters for globalization admit this process will produce more losers than winners any time soon. Lowell Bryan and Diana Farrell predict, "The dichotomy between the losers and the winners is likely to be enormous and to be the source of major social conflict and regional strife."[3] Peter Drucker warns of "a new class conflict between the large minority of knowledge workers and the majority of people."[4]

This means that the losers will be in the majority, and in a democracy, the majority rules. Western democracy, then, will become the tyranny of the losers. This, obviously, invites a backlash that could destroy not only the global market but all that international trade and cooperation have achieved in the past half century. The alternative is an end to democracy and the rule of the market, a global economic oligarchy.

In Chapter 2, we saw that the most vigorous trading nations have also had the most generous social welfare programs, to protect their people from the sharp edges of the market. This social protection has been vital in the winning of broad political support for growing trade and foreign investment. "Social spending has had the important function of buying social peace," according to Dani Rodrik. "The social welfare state is the flip side of the open economy."[5] But the global capital market and the global bond market already are persuading deficit-ridden governments to cut back this welfare spending. This spending can be financed by higher taxes, but with corporations able to dodge these taxes, the entire cost falls not on the global citizens but on those left behind. "Once globalization moves beyond a certain point, the government can no longer finance the requisite income transfers because the tax base becomes too footloose."[6] This means that, as the global economy grows, the pain it inflicts will be felt even more by workers and the poor—the losers. Something has to give.

"Either democracy has to be tamed for the sake of the market, or the market has to be tamed for the sake of democracy," writes David Marquand, a British political scientist. "Society cannot indefinitely tolerate alienation, social fragmentation, and insecurity on the present scale. Globally and nationally, we shall sooner or later have to choose between the free market and the free society."[7]

Global Anarchy

Globalization already has weakened the ability of governments to control their own economies. But the nation-state is not yet outdated and can do much within its borders to affect the future. Japan is doing this already, and Europe is seeking ways to cushion the impact of globalization. Even in this global age, governments still can wield taxes, laws, labor regulations, and corporate codes to ease the transition to this new global era; some of these weapons will be discussed later in this chapter.

But much of the global market, by definition, operates in a global realm that ignores frontiers and scoffs at the abilities of individual governments to regulate it. William Greider writes that the global economy is literally out of control: "Commerce and finance have leapt inventively beyond the existing order and existing consciousness of peoples and societies: [this] wondrous machine, with all its great power and creativity, appears to be running out of control toward some sort of abyss."[8]

No modern nation permits an unregulated economy. Each nation polices its financial markets against fraud, insists that its banking system protect the savings of investors, establishes standards of safety in its factories and health in its products, and levies taxes on businesses to help pay for its civilization. So long as economies remained mostly national in nature, they played by recognized and agreed rules set by national governments that enforced civility, protected society, and kept the law of the jungle at bay.

That is no longer true. The global economy is anarchy on a worldwide scale, fed by a $400 trillion annual war chest. It is bound by no global rules. Instead, it makes its own rules or seeks out places where it can do business with the fewest rules. Capital markets operate in cyberspace, using space-age technology and an unending proliferation of complex speculative instruments. These markets demand that companies cut costs to the minimum, eliminate work-ers, slash wages, produce as cheaply as possible. Forced by these demands and armed with labor-saving technology, these companies jettison workers at home and replace them with Third-World work-ers paid in pennies. When the workers begin to demand dollars instead of pennies, the companies can move on to some other coun-try where labor is cheap, standards low, and laws banning sweat-shop conditions nonexistent.

The sheer fact that these things can be done means they will be done. But the First-World nations have it in their power to control this process to achieve two great aims: first, the preservation of their own civilizations, which have brought so much good to so many peo-ple, and second, the orderly extension of these blessings to the Third World. No nation with any pretense to morality can slam the door on the poorer nations or declare that prosperity, having come this far, will go no further. The wealth must be shared. Fortunately, in a healthy global economy, this wealth will grow, giving everyone a slice of an ever-expanding pie.

The First-World nations are still the engines of the global econ-omy and the repositories of the world's political power. Working together, they can shape the future, but it will require a coopera-tion and enlightened cohesion far beyond anything they have ever shown before.

There is much that each nation can do on its own. But the preser-vation of the First World's many civilizations is possible only if the various nations work together to frame a cooperative global response to the global economic challenge. Much of what I will suggest will be impossible unless the nations cooperate, not only to write new laws but to set up new global institutions to enforce them.

There is today no global law encoding this response, nor any global equivalent to the national institutions that enforce laws and regulations on business. In the United States, these institutions include the Securities and Exchange Commission, Federal Trade Commission, Commodity Futures Trading Commission, Internal Revenue Service, and similar bodies. It is impossible to imagine business in the United States without these regulatory and taxing bodies. Businesses may complain about them, but no honest and decent businessperson would abolish them, for the simple reason that they enable honest and decent people to survive. Without them, business would be no more than mud wrestling.

Sand in the Gears

The first and primary challenge is from the global capital markets, because they are the most developed segment of the global economy, and their power drives all else before it. As Will Hutton writes in *Foreign Affairs*, "The freedoms celebrated by the extraordinarily well-paid denizens of the international dealing rooms now threaten the capacity of the world to sustain a free trade regime and promote economic growth. The world has once again invented an international financial system that is a source of economic instability."[9] These markets trade more in two weeks than is needed for all the world's trade and investment in a year.

All the rest—the other fifty weeks—is speculation. Some of the speculation is useful: hedges against currency fluctuations, for instance, often enable real trade or investment to take place. Some traders estimate that it takes two or three dollars in useful speculation to make one dollar in trade or investment happen. If total world trade and investment amount to about $6.7 trillion per year, this means useful speculation of about $20 trillion. Let's round these figures—trade, investment, and hedging—up to $30 trillion. All the rest, some $370 trillion, is gambling, a speculative economy that outweighs the real economy by 12 to 1.

Commissions and profits on this speculation are tremendous, which is why it grows and why any attempt to control it will be met with some very well-financed opposition. These markets cannot and should not be closed down; those two weeks fuel the world's business. The quarrel is not with the markets themselves but with their speed and size. They are $370 trillion juggernauts, massive waves of money, out of control and steamrolling any nation that gets in their way, as Southeast Asians learned in the autumn of 1997. Even free marketeers such as Alan Greenspan, the president of the Federal Reserve Bank, have admitted that this untethered power frightens them. The future of the global economy demands that these markets be slowed and restricted. Some "sand in the gears," in the words of Nobel prize–winning economist James Tobin, would benefit everyone.

Tobin himself has proposed the most practical immediate solution, the so-called "Tobin tax" on foreign exchange transactions. This would be a tax of about 0.1 or 0.2 percent on all such transactions. Most of these transactions take place at the margin—that is, they are lightning short-term deals intended to take advantage of minuscule differences or "anomolies" in foreign exchange quotations, which are usually around 0.1 percent. Therefore, even a tax this small would erase the gain from most short-term transactions and make them meaningless. A Tobin tax would eliminate much short-term trading and, in so doing, would reduce the mammoth flows of hot money that currently reward short-term speculation over long-term investment and have such an outsize impact on government fiscal policies. A tax of this size would have almost no impact on longer-term flows, so money needed by the real economy will still be there.

Theoretically, a Tobin tax could raise $300 to $600 billion per year—enough to make a serious dent in First-World budget deficits, solve the United Nations' financial problems, or finance many of the world's other needs. Actually, the amount would be considerably smaller. If the tax works, the global financial flows would slow down, and any levy on them would probably raise no more than $150 billion or so—still a useful sum.

Other ideas have been suggested, including a 100 percent tax on short-term speculative profits, proposed by the legendary investor Warren Buffett. The idea behind all of them is the same: to slow down or eliminate speculation by taking away its profit.

The monetary crisis that swept Asia in late 1997 stimulated new thinking on sand in the gears. The crisis itself was no suprise: many bankers knew that countries such as Thailand and Malaysia were living beyond their means. The surprise was the speed and power of the capital markets as they swept through the region, laying waste to whole economies and engulfing countries such as South Korea and Indonesia whose problems were probably solvable, given time. But time is one thing the markets, ever vigilant and ever punishing, will not give. In the wake of the crisis, Michel Camdessus, the managing director of the International Monetary Fund, mused publicly about the need to reduce the amount of money at the markets' command. And even officials of the U.S. Federal Reserve Bank, ever deferential to the markets, suggested privately that raising the "cost of transactions" wouldn't hurt, possibly with a Tobin tax.

Nay-sayers insist a Tobin tax would never work because the markets would simply move to some tax haven, like the Cayman Islands. They're right that all the major trading centers would have to agree to levy this tax. If a big one, like New York or London, refused to go along, the tax would have no chance. But the fact is that the whole future of a stable global economy depends on a number of agreements between the major nations. If they cannot do this, then the game is already lost. The history of diplomacy and international politics shows that governments can agree when the threat is great enough, as it is now.

If traders tried to book their deals through the Cayman Islands, the tax could be levied where the trader is sitting, which is certain to be in one of the major centers. Theoretically, all the traders could move to the Caymans. In fact, this is an expensive proposition, and these small tax shelters could not conceivably support an army of traders. If they tried, the major governments could simply hit deals involving these havens with punitive taxes.

There is a more important point to this objection. It presumes that businesspeople operating in global markets are basically outlaws whose aim is to stay one jump ahead of the tax man. In fact, anyone with experience in dealing with businesspeople, bankers, investors, and other members of the market knows that most of them are honest citizens with no taste for the jungle. If the jungle is all there is, they must play by its rules or perish. But virtually all of them prefer a game with rules, a positive-sum game in which all sides win. Many executives I know are as distressed by the current atmosphere of market-driven downsizing and restructuring as their employees are. They got into business both to make money and to do some good, by providing goods and jobs for society. They are genuinely proud that their efforts put bread on the tables of their employees. Most scorn the raiders of the boardroom or the postpubescent cowboys of the trading rooms. It is my guess that any attempt by the major governments to return some civility and control to global markets would find surprisingly large support within business itself.

A Global Euro

A more long-term goal is to stabilize the major currencies, to reduce the wide swings in their values on which the money markets feed. The European Union has already begun this, through the agreement by most of its members to keep their currencies fluctuating against each other within narrow bands. The aim, as described in an earlier chapter, is to eliminate these fluctuations entirely as a step toward the creation of a single European currency. The birth of the Euro will kill off trading within European currencies and will no doubt put some traders out of business. This is one reason why the framers of the Euro expect a furious attack from the markets when the currencies are aligned. No trader believes the EU can carry this off. Speculators will bet heavily in an attempt to drive the currencies apart; the contest is crucial, and the profits could be huge.

This is why Germany, France, and other prospective members of the Euro have been aligning their economic policies. They hope that if their inflation rates, spending habits, budget deficits, national debts, and other "fundamentals" are coordinated, then their currencies can be coordinated, too. This coordination is written into the criteria that the Maastricht Treaty set for membership.

If there is any future for a world currency, then the Americans, Japanese, Europeans, and other major nations first must coordinate their economic and fiscal policies, as the Europeans have been doing. Paul Volcker, the former Federal Reserve chairman, has called for coordination of this sort within an agreement to limit currency fluctuation.[10] In fact, this is already happening under the impact of global markets, especially the bond markets. Across the nations of the First World, inflation rates, government deficits, national debts, and other major economic indicators are converging.

The fact that the Europeans have been moving toward a single currency proves that it is not beyond the wit or persistence of strong, determined nations. To expand this across the oceans is no small task. It means the United States would have to raise its taxes and the Europeans lower theirs toward some international mean while Japan opened its markets and cut its Ministry of Finance down to size. It would mean that these and other policies would no longer be set solely in Washington or Tokyo, but in cooperation and compromise with other nations. It probably would mean the creation of a form of a global central bank, much as the EU is setting up a European central bank in Frankfurt.

Setting the Rules

This is just the beginning of the international cooperation that is needed and will come if global markets are to be controlled. At the moment, multinational companies move components of products from one country to another, producing here and assembling there, and assign prices to each step according to the tax rates in each country.

Through clever bookkeeping, they can avoid taxes in high-tax countries and pay them in countries that are willing to lower rates for foreign investors or look the other way if the books are cooked. This is tax dodging on a global scale and, like other parts of life in the jungle, is not something that most of these companies can be proud of.

An international corporate tax code, administered by an international form of the IRS, is needed to ensure that companies, as citizens, pay the dues of citizenship. Rodrik has suggested taxation of these footloose corporations "at the global level, with revenue sharing among nations."[11] At the least, the nations of the world should swap tax information much more extensively than they do. Most major industrial nations already do this, and the practice must be extended to the industrializing nations of the Third World, where much of the tax evasion is going on.

This in turn would require companies to open their books and to practice other forms of transparency that the SEC regulations and other American laws force on companies operating within the United States. Again, this would require international laws on corporate reporting, enforced by an international SEC. This SEC could set the rules for global stock and financial trading, as it and the CFTC do now in the United States. Such international rules would prevent repetitions of the Barings incident, in which the Japanese government banned trading in derivatives based on the Nikkei average of the Tokyo Stock Exchange, only to see this trading decamp to Singapore, where Nick Leeson, the rogue derivatives trader, gambled his bank into bankruptcy.

Some of this cooperation and coordination of global institutions is taking place, quietly and behind the scenes. The United States and its allies in the Group of Seven meet regularly to try to coordinate policy, but this coordination is loose and its decisions nonbinding. In Basel, Switzerland, the Bank for International Settlements has set up a code of core principles, nonbinding but effective, for global bank supervision. Stock market regulators around the world, urged on by the U.S. Securities and Exchange Commission, are beginning work on a simple code of global principles to run their markets. American accounting principles are conquering the world, because any foreign company that wants to be listed on the New York Stock Exchange must abide by them. American laws are beginning to dominate the growing practice of private arbitration of international commercial disputes. As they do, U.S. commercial law becomes global commercial law.

The United States and other wealthy nations, meeting at the Organization for Economic Cooperation and Development (OECD) in Paris, are writing a treaty intended to protect First-World corporate investment abroad. This treaty, like much of the other coordination going on, establishes a bill of rights for investors but pointedly excludes protection for workers, the environment, or indeed for the countires where the investment takes place.

There will be more of this, some led by governments, some led by private business, some well planned, some ad hoc. But firm and binding regulation, of the sort that will protect the public, is far beyond the scope of existing institutions.

The International Monetary Fund, created after the war to promote currency stability, now spends most of its time persuading Third-World debtor nations to restructure their economies to protect foreign lenders. Like other UN agencies, it is ill-suited for the task of overseeing the global economy. The OECD exists to study the economies of the leading industrial nations and recommend policy to them. It, too, was created in another time for another purpose but might be the base of a global SEC: at the least, it is a congenial place for the First World to meet to negotiate agreements like the new investment treaty.

Most likely, though, brand-new institutions must be formed, and a new Bretton Woods–type conference must be held to form them. Most of the great international institutions invented after World War II—the IMF, the World Bank, GATT, the OECD—were developed under American guidance. They were born at a time when the United States was the *hegemon*, the one great economic and political power, of the noncommunist world. Once again, the United States is a hegemon, even if this hegemony is limited by the power of Europe and Japan and will be challenged, sooner or later, by China and other Third-World powers. In this atmosphere, the United States must lead but it cannot dictate. If new institutions are to be created, this creation must be a joint production of the United States, the European Union, Japan, and the emerging Third-World nations.

Apart from trade agreements, the history of the ability of the major nations to set rules governing themselves is not bright. There is one exception which proves it can be done. In 1988 the United States, Europe, and Japan agreed that their banks had to keep minimum ratios of capital to loans. Capital is the reserve fund that banks must keep to absorb bad loans; if this ratio is too small, bad loans could force banks to fail. In the 1980s, banks were still in their go-go years of global lending, while the world debt crisis had increased the risk of failure. To prevent this, the major nations, working through the Bank for International Settlements in Basel, set new minimum capital reserve standards. The move was directed mostly at Japan, where banks, informally backed by the promise of a government bailout, were keeping reserves far below prudent levels. The Americans and Europeans pressured the Japanese into accepting the new standards, which exist to this day. One expert, Wall Street analyst Henry Kaufman, wrote in 1992 that the major nations should go further and create "a new official (global) institution . . . that will monitor the behavior of financial institutions and markets, and that will set uniform requirements for capital, for trading, for reporting and for accounting."[12]

Aficionados of the markets would complain that all this global control will reduce their efficiency. Indeed it would; it's the efficiency of these markets that is causing most of the trouble.

With this efficiency comes a turmoil and uncertainty that, as it affects millions of lives, becomes too much to bear. Uncertainty, of course, is endemic to the human condition. Kierkegaard wrote that we must live forward but can only understand backward. We cannot remove uncertainty, but we need to make it tolerable. As the late economist Hyman P. Minsky wrote, "When uncertainty leads to an unsatisfactory result, then it becomes the duty of society in general to protect its citizens against the consequences: a sacrifice of narrow technical efficiency may be called for. The aim of policy is to assure that the economic prerequisites for sustaining the civil and civilized standards of an open liberal society exist. . . . If it is necessary to give up a bit on market efficiency or aggregate income, in order to contain democracy-threatening uncertainty, then so be it."[13]

Beyond the markets, people in all countries will scream that these proposals would rob the United States and other nations of their economic sovereignty. To these patriots, I can only say good morning. That sovereignty they value so highly vanished years ago into the growing global economy. France discovered this when it tried to run its own economic policy in 1983 and ended up in retreat. Japan discovered this in the 1970s when the "Nixon *shokkus*" that destroyed the Bretton Woods system forced it to raise the value of its precious yen. The United States discovered this in 1987, when the decisions of Japanese bond traders caused the Black Monday crash on Wall Street, and again in the 1990s when global bond markets persuaded President Clinton that it was more important to gut the welfare program than to build his own version of a Great Society.

Saving Trade

Trade is a separate problem and one that the world is not close to solving. Periodic rounds of trade talks since the war have lowered tariffs to insignificant levels and have opened markets around the world for goods, many of them produced by First-World nations like the United States. But GATT and its successor, the World Trade Organization, never were able to solve the problem exemplified by Japan, in which a mercantilist country could run an aggressive trade policy without breaking world trade rules, literally destroying whole industries in other countries while these countries were prevented from any defense of their own economies. This situation, which has eroded political support for trade in the West, is about to be magnified by the arrival of China on the world trading scene. China already has signaled that it has learned the Japanese lesson and intends to protect its own vast domestic market while using low-wage labor to attack markets abroad.

If Japan was a problem, China will be a catastrophe. It seems impossible that the world trade system, with all its benefits, can withstand an assault of this sort. Economist Richard Koo maintains, "The free trade system has lasted this long only because China and India are not in it. If China plays the game like the Japanese have, the system is not going to last without safeguards." [14] The major nations must now begin planning new rules to limit aggressive exports of this sort and to demand strict reciprocity—equal access to the markets of China and other developing nations in return for access to Western markets. This is, of course, both protectionism and managed trade, and will be attacked as such by purists who consider anything less than free trade a sin. But trade is an economic issue, not a theological one. The First-World nations have civilizations worth protecting. If the price of that protection is some protectionism aimed at global predators, it seems folly not to pay it. World trade, as I noted in an earlier chapter, is a lot hardier than its defenders claim it is, and will survive this sort of management. What it will not survive is the impoverishment of the First-World nations that created it.

The best solution is continued vigorous trade between countries that are, like the First World, at fairly equal stages of economic development, enhanced by negotiations to open markets that are still closed. The creation of a Transatlantic Free Trade Area (TAFTA), linking the North American and European economics in a free trade zone, would profit everyone. At the same time, regional trade areas—such as the European Common Market, NAFTA, and the South American Mercosur—would bring neighboring countries closer together. Such areas increase trade but are limited if the partners—such as the United States and Mexico—are far apart in economic development. Trade outside these areas should be encouraged, but within rules to ensure that it is not destroyed by a political backlash. The WTO already has escape clauses and safeguards that allow countries to limit imports in order to protect threatened industries. The WTO members could soften the harshest blows of trade by agreeing, formally or informally, to permit wider and easier use of these safeguards.

Beyond that, the trading nations may have to insist on reciprocity, especially toward nations like Japan or China that carry out aggressive trade policies, to force mercantilist nations to open their markets. The American Chamber of Commerce in Japan studied forty-five major trade agreements between the United States and Japan from 1980 to 1996. It concluded that the best results embodied specific goals, numerical targets, and clear measurements, to compel Japan to accept American goods. The Japanese oppose these goals and targets, probably because they *are* so effective, but they are one way to crack a closed and mercantilist economy. Vague agreements reached for reasons of political harmony do little good at all, the study said. The same conclusions will need to be applied to trade with China.[15]

Other rules could provide for a controlled but increasing access to First-World markets for Third-World industries paying vastly lower wages. This would ensure that these industries are allowed to grow, without destroying their First-World competitors overnight.

This is not free trade as taught in the textbooks. Some of it would require a rewriting of WTO rules, or at least an agreement to break those rules. The alternative is worse. It implies that the philosophy of free trade and comparative advantage, created when the Industrial Revolution was just dawning, can still apply to a global economy. Those who believe this will sacrifice the good for the best. Instead, it may be necessary to limit trade in order to save it.

Inventing the Future

The news of the demise of the nation-state is both premature and exaggerated. Within their borders, governments can judge the needs of their people and take steps to meet them.

These needs differ from country to country. The United States is suffering a surfeit of change, individual success, and short-term gain, and must find a way to inject stability, generosity, and the long-term needs of society. Otherwise, it courts chaos.

Europe, based on collective stability and long-term concerns, must accommodate change and find the flexibility to meet the demands of a rapacious global market without succumbing to it. Otherwise, it courts stagnation.

Japan, fixated on protection from a hostile world and an aggressive mercantilism fed by a national paranoia, must find a way to meet that world halfway and to assume its international obligations without upsetting the delicate balance of its insular society. Otherwise, it courts isolation.

Each must find its own future based on its own past. The United States cannot create a Japanese-style society of consensus and conformity, any more than Japan can adopt European or American habits of individualism and citizenship based on events, from the Magna Carta to the Enlightenment, that passed it by. Each is a distinct society, with its own culture and history that, over the centuries, have served it too well to be sacrificed to one great, steamrollering global market. Yet that market exists and is growing, and the only successful societies of the future will be those that find, within themselves, the resources to exploit it.

Japan: One-Way Globalization

The balance of Japan's society will be hard to keep in a globalizing world. Its manufacturing sector is strong and, given its lead in high-tech, high-profit goods, should remain strong. But Japan faces severe pressure from world trade. It is tempting to say that, one of these days, the United States will tire of funding the surpluses that enable the Japanese to maintain full employment. But the United States has made so many empty threats over the years that the Japanese find the American menace "about as frightening as walking through a zoo of caged lions," as one Japanese business leader told me.

The real threat comes from China. The United States cannot possibly take all the exports that China plans to produce, nor accept the
trade deficits that this implies. At that point, China—and also Southeast Asia and India—will seek another market of last resort, and the
obvious candidate is Japan. Japan has too much invested in these
countries and lies too close to China to risk the kind of trade resentments it has built with the United States. Japan will learn that it must
open its markets to Asian goods or retreat into isolation. These foreign goods will lower Japanese prices and cut into the profits that
enable the Japanese economy to employ inefficient workers at high
wages. So long as these Asians do not compete with Japan in services or high-tech goods, Japan can keep its system afloat. But this
won't last forever.

So many foreign commentators have predicted that one threat or
another would spell the end of Japan Inc. that a similar prediction,
like this one, cannot be made with much conviction. In one sense,
Japan's economy is a rigid one depending on closed markets, high
prices, and inefficient labor—all practices that any Western economist
would call a recipe for decline. Yet Japan also remains a marvelously
flexible society, able to accommodate external threats without changing the basic nature of its civilization. A low birthrate and the
approaching decline of the workforce means it should be able to keep
most of its men employed, if not its women. It is positioned to dominate the markets of China and Southeast Asia for cars and other
goods for years to come. It has never sought to turn its economic
might into political power, so it is quite ready to sacrifice diplomatic
clout—through a permanent seat on the U.N. Security Council, for
instance—if the price is surrender to Western trade demands. If an
invasion of Asian goods reduces Japan's trade surplus, it still has its
vast domestic savings as a reserve for investment. This reserve ensures
that, while Japanese industry will make more use of global capital
markets in the future, it will not be ruled by them to the same degree
as are industries in low-savings nations, like the United States.

Japan sees globalization as a one-way process, with Japanese out-
ward investment and exports to the world, and as little inward investment and imports as possible. It intends to change as much as necessary
to stay as it is. It has no intention of becoming like the United States
or, indeed, any other society. It has maintained this policy through
external shocks, including its utter defeat in World War II. The global
economy may finally break up Japan Inc. But don't bet on it.

Europe: Seeking the Balance

Neither Europe's politics nor its treasury can afford continuing double-digit employment. That the unemployed are not yet mutinous is due to a welfare state that ensures joblessness doesn't equal poverty. But the cost of this welfare state already is high and, as the Europeans struggle to reduce budget deficits, no longer supportable. Job creation and economic growth are needed, but are not going to come from the traditional sources of government spending and deficits. France is under pressure to cut back its pervasive government bureaucracy. The traditional German mesh of government, business, and labor is being unraveled by the global market. At the least, nationwide wage bargaining is becoming a thing of the past. But even the captains of German industry say that the nation's Social Market Economy is too valuable to lose. There remains a powerful incentive within most European countries to restrain the market and moderate its effects.

If Japan puts priority on the strength of its nation and the United States on the freedom of markets, Europe mixes the two. This means the struggle there to accommodate the twin demands of globalization and civilization will be especially intense. Can Europe reduce the burdens of its welfare states to enable its economies to compete without adopting protectionism or destroying the balance of obligations between government, business, and workers on which its societies rest? Can it win the race to build a continent-wide market strong enough to stand up to the global economy? Can it share the gains of commerce, as it has in the past, or does the future prosperity of its winners depend on the growing impoverishment of its losers, as in the United States? In a BBC interview, Paul Kennedy observed that the choices are hard:

> What exactly do you do when you have structural unemployment of 18 percent, possibly going up to 20 or 28 percent? If—just to take one example—the German nation finds itself with the choice, in a few years' time, of the continued relocation of industry to lower-wage countries so that Mercedes and BMW and Siemens can survive, *or* severe cuts in the social wage so that it will be competitive in domestically located industry for export market, *or* a return to some forms of protection, which way will it go? Which of the three hard choices would you recommend? And are you sure you know the answer after the surprises and the reverses in the past decade in international affairs? Who is putting his money on the table or

her money on the table for what the international economic order—let alone the international power-political order—will be in the year 2010?[16]

It is vital that Europe keep a strong welfare state, because the safety net it provides makes the switch to a global economy possible. A society like Europe, traditionally open to trade, can accept the instability of globalization only if it is offset by the stabilizing force of unemployment pay and other benefits.

The unemployment crisis in Europe is prompting a stream of fresh, even visionary, ideas. Two German politicians, Gerhard Schröder and Kurt Biedenkopf, issued a paper calling for more part-time work, more flexible hours, even more domestic work, all in an effort to increase jobs. Jacques Attali, the former president of the European Bank for Reconstruction and Development, predicts a new era of nomadic labor, as workers roam the world, going wherever the jobs are. Claus Offe, director of the Center for Social Policy Research at the University of Bremen, believes that society never again will create enough jobs. Therefore, he says, persons who drop out of the workforce and choose a life of unemployment should be paid for not working, "at a level commensurate with a modest way of life," because they have opened up a place for someone who wants to work. This is similar to unemployment pay, but would not carry the aura of failure and, presumably, would be permanent.

Despite pledges of free trade, the chances seem good that, over the next few years, Europe will look inward, finding growth within itself. This is possible because the continent offers so much room for growth. Some existing EU members—Greece, Portugal, Spain, and Ireland—still have far to go before they catch up with the more prosperous nations of the north. In the meantime, Poland, which is as big as France, plus the Czech Republic, Hungary, and possibly the Balkan and Baltic nations, will get EU membership. East Germany became an EU member at the moment of reunification with West Germany. All these countries, cruelly retarded by their experience with communism, are basically North European societies, more attuned than Greece or Portugal to industrial and commercial development. If their development is rapid, as seems likely, Europe's growth problems could be solved for the next generation.

Europe would seem to have an obligation to the Third World, particularly to Africa, because of its history of colonialism there. There is a great deal of rhetoric in Europe about the need to bring these formerly colonial countries into the global economy. But the reality does not match the rhetoric. Of all the areas of the Third World, sub-Saharan Africa seems last in line for foreign investment, and there is no European rush to invest there. Europe's one big spasm of colonial responsibility, the Lome Agreement, was signed in 1975 to give exports from former colonies in Africa, the Pacific, and the Caribbean preferential treatment on European markets. It fell far short of its ambitions and may not be renewed when it expires in 2000.

America: Regaining Stability

Japan so far has managed to keep the global economy at bay. Europe has been preoccupied with the development of its own unity, the end of communism, and the reuniting of Germany, and is only beginning to sense the threat this economy presents to its civilization. The impact has been greatest in the United States, and potential solutions have been most debated there.

Some steps seem clear. Whether the decline in median wages is caused by trade, technology, vanishing industry, or a combination of many factors, it has been accelerated by the collapse in the floor under the lowest wages. A decent minimum wage props up all other wages. When the minimum wage is allowed to decline, this prop is removed, and all wages decline with it.

Instead of downsizing workers by the thousands, American business, working with its employees, could adopt the European and Japanese patterns of keeping workers on the job on short hours or four-day weeks at reduced pay when demand is low. This is not as good as a full-time job at full pay, but it is less demoralizing than unemployment, preserves health insurance and other benefits, reduces the instability in society, and ensures that the workers and their experience are available to the company when demand goes up again.

The decline in wages and the increase in stability has also been paralleled by the decline in unions. Unions exist partly to increase wages but mostly to ensure job security. In a time of insecurity, it seems certain that workers will seek some form of solidarity—perhaps in traditional unions, perhaps in other forms of employee associations. Because more employees work in smaller and relatively volatile companies, these unions or associations will focus on entire industries or job categories, not on single huge corporations, as did the unions of old. Unions in the past contributed to industrial stability and professionalism, two missing qualities today; new unions or associations can help restore those qualities. Government must lead the way by strengthening labor rights and laws, protecting workers who try to organize, and tilting the balance of power back toward labor.

The decline in wages at the bottom has been accompanied by the unprecedented increase of wages, bonuses, and stock options at the top, creating an inequality that is no less than a national disgrace. One would hope that corporations would come to their senses and call a halt by capping wages and bonuses and limited options so that executive income, now running at 140 times more than average income, returns to some reasonable multiple. Short of that, the only solution is a sharp increase in maximum tax rates, clearly punitive and aimed at punishing this disregard for common decency. The practice of stock options could be outlawed. Intended to ensure that the fortunes of executives rise and fall with the fortunes of their companies, they now are widely abused, with companies making up losses, and have led to the explosion in income that has become such a corrosive feature of American society.

Stock options became popular after the government set a $1 million limit on executive salaries that companies could deduct from their corporate tax. This so-called cap has backfired to the point that salaries now are barely one-fifth of total pay. A new cap is needed on the size of total compensation—salary, bonuses, options, and perks—that can be deducted.

Short of this, executives should be required to hold stock options for several years before exercising them, to promote long-term thinking; otherwise, gains from these options could be taxed at 100 percent. So could golden handshakes given to short-term executives. There is no place in a fair society for the $90 million severance package paid to former Disney president Michael Ovitz after an apparently unsuccessful year on the job.

Economist Edward N. Wolff has called for an American "wealth tax" that would tax accumulated wealth of $100,000 or more, not counting household effects, pensions, annuities, and one modest car. Only those with a net worth of more than $750,000 would pay as much as $1,000 per year, Wolff said. He calculated the tax would have raised $43 billion in 1989, about four times the amount raised by gift and estate taxes, which are "so porous that some describe [them] as a 'voluntary' tax." Other nations, including Germany, the

Netherlands and Switzerland, have such taxes, he said. Apart from helping to balance the budget, Wolff continued, a wealth tax would be an expression of simple equity—the idea that those who have gained from society have an enhanced responsibility to support it.[17]

Education and training are cited often as the panaceas for the jobs crisis. With the advent of the information society, the best-paid workers are the "symbolic analysts," those who can manipulate the symbols of this computerized era and cope with the demands of technology. From President Clinton on down, leaders who understand the dilemma of falling wages and the pain of insecure lives say that the solution lies in higher training, so that everyone will be able to share in the boons of the new global economy.

No one could argue the value of education, if only because it helps those who have it to understand what happened to them when their jobs disappear. But education and training will not save American workers. This is the "Lake Wobegon solution," the notion that everyone can be above average. In any society, there are going to be workers with more brains and skills, and workers with fewer brains and skills. The problem with the American economy in the past twenty years has been, first, the erosion of jobs for the less skilled as industry went overseas and, then, the downsizing of the more skilled because technology took their jobs. With the two groups fighting for the jobs that were left, business pursued a race to the bottom, bidding wages and working conditions ever lower in the certain knowledge that there would always be takers.

At the same time, there is evidence that jobs in the new, high-tech information economy often require less training and education, not more. A celebrated survey by the McKinsey Global Institute noted that manufacturing in Toyota plants in Japan, where productivity and efficiency are as high as anywhere in the world, was designed to stress "ease of assembly and low complexity." Toyota, the institute reports, "attempts to specify [designs] so that they are easier to produce and assemble." In other words, the jobs at Toyota are becoming easier, not harder, and require fewer skills, not more.[18] The British economist Simon Head says he checked this out at other Japanese factories and was told that skills ranked well behind team spirit in the list of employee virtues. Looms in the old textile mills of the American South were dirty and dangerous, but they required considerable skill to run. They have been replaced by automated

looms housed in clean, quiet rooms as big as a football field and operated by employees who need to learn and remember only which but-
tons to push on a computerized panel. Head continues:

> These aspects of lean production help to explain why the rising produc-
> tivity of blue-collar workers is not being matched by the rising value of
> their paychecks. Corporations that can achieve higher productivity while
> dispensing with entire categories of skilled labor are unlikely to pass those
> savings on to their remaining, and less-skilled, workers.[19]

Or, he might have added, to more-skilled workers who have been
forced to take low-skilled, low-paying jobs to survive.

The sheer cost of proper education and retraining is likely to keep
it from happening. Ethan Kapstein has figured that the total bill for
retraining the 34 million unemployed persons in the OECD countries
would be $238 billion, assuming an average cost of about $7,000.
This, of course, doesn't count the cost of those who will become
unemployed or need new training to remain employed. The bill for
the United States alone would be $49 billion.[20] No government, fight-
ing deficits, is likely to spend that kind of money. Nor are corporations likely to spend it. As Head notes, the supposedly low state of
America's schools has not kept these corporations from achieving
high productivity and record profits. Besides, for the same money,
they can train cheaper workers elsewhere.

Education is good in itself. But we should not delude ourselves
that we have solved the problem when we educate the young for jobs
that don't exist or train them for an economy that no longer needs
the skills they are learning. The retention and creation of good, high-
skilled jobs, underpinned by a base of solid, less-skilled jobs, is the
only route to a healthy society. When these jobs are plentiful, education will mean something.

Finally, Americans must restore the sense that corporations and
their employees have interests in common. This existed once. It was
assumed that, when companies prospered, so did their employees.
This is no longer true. As wages fall and jobs disappear, corporate
profits and stock prices rise, often for the same reason: globalization
means that companies can do best for themselves by abandoning their
home base and the workers there and moving overseas. What's good
for General Motors or any other corporation is not necessarily good
anymore for America.

There are several ways to restore this sense of identity, which is crucial if the United States is to have a decent economic life. The curtailing of global financial markets, which force corporations to put the bottom line above all else, would help. Laws that penalize companies for moving overseas could slow the exodus. Wage policies that reduce inequities would signal management's intention to improve relations. So would an end to union-busting tactics and a willingness by management to engage employees in framing the conditions of their work lives.

The Stakeholder Economy

More than anything else, the adoption of the kind of "stakeholder" mentality that still exists in Germany and Japan would restore civility to the American workplace. At the moment, corporate practice and American law give primacy to "shareholder rights"—the view that, because the shareholders put up the money, they take all the risks and deserve all the rewards. "Chainsaw Al" Dunlap, whose gleeful downsizing at the companies he has run has become a caricature of capitalist rapacity, described shareholder rights in the bluntest possible way when he said, "The point of business is to make a profit. The responsibility of the CEO is to deliver shareholder value. Period. It's the shareholders who own the corporation. They take all the risk. And how does the CEO maximize value? He does that by focusing on profit."[21]

Dunlap has become notorious for the vigor with which he defends what is, in fact, common American business practice. Under American law, executives and boards could be sued by shareholders if they didn't maximize shareholder value in this way. The global economy has raised the cost for anyone else caught in this process—employees, suppliers, communities. In short, the stakeholders.

Margaret Blair of the Brookings Institution argues that corporations have a social role that goes beyond the rights of shareholders. This idea, which is obvious to Europeans and Japanese, is a radical concept in the United States, where it is sometimes argued on moral grounds but not as a matter of economic policy or law. Blair, however, insists that American law on shareholder rights violates common sense. Most investors, she notes, take very little risk. Most own only a tiny percentage of any company; even the biggest institutional investors, like pension funds, seldom own more than 1 or 2 percent. Moreover, most investors hedge their bets by spreading investments over many companies. If a company goes broke, the investors lose their investment, but that's all. Under the laws of limited liability, no investor risks his or her house, car, or children's education, regardless of the actions of the company he or she "owns." In fact, by the time the company goes broke, most investors will have sold out and moved on. An investor's stake in any company is moved easily, and any risk can be undone with a telephone call to a broker. More than half the stock of an average U.S. firm now changes hands in less than a year.[22]

In addition, Blair argues, investors may own a company but cannot behave like owners. Any shareholder who marched into a company and tried to dictate a new product line or design would be tossed out. This shareholder's "rights" of ownership extend no farther than the right to go to the annual meeting and ask an embarrassing question, which will be ignored.

The real risk, Blair says, lies with those who have literally bet their lives on the company—the employees who have devoted ten or twenty years to it, the community that relies on it for its jobs and tax money, the small suppliers who would go broke without it. These are the stakeholders. Some are managers with more real power to dictate policy than the so-called owners. Others are workers who know much more about how a company is run, or should be run, than the owners. All of these stand to lose a lot—the house, the car, the education—if the company fails. Unlike investors, employees and suppliers can jump ship only with great difficulty, and at their risk; so many jobs involve skills learned after years with one employer that the average downsized employee typically earns 14 percent less at his or her new job, a pay cut that gets worse the longer the employee held the old job.[23]

Employee stock ownership plans (ESOPs) are making owners of many employees. But even these employee-owners have no power; only about 4 percent of companies that distribute stock to employees let them elect a representative to the board or give them a real voice in management. Employee-owned companies, like UAL Corporation, the parent of United Airlines, are still fairly rare, although some high-tech firms, finding that their assets lie mostly inside the skulls of their employees, are giving these employees real rights and powers to keep them from taking these assets out the door.

Blair feels American law is flexible enough to accommodate stakeholder rights, but other experts feel a change in corporate laws is necessary. Whoever is right, real progress toward a stakeholder society must be preceded by a revolution in Americans' attitudes toward the corporations that dominate their economy.

The Prosperity of Nations

At the heart of the debate over the global economy is the struggle of democracy and capitalism. In theory, they are meant to go together, indeed, to be inseparable. But democracy's priorities are equality before the law, the right of each citizen to influence the decisions that govern his or her life, the creation of a civilization based on fairness and equity. Capitalism's priorities are inequality of return, profit for the supplier of capital, efficiency of production and distribution, the bottom line. At its best, capitalism creates wide prosperity, general comfort, and public stability; in effect, it makes democracy possible. At its worst, it can steal this prosperity, erode this comfort, and upset this stability, threatening the very democracy it helped create.

Over the past fifty years, democracy and capitalism have been able to work together to create one of the golden ages in the world's history. A confluence of forces—the enlightened leadership of the United States, the enormous economic spur that came from the rebuilding of Japan and Europe, the competition with communism that inspired the West to stress all that was best in its society, the expansion of trade and prosperity between the world's most sophisticated societies—permitted the simultaneous flowering of economic well-being and democratic civilization. These forces no longer rule, or have weakened. A new confluence of forces will propel the world into the next century, and the same happy result is by no means guaranteed.

Edward Mortimer, writing in the *Financial Times* of London, said that most people need a balance between democracy and the market. Asked to be full-time citizens or full-time consumers, he said, "most of us don't want to be either of these things":

> We want to be assured of a minimum standard of government, and a reasonable choice of goods and services with some protection of consumers against unsafe products or outright fraud. We want the chance to vote a corrupt or incompetent government out of office, and the chance to

switch suppliers if a product is unsatisfactory. But we have other things
to do in life, and we want to get on with them.

Too much democracy kills the market, because "the people," or an
authority acting in their name, make all the decisions collectively, leaving
nothing to the individual. But too much market may also kill democracy.
If every choice is left to the market, the right to vote becomes meaningless, because the people you elect have no power to change anything. No
doubt the market is a necessary condition for democracy, as water is for
life. But you can also drown.[24]

The global economy wants everyone to be consumers first and
citizens second. But to be consumers, we must first be producers, or
we earn nothing and lose the means to share in the market's bounty.
By eroding our ability to produce, the global economy is undermining the economic basis of our democracy. Even more, it saps the valid-
ity of the nations that command the loyalty of most of us and give
us our identity: we are Americans or French or Germans or Japanese before we are citizens of the world. Our civilizations have nurtured the lives of everyone fortunate enough to share them, and they
are worth preserving.

The global economy is a reality and cannot be denied. But uncontrolled, it can destroy these civilizations, to the point that we will
wake one day to discover that we are neither consumers nor producers nor citizens at all.

The French, as you'd expect, worry about this matter of civilization. It is what a French government official had in mind one
afternoon when he told me, "We must balance the prosperity of our
industry with the prosperity of our culture. What's at stake, really?
It is the prosperity of nations, which means the people. It's about the
creation of wealth. If it comes through the prosperity of a corporation or company, that's fine. But it's always a question of how and
for whom the company is getting rich. The responsibility of government is to try to manage some balance between all these interests. We must keep things working, if not perfectly, then in a way
through which everyone finds some interest."

We live at a moment when the great forces of economic revolution, government power, and the integrity of civilizations are creating nothing less than the world of the twenty-first century and
beyond. The shape of this world depends on striking this balance
now, so that we may face this future with confidence.

ENDNOTES

Chapter 1

1. Spokesman, Bank for International Settlements, Basel, 1996.
2. Cited in Michel Albert, *Capitalism vs. Capitalism* (New York: Four Walls Eight Windows, 1993).
3. Lowell Bryan and Diana Farrell, *Market Unbound* (New York: John Wiley & Sons, Inc., New York, 1996).
4. Interview, July 3, 1996.
5. Ibid.
6. Interview, July 4, 1996.
7. David Marquand, "The Great Reckoning," *Prospect* magazine, July 1996.
8. Telephone interview, February 1997.
9. "Eurosclerosis: The Misdiagnosis," *The American Prospect*, January–February 1997.
10. Edward N. Luttwak, "America's Security Blanket," *Washington Post*, National Weekly Edition, December 5–11, 1994.
11. Robert Reich, *The Work of Nations* (New York: Knopf, 1991).
12. Stephen Roach, "Lessons in Restructuring," *Financial Times*, Oct. 22, 1996.
13. Peter Drucker, "The Age of Social Transformation," *Atlantic Monthly*, November 1994.
14. Interview, Paris, July 9, 1996.
15. Interview, Paris, July 19, 1996.
16. Interview, Tokyo, June 19, 1996.
17. "The Top 200: The Rise of Global Corporate Power," by Sarah Anderson and John Cavanagh, Institute for Policy Studies, Washington, Sept. 25, 1996.
18. Bryan and Farrell, *Market Unbound*.
19. Cited by Robert L. Heilbroner in introduction to *The End of Work*, by Jeremy Rifkin (New York: G. P. Putnam's Sons, 1995).
20. *Network*, copyright 1976 by Metro-Goldwyn-Mayer, Inc., and United Artists Corp.

Chapter 2

1. Interview, March, 1988.
2. Sarah Anderson and John Cavanagh, "The Top 200: The Rise of Global Corporate Power," Institute for Policy Studies, Washington, D.C., 1996.

3. Paul Kennedy, "Globalization and its Discontents," 1996 Analysis Lecture on Radio 4, British Broadcasting Corp., May 20, 1996.
4. Interview, June 18, 1996.
5. Greg Mastel and Andrew Z. Szamosszegi, "China's Growing Trade Surplus: Why It Matters," *Washington Quarterly*, Spring 1997.
6. Interview, April 1988.
7. Peter Huber, "Cyberpower," *Forbes*, Dec. 2, 1996.
8. William W. Lewis and Marvin Harris, "Why Globalization Must Prevail," in *The McKinsey Quarterly Reprint Series*, McKinsey Global Institute, 1992.
9. John Maynard Keynes, "National Self-Sufficiency," in *The Collected Writings of John Maynard Keynes*, vol. 21, 1933.
10. For details on the Euro, see Chapter 6.
11. Lowell Bryan and Diana Farrell, *Market Unbound* (New York: John Wiley & Sons Inc., 1996); and R. Taggart Murphy, *The Weight of the Yen* (New York: W. W. Norton & Co., 1996).
12. Bryan and Farrell, *Market Unbound*.
13. Huber, "Cyberpower."
14. James Annable, "The Rationalizing Economy: Macroeconomic Consequences," *Economic Issue Backgrounder* (First Chicago NBD Corp.), January, 1996; and James Annable, "Insecure Executives Make the Economy Grow," *Wall Street Journal*, April 28, 1997.
15. Bryan and Farrell, *Market Unbound*; and *Wall Street Journal*, April 10, 1997.
16. Dani Rodrik, "Has Globalization Gone Too Far?" Institute for International Economics, Washington, D.C., 1997; Peter Katzenstein, *Corporatism and Change: Austria, Switzerland and Politics of Industry* (Ithaca, N.Y.: Cornell University Press, 1984); and interview with Stephan Leibfried, Bremen, November 5, 1995.
17. Ian Angell, "The Signs Are Clear: The Future Is Inequality," *The Independent* (London), September 25, 1966.
18. Yves Dezalay and Bryant Garth, "Merchants of Law as Moral Entrepreneurs: Constructing International Justice from the Competition for Transnational Business Disputes," *Law & Society Review* 29(1) (1995).
19. Bryan and Farrell, *Market Unbound*.

Chapter 3

1. Richard J. Barnet, "The End of Jobs," *Harper's*, September 1993.
2. Interview, Paris, May 24, 1994.
3. Interview, Geneva, May 26, 1994.
4. Hans Magnus Enzensberger, *Civil War* (London, Granta Books, 1994).
5. Niels Thygesen, Yutaka Kosai, and Robert Z. Lawrence, *Globalization and*

Trilateral Labor Markets: Evidence and Implications (New York: The Trilateral Commission, December 1996).

6. Bureau of Labor Statistics; Bureau of the Census; and Economic Policy Institute, "The State of Working America" (Armonk, NY: M. E. Sharpe, 1994).

7. Organization for Economic Cooperation and Development, *Employment Outlook 1996* (Paris: OECD, 1996).

8. Interview, Chicago, September 1996.

9. Interview, Bonn, July 2, 1996.

10. Interview, Chicago, June 1, 1996.

11. OECD, *Employment Outlook 1996.*

12. Susan N. Houseman, "External and Internal Labor Market Flexibility, an International Comparison," in *The Human Resource Management Handbook,* David Lewin et al., eds. (Greenwich, CT: JAI Press, 1997).

13. Ibid.

14. Abraham and Houseman, "Job Security in America," *Brookings Review,* Summer 1993. See also Houseman and Abraham, "Labor Adjustment Under Different Institutional Structures," in *Institutional Frameworks and Labor Market Performance,* edited by Buttler et al. (London: Routledge, 1995).

15. Charles Morris, "The Job Engine Sputters," *New York Times,* March 18, 1997.

16. Richard Brown, interview with author, Toulouse, France, June 12, 1996.

17. William Dawkins, "Japan's Silent Knife," *Financial Times,* Nov. 17, 1995.

18. Interview with Kiyoharu Matsuura, Japanese Trade Confederation (Rengo), Tokyo, June 19, 1996.

19. Policy Planning and Research Department, Ministry of Labor, *Monthly Cash Earnings, 1970–94* (Tokyo: Ministry of Labor).

20. Supplied by a spokesman for Fujitsu Ltd., Tokyo, June 18, 1996.

21. Lawrence Mishel and Jared Bernstein, "The State of Working America."

22. Robert Reich, speech to Low Wage Workers Conference, Washington, D.C., February 16, 1995.

23. Interview with Andrea Meltzer, Chicago, June 1995.

24. Interview, Chicago, June 1995.

25. Susan N. Houseman and Machiko Osawa, "The Growth of Part-Time Employment in Japan," manuscript, March 1996.

26. Ibid.

27. Interview with Kiyoharu Matsuura, Tokyo, June 19, 1996.

28. Houseman, "External and Internal Labor Market Flexibility."

29. Interview with Richard Brown, Human Relations Director, Airbus, July 12, 1996.

30. A good summary of this argument is by Robert Z. Lawrence in Thygesen et al., *Globalization and Trilateral Labor Markets* (New York: The Trilateral Commission, 1996).

31. Peter Drucker, "The Age of Social Transformation," in *Atlantic Monthly,* November 1994.

32. Michael Dunkerley, *The Jobless Economy? Computer Technology in the World of Work* (London: Polity Press, 1996).
33. Adrian Wood, "How Trade Hurt Unskilled Workers," *Journal of Economic Perspectives*, Summer 1995.
34. Robert Z. Lawrence in Thygesen et al., *Globalization and Trilateral Labor Markets*.
35. Dani Rodrik, "Has Globalization Gone Too Far?" Institute for International Economics, Washington, D.C., 1997.
36. Alan Ehrenhalt, "Keepers of the Dismal Faith," *New York Times*, February 23, 1997.
37. David Howell, "Institutional Failure and the American Worker: The Collapse of Low-Skill Wages," Public Policy Brief No. 19, Jerome Levy, Economics Institute, 1997.
38. Speeches, February 16, 1995, and September 4, 1996.
39. Gary Burtless, "International Trade and the Rise in Earnings," *Journal of Economic Literature*, June, 1995.
40. David E. Bloom and Adi Brender, "Labor and the Emerging World Economy," *Population Bulletin* (Population Reference Bureau, Inc.), October 1993.
41. Benjamin I. Page, "Trouble for Workers and the Poor: Economic Globalization and the Reshaping of American Politics," presentation at a conference at the University of Montreal, October 6–8, 1996.
42. Burtless, "International Trade and the Rise in Earnings."
43. Rebecca Blank, "Eurosclerosis: The Misdiagnosis," *American Prospect*, January/February 1997.

Chapter 4

1. Felix Rohatyn, "Requiem for a Democrat," speech at Wake Forest University, March 17, 1995.
2. Reuters, March 8, 1994.
3. Greg J. Duncan et al., "W(h)ither the Middle Class? A Dynamic View," in *Poverty and Prosperity in the USA in the Late Twentieth Century*, edited by Dimitri B. Papadimitriou and Edward N. Wolff (New York: Macmillan, 1993).
4. Greg J. Duncan, Timothy Smeedling, and Johanne Boisjoly, "Economic Mobility of Young Workers in the 1970s and 1980s," *Demography* 33(4), November 1996.
5. Bureau of the Census, *Income and Job Mobility in the Early 1990s* (Washington, D.C.: Bureau of the Census, March 1995).
6. Robert C. Topel, "Specific Capital and Unemployment: Measuring the Costs and Consequences of Job Loss," in *Studies in Labor Economics in Honor of Walter Y. Oi*, edited by Allan H. Meltzer and Charles I. Plosser (Amsterdam: North Holland, 1990).

7. "Redefining the Middle Manager" (New York: The Conference Board, 1995).

8. "The Middle Class," *Lutheran Brotherhood Reports* (Minneapolis, Minn., December 22, 1993).

9. "Beyond Downsizing," WTTW Channel 11 (Chicago), April 2, 1997.

10. G. J. Meyer, *Executive Blues: Down and Out in Corporate America* (New York: Franklin Square Press, 1995).

11. Peter Drucker, "The Age of Social Transformation," *Atlantic Monthly*, November, 1994.

12. Robert D. Putnam, "Bowling Alone: America's Declining Social Capital," *Journal of Democracy*, January, 1995.

13. Alan Ehrenhalt, *The Lost City: The Forgotten Virtues of Community in America* (New York: Basic Books, 1995).

14. Robert J. Samuelson, *The Good Life and Its Discontents: The American Dream in the Age of Entitlement, 1945–1995* (New York: Times Books, 1995).

15. William Julius Wilson, *The Truly Disadvantaged* (Chicago: University of Chicago Press, 1987); and Nicholas Lemann, *The Promised Land: The Great Black Migration and How It Changed America* (New York: Doubleday, 1991).

16. Sam Roberts, *Who We Are: A Portrait of America Based on the Latest U.S. Census* (New York: Times Books, 1993).

17. James P. Smith, *Unequal Wealth and Incentives to Save* (Santa Monica, Calif. RAND, 1995).

18. Dr. Harold Visotsky, interview with author, Chicago, March 1996.

19. David Leonhardt, "Two-Tier Marketing," *Business Week*, March 17, 1997.

20. Robert Reich, *The Work of Nations: Preparing Ourselves for 21st-Century Capitalism* (New York: Knopf, 1991).

21. Organization of Economic Cooperation and Development, *Employment Outlook* (Paris: OECD, 1996).

22. Edward N. Luttwak, "America's Security Blanket," *Washington Post*, National Weekly Edition, December 5–11, 1994.

23. Stephen Roach, "America's Recipe for Industrial Extinction," *Financial Times*, May 14, 1996.

Chapter 5

1. David Roche, "Magical Fiction," *Independent Strategy* (newsletter), Feb. 20, 1997.

2. Michael Lev, "Taxis and the Toppling of Japan, Inc.," *Chicago Tribune*, May 4, 1997.

3. Samuel P. Huntington, *The Clash of Civilizations and the Remaking of World Order* (New York: Simon & Schuster, 1996).

4. Interview, Chicago, Jan. 27, 1997.

5. Karel van Wolferen, *The Enigma of Japanese Power* (Rutland Vt.: Charles E. Tuttle Co., 1996).

6. R. Taggart Murphy, *The Weight of the Yen* (New York: W. W. Norton & Co., 1996).

7. Eisuke Sakakibara, *Beyond Capitalism* (Lanham, Md.: University Press of America, and Washington, D.C.: Economic Strategy Institute, 1993).

8. van Wolferen, *The Enigma of Japanese Power.*

9. Robert M. Orr, Jr., speech in Tokyo, April 13, 1994.

10. van Wolferen, *The Enigma of Japanese Power.*

11. Ibid.

12. Murphy, *The Weight of the Yen.*

13. For example, see "The Unhappy Alliance," in *The Economist*, February 17, 1990, and "Whispering Reform," in *The Economist*, January 11, 1997.

14. Sakakibara, *Beyond Capitalism.*

15. Eamonn Fingleton: *Blindside: Why Japan Is Still On Track to Overtake The U.S. by the Year 2000* (Boston: Houghton Mifflin, 1995).

16. James Fallows, *Looking at the Sun* (New York: Pantheon, 1994).

17. Interview, Tokyo, June 20, 1996.

18. William L. Givens, "The U.S. Can No Longer Afford Free Trade," *Business Week,* November 22, 1982.

19. Anderson and Cavanaugh, "The Top 200."

20. Toyoo Gyohten, *Business and the Contemporary World*, Winter, 1992.

21. Murphy, *The Weight of the Yen.*

22. Patricia Hagan Kuwayama, "Success Story," *Wilson Quarterly*, Winter, 1982.

23. Stefan Wagstyl, "Elusive Key to Japan's Closed Shop," *Financial Times*, February 27, 1989.

24. See Murphy, *The Weight of the Yen*, for a good discussion of this.

25. Organization for Economic Cooperation and Development, OECD *Economies at a Glance: Structural Indicators* (Paris: OECD, 1996).

26. *The Economist*, "Rising Surplus, Rising Wrath," March 22, 1997.

27. Interview, Tokyo, June 12, 1996.

28. Murphy, *The Weight of the Yen.*

29. Carol Lufty, "The Lady Vanishes," *New York Times Magazine*, March 30, 1997.

30. Kenneth S. Courtis, "Business & the Contemporary World," Winter, 1992; *Asahi Evening News*, May 13, 1996; interview with author, Tokyo, June 19, 1996.

31. Interviews of Fujitsu officials with author, Akashi, June, 17, 1996.

32. Interview, Tokyo, June 20, 1996.

33. Fingleton, *Blindside.*

34. Kuribayashi Yoshimitu, *Okurasho: Fushin no Kōzu* (Tokyo: Kodansha, 1992). Cited in R. Taggart Murphy, *The Weight of the Yen* (New York: W. W. Norton, 1996).

35. Interview, Tokyo, June 10, 1996.

36. Murphy, *The Weight of the Yen.*

37. Interview, Tokyo, June 18, 1996.

38. Akio Mikuni, interview, Tokyo, June 18, 1996.
39. Interview, Tokyo, June 13, 1996.
40. Fallows, *Looking at the Sun.*
41. Sakakibara, *Beyond Capitalism.*

Chapter 6

1. Interview, Frankfurt, July 3, 1996.
2. Interview, Bonn, July 1, 1996.
3. Horst Teltschik, interview with author, Munich, July 5, 1996.
4. John Plender, *A Stake in the Future* (London: Nicholas Brealey Publishing, 1997).
5. Interview in *Woman's Own* (London), October 31, 1987.
6. Dasa statement, October 23, 1995.
7. Michel Albert, *Capitalism vs. Capitalism* (New York: Four Walls Eight Windows, 1993).
8. I am indebted to Michel Albert for his concise and learned description of the German and French economies, *Capitalism vs. Capitalism*, chs. 6, 12.
9. *Headline* (Daimler-Benz internal newsletter), March 28, 1996.
10. Harold Perkin, *The Third Revolution: Professional Elites in the Modern World* (New York: Routledge, 1996).
11. Albert, *Capitalism vs. Capitalism.*
12. Interview with author, Munich, July 5, 1996.
13. Wolfgang Münchau, "Breakdown of Consensus," *Financial Times*, October 21, 1996.
14. Klaus-Peter Klaiber, interview with author, Bonn, July 1, 1996.
15. Interview, Munich, July 6, 1996.
16. Marc Blondel, interview with author, Paris, July 10, 1996.
17. Interview, Paris, July 8, 1996.
18. Roger Cohen, "For France, Sagging Self-Image and Esprit," *New York Times*, February 11, 1997.
19. Klaus Schwab and Claude Smadja, "Start Taking the Backlash Against Globalization Seriously," *International Herald Tribune*, February 4, 1996.

Chapter 7

1. George Soros, "The Capitalist Threat," *Atlantic Monthly*, February 1997.
2. Bureau of Labor Statistics, Washington D.C. (various publications).
3. Interview, Tokyo, June 12, 1996.
4. Interview, Tokyo, June 11, 1996.
5. Associated Press, April 7, 1995.

6. Jennifer Reingold, "Executive Pay," *Business Week*, April 21, 1997.

7. Towers Perrin, "Worldwide Total Remuneration," New York, 1996.

8. Interview, Tokyo, June 20, 1996.

9. Interview, Paris, July 10, 1996.

10. Interview, Cologne, July 2, 1996.

11. Dominique Mariette and Colette Menguy, "Les salaires des patrons toujours tabous," *La Tribune Desfosses*, July 11, 1996.

12. Henri Gibier, "France, tes impôts chassent tes talents," *L'Expansion*, Paris, June 17, 1996, citing figures from Arthur Andersen.

13. Interview, Paris, July 11, 1996.

14. Sarah Anderson and John Cavanagh, "CEOs Win, Workers Lose" (Washington, D.C.: Institute for Policy Studies, April 24, 1996).

15. Reingold, "Executive Pay."

16. Towers Perrin, "Worldwide Total Remuneration."

17. John M. Abowd and Michael L. Bognanno, "International Differences in Executive and Managerial Compensation," in *Differences and Changes in Wage Structures*, edited by Freeman and Katz (Chicago: University of Chicago Press, 1995).

18. *Chicago Tribune*, June 2, 1996.

19. "The Road to Riches Is Paved with Options," *New York Times*, March 30, 1997.

20. Reingold, "Executive Pay."

21. Ibid.

22. *Business Week*, July 3, 1995.

23. Lawrence Mishel and Jared Bernstein, "The State of Working America 1994–95" (Armonk, N.Y.: Economic Policy Institute, Sharpe, 1994).

24. Edward N. Wolff, *Top Heavy*, Twentieth Century Fund report (New York: The New Press, 1996).

25. All figures from Bureau of Labor Statistics.

26. Burtless, interview, Washington, September, 1995.

27. Interview, Chicago, February 1996.

28. Edward N. Wolff, "Time for a Wealth Tax?" *Boston Review*, February/March 1996.

29. Wolff, *Top Heavy*. See also James M. Poterba and Andrew A. Samwick, "Stock Ownership Patterns, Stock Market Fluctuations, and Consumption," *Brookings Papers on Economic Activity* 2 (1995).

30. James P. Smith, "Unequal Wealth and Incentives to Save," a RAND report, Santa Monica, Calif., July 24, 1995.

31. Ibid.

32. Timothy M. Smeeding and Peter Gottschalk, "The International Evidence on Income Distribution in Modern Economies: Where Do We Stand?" presentation at the annual meeting of the Population Association of America, New Orleans, 1996.

33. Mishel and Bernstein, "The State of Working America 1994–95."

34. Robert Reich, "The Menace of Prosperity," *Financial Times*, March 3, 1997.
35. David Marquand, *Prospect* magazine, London, July 1996, citing Harold Perkin, *The Third Revolution: Professional Elites in the Modern World* (London: Routledge, 1996).

Chapter 8

1. Interview, Corydon, Iowa, September 1992.
2. Interview, Ames, Iowa, September 1992.
3. "The Future of the Auto Industry: It Can Compete, Can It Survive?" (Washington, D.C.: Economic Strategy Institute, 1992).
4. McKinsey Global Institute, "Manufacturing Productivity" (Washington, D.C.: McKinsey Global Institute, 1993).
5. Yutaka Kosai, in *Globalization and Trilateral Labor Markets* (New York: The Trilateral Commission, 1996).
6. A. J. Liebling, "Two Pounds for a Dime," *New Yorker*, November 2, 1946.
7. Stephen Roach, "Lessons in Restructuring," *Financial Times*, October 22, 1996.
8. Dominique Moïsi, "New Vision of the Future," *Financial Times*, March 21, 1997.
9. Richard Koo, "Japan and International Capital Flows" (Nomura, April 1996).
10. "America Still Works," *Harper's*, 1995, reprinted in *The National Times*, August 1996.

Chapter 9

1. Interview with Kenneth Courtis, Deutsche Bank, Tokyo, June 11, 1996.
2. These statistics are taken from a variety of publications of the Organization for Economic Cooperation and Development, Paris; the European Union, Brussels; and the Bureau of the Census, Washington, D.C..
3. Interview, July 2, 1996.
4. William Drozdiak, "French Won't Give Up 'Womb-to-Tomb' Perks Quietly," *International Herald Tribune*, June 25, 1996.
5. Paul A. Summerville, "Japan's Chronic Labor Shortage," *Business & The Contemporary World*, Winter, 1992.
6. Interview with Martin Seeleib-Kaiser, Center for Social Policy Research, Bremen, Germany, November 4, 1995.
7. Summerville, "Japan's Chronic Labor Shortage."
8. McKinsey Global Institute, "Manufacturing Productivity" (Washington, D.C.: McKinsey Global Institute, October 1993).
9. Robert Kuttner, "If It Ain't Broke, Don't Tinker," *Business Week*, Feb. 20, 1995.

10. Henry Aaron and Barry Bosworth, "The Budget Meets the Boomers," *Brookings Review*, Fall 1996.
11. U.S. Department of Labor, Bureau of Labor Statistics, *Employee Benefits in Medium and Large Private Establishments, 1993* (Washington, D.C.: Department of Labor, 1994).
12. Peter Martin, *Financial Times* (London), September 19, 1996.
13. James P. Smith, *Unequal Wealth and Incentives to Save* (Santa Monica, Calif.: RAND, 1995).
14. U.S. Department of Commerce, Bureau of the Census, *Homeownership Rates* (Washington D.C.: Department of Commerce, 1995).
15. Interview, Frankfurt, July 4, 1996.
16. Interview, Bremen, November 4, 1995.
17. Oswald von Nell-Brunning, *Drei Generationen in Solidaritat* (Köhn: J. P. Bachem, 1981).
18. David Stockman, *The Triumph of Politics: The Inside Story of the Reagan Revolution* (New York: Avon, 1987).

Chapter 10

1. Robert Kuttner, *Everything for Sale* (New York: Knopf, 1997).
2. Robert Heilbroner, *The Nature and Logic of Capitalism* (New York: W. W. Norton, 1985), cited in Kuttner, *Everything for Sale.*
3. Lowell Bryan and Diana Farrell, *Market Unbound* (New York: Wiley, 1996).
4. Peter F. Drucker, "The Age of Social Transformation," *Atlantic Monthly*, November 1994.
5. Dani Rodrik, *Has Globalization Gone Too Far?* (Washington, D.C.: Institute for International Economics, March, 1997).
6. Ibid.
7. David Marquand, "The Great Reckoning," *Prospect* (London), July 1996.
8. William Greider, *One World, Ready or Not: The Manic Logic of Global Capitalism* (New York: Simon & Schuster, 1997).
9. Will Hutton, "Relaunching Western Economies," *Foreign Affairs*, November/December 1996.
10. Paul Volcker, "Toward Monetary Stability," *Wall Street Journal*, January 24, 1996.
11. Rodrik, *Has Globalization Gone Too Far?*
12. Henry Kaufman, "It's Time to Think Big," *International Economy*, November/December 1992.
13. Hyman P. Minsky, "Uncertainty and the Institutional Structure of Capitalist Economies," Working Paper No. 165 (Jerome Levy Economics Institute, April 1996).
14. Interview with Richard Koo, Nomura, Tokyo, June 18, 1996.

15. American Chamber of Commerce in Japan, *Making Trade Talks Work: Lessons from Recent History* (Tokyo: The American Chamber of Commerce in Japan, 1997).
16. Paul Kennedy, "Globalization and Its Discontents," 1996 Analysis Lecture on Radio 4, BBC May 20, 1996.
17. Wolff, *Top Heavy*.
18. McKinsey Global Institute, "Manufacturing Productivity" (Washington, D.C.: McKinsey Global Institute, October 1993).
19. Simon Head, "The New, Ruthless Economy," *New York Review of Books*, February 29, 1996.
20. Ethan Kapstein, "Workers and the World Economy," *Foreign Affairs*, May/June 1996.
21. "America Still Works," *Harper's*, 1995, reprinted in *The National Times*, August 1996.
22. Carrie R. Leana, "Why Downsizing Won't Work," *Chicago Tribune Magazine*, April 14, 1996.
23. Margaret M. Blair, *Ownership and Control* (Washington, D.C.: The Brookings Institution, 1995).
24. Edward Mortimer, *Financial Times*, (London), February 20, 1996.

INDEX